COVENANT-MAKING

Covenant-Making

THE FABRIC OF RELATIONSHIP

· · · · ·

Edited by
Charles J. Conniry Jr.
Laura K. Simmons

with an afterword by
Leonard Sweet

☙PICKWICK *Publications* · Eugene, Oregon

COVENANT-MAKING
The Fabric of Relationship

Copyright © 2014 Wipf and Stock. All rights reserved. Except for brief quotations in critical publications or reviews, no part of this book may be reproduced in any manner without prior written permission from the publisher. Write: Permissions, Wipf and Stock Publishers, 199 W. 8th Ave., Suite 3, Eugene, OR 97401.

Pickwick Publications
An Imprint of Wipf and Stock Publishers
199 W. 8th Ave., Suite 3
Eugene, OR 97401

www.wipfandstock.com

ISBN 13: 978-1-62564-224-0

Cataloging-in-Publication data:

Covenant-making : the fabric of relationship / edited by Charles J. Conniry Jr. and Laura K. Simmons.

xii + 186 p.; 23 cm—Includes bibliographical references.

ISBN 13: 978-1-62564-224-0

1. Covenants—Biblical teaching. 2. Covenant theology. 3. Shelton, Larry. I. Conniry, Charles J., Jr. II. Simmons, Laura K. III. Title.

BT155 C565 2014

Manufactured in the USA.

New Revised Standard Version Bible, copyright 1989 by the Division of Christian Education of the National Council of Churches of Christ in the USA.

Holy Bible, New Living Translation, copyright 1996, 2004 by Tyndale Charitable Trust.

Common English Bible. All rights reserved. No part of these materials may be reproduced or transmitted in any form or by any means, electronic or mechanical, including photocopying and recording, or by any information storage or retrieval system, except as may be expressly permitted by the 1976 Copyright Act, the 1998 Digital Millennium Copyright Act, or in writing from the publisher.

Daniel L. Brunner's chapter is reprinted with permission from *Quaker Religious Thought*.

Contents

List of Illustrations and Tables | vii

Foreword | ix
Charles J. Conniry Jr.

Introduction | xi
Laura K. Simmons

Chapter 1: The Man behind the Curtain: Who is This Covenant Theologian? | 1
MaryKate Morse

Chapter 2: Finding a Home in Shelton's Vision of the Atonement | 18
Steve Sherwood

Chapter 3: Participation and Dignity: Implications of a Covenant Theory of the Atonement for the Mission of the Church | 28
David R. Wilson

Chapter 4: Creation's Cry against Shallow Shalom: The Uneasy Relationship between Covenant Theology and Creation Theology in the Conflict between True and False Prophets | 53
Steve Delamarter

Chapter 5: Did Jesus or Custer Die For Our Sins? Exploring the Mission of Covenant among Non-Western Indigenous Cultures | 74
Randy S. Woodley

Chapter 6: The Salvation of a "Sinister Kid" | 86
Robert W. Wall

Chapter 7: The Kerygmatic Covenant: A Unifying Center for the New Testament? Literary and Historical Considerations | 106
Eugene E. Lemcio

Chapter 8: Rehabilitating Good Works: The Meaning of ἔργον | 116
Kent L. Yinger

Chapter 9: Suffering, Creation, and Luther's *Theologia Crucis* | 126
Daniel L. Brunner

Chapter 10: Covenantal Responses after Nine Minutes of Horror in Newtown | 135
Susie C. Stanley

Chapter 11: Marriage as a Metaphor for God's Covenant Love and Faithfulness | 146
Clifford W. Berger

Chapter 12: Theologians *in* Covenant: What They Do, Why They Do It, and What Gets in Their Way | 161
A. J. Swoboda

Afterword | 173
Leonard I. Sweet

Bibliography | 177

Illustrations and Tables

Figure 01 | 101

Table One: The Sinaitic Covenant and a "Kerygmatic" Covenant of the New Testament | 107

Table Two: The Unifying Kerygma of the New Testament | 114

Foreword

THE "RIPPLE EFFECT" IS described as ever-expanding influence caused by an event or action. Thus conceived, the Incarnation is creation's supreme ripple-making event. The ripples from that moment not only extend to the present day by virtue of the Incarnation's enormity, but also provide the metaphorical framework within which to construe our place and influence as followers of Jesus Christ. The Kingdom of God is about ripples and the people of God's Kingdom exercise leadership by making ripples after the manner of the Incarnation.

On May 15, 2013, Dr. R. Larry Shelton retired from his teaching post at George Fox Evangelical Seminary, completing forty-five years of distinguished ripple-making in Christian higher education. All along the way, Larry has modeled the convergence of academic reflection, which is proper to the academy, and hands-on engagement in pastoral ministry. In tandem with his work as a professor, Larry has served with distinction in several pastoral settings, modeling the dynamic interplay of academic reflection and ministry practice . . . praxis-based ripple making at its best!

It would be a ponderous exercise to recount forty-five years of scholarly production. Among the most important of his contributions, however, is his 2006 book, *Cross and Covenant: Interpreting the Atonement for 21st Century Mission*, which in many ways embodies the culmination of a lifetime of theological reflection.

Yet to view Larry as an erudite scholar with specialized research interests in Wesleyan theology and covenant atonement—and their practical intersection with the church and world—is to capture only a sliver of the Larry's influence. He is a devoted husband, father, father-in-law, grandfather, and friend. He loves to hike, fish, and hunt . . . and he enjoys sharing his passion for the outdoors with everyone who comes into his gravitational pull.

I count it an honor to be one of Larry Shelton's friends. Early on in my time at George Fox Larry invited me into his world as a trusted colleague and friend. We have spent countless hours camping, boating, fishing, and sharing our souls. Being Larry's friend has been one of the greatest blessings of my life.

We created this book in secret, far from the watchful gaze of the one in whose honor we created it. It is, in a word, a Festschrift: a "celebratory publication" that is written in honor of a respected scholar—and presented during the honoree's lifetime. Had we delayed too long, this piece would have ended up a Gedenkschrift (a memorial publication). I am glad we did not wait. Larry deserves to enjoy the accolades of his comrades while he still has many years of fruitful ripple-making left!

Each contribution in this piece reflects a different facet of covenant relationship, which is arguably one of the most important contributions Dr. Shelton has made to his disciplinary field, to the churches he has served, to his colleagues and friends, and to his family. Larry Shelton is a ripple maker, and only eternity will reveal the extent to which his influence has reached.

This book is a labor of love, fashioned by those over whom Larry's ripples have washed. In the final analysis it represents only a small sample of his widespread influence. Still we offer this work with deep gratitude for a life well lived . . . and with the prayer that the ripples of our distinguished honoree will continue long after the last chapter of his life has been written.

Charles J. Conniry Jr.
September 27, 2013

Introduction

Laura K. Simmons

A FESTSCHRIFT IS AN odd endeavor. We recruit colleagues and friends of a scholar to write about topics where their specialties may dovetail with those of the honoree (or not). Then we knit those contributions together into what we hope will be an attractive tapestry. In the rare air of the academy, this can result in groundbreaking volumes advancing a field of study further than it might have progressed in the work of those scholars individually.

Our honoree, Dr. Larry Shelton, is not your typical academic. This is a man who, as you will see in the coming pages, invested his life in numerous endeavors: he has been a pastor, a teacher, a scholar, a role model, a colleague, and a friend to those whose words fills these pages. His multifaceted legacy makes itself known in a number of ways. It is not common to encounter a bibliography ranging from Aristotle to C. S. Lewis—but we've got one. A volume of academic essays might not normally contain biblical, theological, *and* practical approaches to a theme—this book does. One might never find so many pastor-academics coming together to create a tribute to one of their own, but a fitting tribute to someone as gifted as Larry Shelton requires a concerted effort.

Shelton may be best known among academics for his covenant theology, expressed in *Cross and Covenant* (Paternoster, 2006). His students have been influenced by how Shelton's theology interfaces with his personal story of living with a heart transplant for nearly two decades. Churches, denominations, and other Christian institutions remember his leadership and pastoral touch as much as his scholarship. Even in retirement, Larry Shelton will serve a growing church in his community as distinguished theologian in residence, mentoring the pastoral team and providing theological leadership. MaryKate Morse's opening chapter describes the broad landscape of Shelton's life and influence, to help set the stage for the contributions that follow. Steve Sherwood reminds us of the stakes in getting our theology right as he describes how today's young people experience traditional atonement theologies.

Steve Delamarter and Randy Woodley explore how communities (Israelite and indigenous) make sense of the idea of covenant. Rob Wall, Gene Lemcio, and Kent Yinger shine a close lens on biblical and theological aspects of covenant. David Wilson explores how Shelton's theology might influence ministry among postmoderns. Dan Brunner unpacks the implications of covenant theology for our relationship with the created order. Susie Stanley and Cliff Berger apply the idea of covenant to practical matters of great import for our nation and the individuals who populate it.

And A. J. Swoboda concludes this collection with a very personal description of how theologians can form or de-form their students, a fitting tribute to a man who formed him, first as a student, then as a colleague. One of Swoboda's cautionary reminders is that all too often, theologians remain disconnected from the lived experience of faithful people. If that had been Larry Shelton's approach, this would be a significantly less interesting volume.

We are most grateful to Larry's friends and colleagues who have contributed their unique perspectives on his life and legacy here. What is hard to capture on the page is Larry Shelton's joyful storytelling, steadfast support, and thoughtful mentoring. For those, you'll have to get to know him yourself.

1

The Man behind the Curtain

Who Is This Covenant Theologian?

by MaryKate Morse

In the classic story, *The Wizard of Oz,* Dorothy and her friends travel to the Emerald City to have an audience with the Great and Powerful Wizard. They each have a request and each meets the Wizard, who appears to them in a variety of astonishing and terrifying forms. The Wizard has a reputation for his wisdom and his ability to work wonders, and they believe he can solve their problems. In the end, they discover that the real Oz behind the curtain is an ordinary man from Omaha, Nebraska.

The Wizard is akin to the world of academics. He has an impressive name: Oscar Zoraster Phadrig Issac Norman Henkel Emmannuel Ambroise Diggs. Academics cultivate impressive "names" by detailing their accomplishments in curricula vitae (CV). William H. Bergquist and Kenneth Pawlak, in their book *Engaging the Six Cultures of the Academy,* note that the academy culture is a world "with a strong emphasis on often subtle but nevertheless quite powerful competition and striving for prestige and dominance."[1] Academicians cultivate their CVs and use them as brands for their accomplishments and status.

Though the curricula vitae become a testimony to greatness and wonders, they do little to reveal much about the true character of the academic behind the curtain. This can create an unhealthy and false self, which is

---

1. Bergquist and Pawlak, *Engaging the Six Cultures of the Academy,* 33.

presented to students and faculty while the true self stays hidden behind the curtains. This is especially troubling for those who are Christian academics and who desire to emulate the servant leadership of Jesus. The purpose of this chapter is to pull back the curtain and reveal one academic, Dr. Larry Shelton, born in Hooper's Creek, North Carolina, on January 10, 1942. He is an accomplished academic who has put more value on moral authenticity than accomplishments in the academy; thus, he has influenced with his life and not just his words.

Larry Shelton has served in Christian higher education for 45 years, beginning as an Assistant Professor of Religion at Azusa Pacific University in California and ending his teaching career as the Richard B. Parker Professor of Wesleyan Theology at George Fox Evangelical Seminary. Throughout his career he had a unique trifecta of callings. He not only excelled as a scholar, but as a teacher and academic administrator, and as a church pastor.

Shelton is an ordained elder in the Free Methodist church, having served in various pastoral roles including ministry with the Foursquare church, while he worked full-time as a theologian and professor. Shelton also served tirelessly in various administrative roles as a Board member for several Christian camps, in various Free Methodist district positions, and in service to various Christian colleges and universities as department chair or dean. He is committed to promoting those whose voices are marginalized, such as women called to ministry and Latino and Native American leaders and scholars. He is also a devoted husband and father.

From the beginning, Shelton showed promise as a scholar. He graduated as the class valedictorian from Pfeiffer College, where he majored in English and minored in psychology. He received a Master of Divinity and a ThM in Biblical Liturature from Asbury Theological Seminary, studying under George Turner and Robert A. Traina and graduating number one in his class. He went on to complete a ThD in Historical Theology at Fuller Theological Seminary. Calvin Shoehoven and Geoffrey W. Bromiley were his advisors, with Bromiley serving also as his mentor. Shelton graduated with a doctoral major in the History of Hermeneutics, primarily under the guidance of Bromiley, and he completed a doctoral minor in New Testament Theology under George Eldon Ladd. He also completed a minor in Christian Ethics under Lewis B. Smedes. Shelton finished his doctorate in five years, writing his dissertation on Martin Luther's Concept of Biblical

Interpretation in Historical Perspective. He published three articles out of that material, and it formed the backbone of his academic work.

Shelton's scholarship includes an important book on covenant theology titled *Cross and Covenant: Interpreting the Atonement for 21st Century Mission* (Paternoster, 2006). His scholarship is purposed towards the church. David Wilson wrote in a review of the book, "*Cross and Covenant* is a fresh and thought-provoking contribution to contemporary soteriology and mission. It is not, however, merely the outline of yet another theory of the atonement. Larry Shelton's own exegetical and biblical-theological intent persists in its implications for mission and praxis where the focus of theology remains in the life of the church as God's covenant community."[2]

Academics lead with their research and teaching; Shelton has led as a theologian, pastor, and administrator. Much of the current leadership literature and research understands the flawed approach of focusing on the "great man or woman," "the Wizard," and his or her accomplishments. This has proven to be an insufficient understanding of leadership illustrated by the many spectacular moral failures of prominent leaders, pastors, and academicians. When the "great-man-or-woman show" collapses, we see that the person behind the curtain is deeply flawed.

Howard Gardner, professor at Harvard Graduate School, wrote in *Five Minds for the Future* about the importance and nature of the ethical mind. His premise is that because we are living in times of tremendous change and global challenges, we need leaders in business and schools who have the capacity to learn and think differently than leaders have in the past. He proposes five particular cognitive abilities, one of them being the ethical mind.[3] He and his research team found that leaders with an ethical mind:

1) Had parents who raised their children in an environment where morals and open-mindedness were normative;

2) Had values that were not undermined during their school and early adult years;

3) Believed in the mission of their organizations and were able to overcome odds for the benefit of the organizations;

---

2. Wilson, "Cross and Covenant," 222–24.

3. The other four minds are the disciplinary mind, the synthesizing mind, the creating mind, and the respectful mind. See Gardner, *Five Minds*.

4) Had mentors or were influenced by anti-mentors (persons they didn't want to emulate);

5) Were able to speak truth to power, consulting with others and being prepared to resign or be fired in the process; and

6) At the end of the day would do the right thing to contribute to improving conditions in the world.[4]

I spent seven hours interviewing Larry Shelton; the interviews were taken verbatim and checked for accuracy with him. He thought the interviews were in preparation for my part in his retirement party.[5] I began asking him to tell the story of his life and then I concluded with some specific questions about theological education, the church, and his legacy. From these interviews, I will illustrate each of the above six points by using representative stories from Shelton's life to illustrate his ethical mind; he is a covenant theologian who speaks and walks as one.

Has an Ethical and Open-Minded Upbringing

Bernard Bass and Ronald Riggio, in *Transformational Leadership*, reviewed the research literature on the correlation of one's family upbringing to having a transformational leadership style.[6] They wrote, "Highly transformational executives came from families who stressed high standards of excellence along with strong, supportive homes."[7] Persons who grew up with moral and spiritual values as a consistent part of their home life are less likely to act unethically as leaders. Shelton was the only child in a family of ministers in the Wesleyan Holiness tradition:

> My life story begins before I was born. Dad grew up in the Appalachian Mountains in Eastern Kentucky in a family of 8. His

4. This synopsis is condensed from Fryer, "The Ethical Mind."

5. I do interviews for persons who want to preserve their story and legacy, so this was my gift to him upon his retirement. I asked Dr. Shelton if I could use parts of his story for an article, and I checked to make sure some stories were okay to tell.

6. Transformational Leadership theory is the most researched, standardized, and reviewed leadership theory found in all parts of the globe and in all types of professions. A transformational leader exhibits idealized influence, inspirational motivation, intellectual stimulation, and individualized consideration. For further information, see Bass and Stogdill, *Handbook of Leadership*.

7. Bass and Riggio, *Transformational Leadership*, 144.

mother died when his youngest sister was 11 days old. Father was a mountain preacher and circuit rider, a farmer and brick maker. His mother died during the depression and the family was destitute. My dad, Raymond Samuel Shelton, began preaching when he was 16 in the mountains. He went to God's Bible School in Cincinnati. My dad was in the Pilgrim Holiness tradition. My mother was born in Hendersonville, NC. She grew up and went to college at Marion College Wesley Methodist, and became a teacher. She was a devoted Christian and committed to the church her whole life. She was a leader, an ordained deaconess in the Wesleyan Methodist Church.

We lived in Winnsboro, South Carolina. We went to different churches and my dad preached from point to point. My mother sang and played the piano. I grew up in the very inner belly of the church and that's really the core of the life that I knew. And though the church I grew up in was part of a very legalistic holiness movement known for its notion of separateness, I learned how to find ways around the legalism.

I was an only child. It was a lot of pressure, though I didn't perceive it. I was inwardly motivated. I wasn't greatly athletic, but I could hold my own. In wrestling I always won my weight class in Physical Education, but I couldn't go out for a team because competitive sports were worldly. I remember in 9th grade I realized that I couldn't go to football or baseball games because they were worldly amusements. But if there was a practical purpose connected to education that required me to go, then I could go. So I decided to join the band so I could go to the ball games. I decided to play the clarinet and learned to play. For 3 years I played in the HS band and went to most of the games and had a great time.

When I was a senior and was going to order class rings, it was worldly apparel, so it became an issue for those in our church. We had an active youth group and my mother was the force behind it. We couldn't get the rings. I found out that they had class pins. The issue wasn't the gold but wearing something around the finger, so we proposed to church elders that we order class pins and they approved it.

During the summer between high school and college I came to a real faith renewal. I began to realize that I needed to rethink my values. God was working with me in different ways. I made a definite recommitment to the calling God wanted for my life. I needed to go in the direction of becoming a minister. My mom and dad were ecstatic: "Thank you Jesus, the prodigal has come home." I always knew what they preferred and what they sensed about my direction, but they never did try to interfere or influence my choices even after I entered the ministry.

Larry Shelton was beloved of his parents and they did not try to force him in any one direction professionally, though they had high expectations for his spiritual and moral behavior. They showed a level of openness in allowing him to pursue his calling, even though the environment promoted an overly legalistic and rigid understanding of what was right and wrong. Despite that, his parents loved and encouraged him. In this setting Shelton credits his parents with influencing him to be a man of integrity and to give his life in service to others.

Overcomes Integrity Challenges during School and Early Adult Years

Iain Mangham, the former head of the School of Management at the University of Bath in a chapter on "Leadership, Ethics, and Integrity," concluded from his experience and research that integrity and selflessness were "crucial qualities of leadership."[8] Referring to the work of Joseph L. Badaracco and Richard Ellsworth (1989), Mangham noted that these leadership scholars and practitioners believed that integrity was "at the very heart of understanding what leadership is. For them, integrity suggests wholeness and coherence. It also suggests 'rightness, a sense of moral soundness.'"[9]

> I learned a major life lesson at Pfeiffer College. I became more focused than I might have been on grades. I wanted the highest grades I could get to go onto seminary and maybe on to a doctorate. Part of my value system was to get straight A's. One semester I took a literature class, World Literature, and the second semester I was to take the American Novel. The professor was extremely rigorous. On the first exam I made a B+, and it rocked my world. I had to buckle down. I did make an A, but I made the decision that for the sake of my GPA I didn't think I could make an A the second semester, so I took a different course. It really gave me a sense of shame that I had let my values to get grades supersede my path for a life-changing, phenomenal course. I shouldn't have worried about grades, but instead focused on the quality of the course. It changed a value in me that reshaped my educational

---

8. Mangham, "Leadership, Ethics, and Integrity," 44.
9. Ibid.

journey—don't ever avoid anything simply to get a better grade, which is an absolute distortion of educational values. It was a deep life lesson.

After college I applied to seminaries and went to Asbury and thought it most closely supported my theological direction. I was still in the holiness movement, though I had very strongly rethought the legalistic issue through college years, and I came out with moderate views on legalism. I was bothered by the inconsistences of external issues like women not cutting their hair or wearing makeup and jewelry, yet men could have expensive watches and suits and cars. The issue of consistency was a theme that mattered to me.

Asbury was really transformational for me. There I encountered inductive Bible study for the first time. I took a course from Robert A. Traina on Romans and another course on the Theology of the Reformation by Kenneth Kinghorn, and I had a gestalt. Somehow, working through Romans 7 on justification by faith and faith alone and studying Luther hit me about midnight one night, and I couldn't go to bed. I was still sitting in my chair at daylight and I was almost in shock. I didn't sleep well for two weeks. One thing after another would hit and things connected, and questions answered, like fireworks going off in my brain. It was probably the most transformational experience I've ever had in my life. My faith took new shape understanding relationship issues, how the text works, what faith is all about. It wasn't subject matter but a whole new methodology of looking at truth through God and Christ's interpersonal relationship and not through propositions. That put me on a completely different path that I was able to follow.

In January 1968 I started teaching in the School of Religion at Azusa. I hit it off with students and had a good time. I was also hired as the Youth Pastor at Reese Memorial Pilgrim Holiness church, which was two blocks from Pasadena College. Vangie and I were right in the middle of the Jesus Movement, and the church gave us a two-story building to start a coffee house. We made bean bags to sit on. We had carpet and black lights. We'd bring in music groups and the thing grew to about 100–120 kids on Friday night, many right off the street. The coffee house was a powerful force. Kids were getting saved every week. Eventually it raised the hackles of the traditional church members—one of the guys on the board was not a fan of the youth programs. He challenged me, "Larry, what are you going to do if some Sunday morning, we start getting all these hippies walking down the aisle of our church?" I said, "Richard, if you're going to sit beside them in heaven, you might as well get used to sitting beside them now."

Larry Shelton throughout his life has been a man of integrity. Though the legalistic environment of the holiness tradition was troubling to him, he did not waver from a deep sense of purpose to be of service of God, not just in his actions but with an internal compass to walk the talk, especially under pressure to succeed and to conform.

Believes in an Organization's Mission and Is Able to Overcome Odds

Gary Yukl, author of *Leadership in Organizations*, reviews the research and concludes that successful leaders "are more interested in building up the organization than in personal aggrandizement or domination over others."[10] Their personal interests are subordinated to helping an organization fulfill its mission and to building effective relationships. Jim Collins, in his widely read book *From Good to Great*, refers to these humble and mission-oriented leaders as exemplary Level Five leaders.[11] Bennis and Thomas, well-known leadership experts and coaches, note that the essential skills needed today include integrity with a strong set of values, commitment to an organization's mission, as well as an adaptive capacity, which is "an almost magical ability to transcend adversity, with all its attendant stresses, and to emerge stronger than before."[12] Even as a young man, Shelton showed promise as a leader and was willing and able to help an organization grow, even at personal cost. He believed in their missions, whether camps or colleges.

> During my sophomore year at Pilgrim Bible College, I was the district youth president. One thing we accomplished was to purchase a youth camp. It was just a piece of land that had a lake and seven acres. I gave leadership to the Board that developed it, and then I left and went to seminary before it was totally developed. We contacted a professor at North Carolina State in public recreation, and he designed the youth camp for us, and we began to implement the plan. It's still being developed. It's a major conference center in the south, and now it has 100 acres in prime area in NC, very

---

10. Yukl, *Leadership in Organizations*, 202.
11. Collins, *Good to Great*.
12. Bennis and Thomas, *Geeks and Geezers*, 121.

rural (though accessible at the time) known as the NC Wesleyan Youth camp.

My first year teaching at Azusa was hard because I was trying to dig out as I went. I had large classes, 30–50 college students, and I clicked with the students. I spent a lot of time with them interacting with them. We developed some close relationships. After the second year, the graduation guest was Dale Evans Rogers. When the awards came, I'd been selected by students as Teacher of the Year and Dale Evans came up and gave me a hug. I was blown away. I had seven years there with a very productive and effective ministry to students. I taught inductive Bible studies, church history, and biblical theology—general education Intro to Religion. I'd have 100 students in general-education courses; it was a stimulating time.

By about September 1970 I was approached by administration to become the Director of Spiritual Life for the University. I accepted and did it for three years; it was a chaplain-type role. It was during the Jesus Movement and in '72 the college revivals broke out across the country. They started at Asbury in the college chapel. Students came forward and confessed and there was a full-blown student revival. Asbury Chapel went on for 2–3 nights and days.

I got in touch with the Asbury chaplain, and I invited someone to come out to share at Azusa. We had chapel Monday, Wednesday, and Friday. I introduced the student body president from Asbury; he began to tell us about the blessings, the work of the Holy Spirit, lives transformed. We had a simple invitation and students lined up. Chapel continued on and we shut down classes for the day. Students were confessing and praying. It went on into the dorms and for the rest of the week and across campus. Many went back to home churches and shared and revivals happened in churches. It spread through 150 colleges in the US.

Shelton finished his doctorate, and he and Vangie adopted their daughter, Anna, all the while teaching and serving in a church.

Emotionally exhausted, I was ready for a change. We received an invitation from a Wesleyan church in High Point, North Carolina. The Senior Pastor, Dr. Adrian Grout, a person of dignity and an outstanding preacher, had been the pastor for 36 years. In the early '70s, they needed someone to build staff. I was invited to develop the staff there at High Point Wesleyan. It was one of the largest Wesleyan churches at the time, with 600–700 attendees (which is large for holiness standards), and *Christian Life* named it one of the ten fastest-growing churches in America.

I went. I felt it was the right thing to do, and Allison was born at High Point. For three years we had a profound, far-reaching ministry. Vangie got her baptism as a ministry leader. I hired seven people and built the music, educational, and youth ministry until it became the second-largest church in the denomination.

At the same time John Wesley College in Greensboro, a Bible college, hired me as a half-time religion professor. After two or three years, they asked me to be the dean. So I worked at church and I taught. I got the college stabilized. It was located on a very valuable piece of property; I found new campus property at High Point, and I sold their current property and bought the new one and it canceled all their debts. I helped John Wesley Bible College get its accreditation and I got the campus moved to its High Point location, which saved their lives. They are still going strong and they're keeping current. The whole ministry at High Point was many-faceted, but it did wear us out.

Larry Shelton is very visionary, and when he believes in something, he puts time, energy, and talents into taking an organization to the next level. Even as a young college student, he was involved in camping ministries, churches, or Christian schools. At each place, he helped the organization flourish, often with little fanfare for his accomplishments.

Is Influenced by Mentors

Mentors have become a recognized component in the development of successful leaders. Jennifer Dziczkowski reviewed the literature on mentoring and leadership development and noted that "Many of the world's finest and most successful leaders have trusted mentors. Mentoring has emerged as a means to cultivate the leadership skills of current and future leaders."[13] Mentoring increases self-esteem, self-awareness and insight, improves professional skills, and reduces stress. The most effective leaders have mentors and are mentors. Larry Shelton had several mentors throughout his life who influenced him and whom he trusted and admired. He also became a mentor to others.

At Pfeiffer College, I took speech classes and oral interpretation—Bob Grubbs was the professor in that area. I was going to go into

13. Dziczkowski, "Mentoring and Leadership Development," 351.

ministry so they were good classes. Bob Grubbs had a very strong influence on me. He was a great guy. He tapped into the intellectual side of my faith issues and challenged me to think along the lines of my own self-identity. What is truth? What is reality? How do you evaluate the world around you? He stimulated a dialogue about the meaning of life.

My English professors were also excellent models for me. For the first time, in my literature classes I really faced a truly superior level of intellectual activity. They were superb intellectuals. Though not necessarily faith-oriented, they offered a real challenge to me to understand the level of discourse, the meanings and concepts being discussed and analyzed in lit classes. They gave me a very strong interest in liberal arts and intellectual issues—concerns about the meaning of life and philosophical issues.

It put an exclamation point at the end of my legalistic tendencies when I got to Asbury. There you had people who reflected a depth of spirituality and character that was way more sophisticated than I was accustomed to. A number of world-class leaders in spiritual development came to visit and we were exposed to them. One of those was E. Stanley Jones, a great missionary to India. He had a three-day retreat he called a Christian Ashram, and I had the opportunity to go through the Ashram under his guidance. There was a specific structure; during the open-heart period we would tell our stories and at the end was the period of the overfollowing heart. It was my first experience with everyone going around and being brutally honest with unloading their heart. He was tremendously redemptive in how he led it.

I was also exposed to women in Pilgrim Holiness and Wesleyan women in ministry, but at Asbury I was exposed to a whole new level of world-class women in theology and teaching who came through Methodism. I was thoroughly impressed with these women and others. The professors I had were phenomenally mature and it challenged me at a whole deeper level of intellectual curiosity and compassionate ministries all integrated together.

Teaching at Azusa, I was John Wimber's first theology professor after he converted. We formed a bond through his college years. He took several courses from me and the mentoring was both ways. I came out of such an innocent background. He was at Yorba Linda Friends for several years. He had me down to do teaching at his church. Every Sunday he did an introduction of new believers, and he had 10–15 every Sunday brought before congregation. He began a network of small groups that was estimated at 2000 people. We stayed in touch for a long time.

Shelton commented that what kept him going through various hardships over the years were his faith and his friends. He has deep and loyal friends that he has kept throughout his life, and he is a mentor and friend to many both colleagues and students. He believed in the bonds forged in community with mentors and friends.

Is Able to Speak Truth to Power Despite the Risk

Edwin Friedman, in his ground-breaking book *A Failure of Nerve*, wrote about the well-differentiated leader who was able to stay non-reactive in the face of adversity and still do the right thing for the sake of the organization. He writes, "I mean someone who can manage his or her own reactivity to the automatic reactivity of others, and therefore be able to take stands at the risk of displeasing."[14] Very little is as hard in leadership as speaking truth to power when job security, status, or future possibilities are at stake. Shelton's moral courage was life-long.

> David McKenna from Seattle Pacific wanted me to be the dean of the School of Religion at Seattle Pacific University in Washington. I had a very good interview and was hired. The challenge and the opportunity were overwhelming. The religion department was getting at cross purposes with the university's goals and objectives. He wanted me to straighten out the situation. If I knew what I know now, I'm not sure I would have jumped at the situation. Biblical scholars and theologians don't like to be straightened out. I started in September of 1978. I was to reorganize the School of Religion.
>
> The Seattle Pacific School of Religion had very great potential to develop as a real player in theological education and scholarship. It was also a real professional opportunity for me. Despite philosophical and personality conflicts, we were able to function together fairly well. We hired four to five new faculty. Ultimately with maturity I was learning how to get along with the diverse faculty and how to deal with the whole issue of turning a traditional theological view into more contextualized theological thinking. It was a real challenge. Some of the things threatening to happen were a significant threat to the school. I was also teaching probably a 60% load. All that stress went a long way towards making my heart transplant necessary. It was so stressful.

14. Friedman, *A Failure of Nerve*, 14.

Later Dr. David LeShana asked me to consider coming down as academic dean to Western Evangelical Seminary in Oregon. I served under him at Seattle Pacific, so we knew each other. He also wanted me to teach theology. I came to WES in 1994 and there was way more water under the bridge than was divulged to me. I knew the seminary had to be on firm ground. It was on probation with the Association of Theological Schools, and there were firings and economic instability. My job was to get it off probation. We developed and submitted 3 new degree programs—Certificate in Spiritual Formation, Masters of Arts in Christian Ministries, and a cohort Master of Ministry Leadership. We got a couple of notations off the record. Then LeShana told me that in order to get financially solvent, we would have to merge with George Fox University.

A small committee was put together with a couple of board members and the two presidents of George Fox and the seminary. The meetings went on for a year. Very few people knew what was going on. I fortunately found out that they were not going to issue contracts for the current faculty. The Counseling program was going to have another life, but in the merger they were going to revamp the seminary. The committee decided that they were going to open up the seminary positions and offer first dibs to George Fox religion faculty, and then have a search for what was left. That crossed a line for me. The identity, mission, and faculty of the seminary were going to be dismantled for parts.

In the next larger meeting of the Oversight Committee, I brought it up. When it became known to a wider group, people protested and said this was wrong. So the seminary got a second life, but that was it for me; I crossed the line. During this same time period, I was having heart transplant surgery in Seattle. I was in the hospital room and I got out of the hospital and dressed and went across town to make a video on observations and recommendations on the merger issues to be delivered in time for a George Fox board meeting coming up. I paid out all my chips trying to save the seminary in February 1996.

When I was back at the seminary after my transplant, the president and the academic dean came over to the Portland Center (which housed the seminary), and they were walking around. I ran into them in the lobby downstairs, and they confronted me. They said, "We don't feel you can continue as dean of the seminary after your contract expires this summer." They said I was against the merger. I wasn't against it, but I was against collapsing the seminary into GFU without any identity and dismissing the

> faculty. They said in the end, "You can't function effectively and relate to GFU, so we'll end your contract as dean"; they fired me on the spot. It took a while to chew through that one. Eventually you just realize that it's counter-productive. "What's past is past. You need to move on." I cared about the mission of the seminary; it was worth the cost.

Larry Shelton has been willing to speak truth to power, even if it meant losing his job or his status. Both at Seattle Pacific and George Fox University, he tackled some daunting challenges, which threatened his job and his health. His persistence in speaking truth to those in power is illustrated in his life.

At the End of the Day Does the Right Thing to Improve the Lives of Others

Those leaders who live selflessly and who notice and empower others to improve their lives and their condition in the world are ethical leaders. Michael Fullen, a professor and management expert, in his *Leading in a Culture of Change*, calls it moral purpose. When a leader has moral purpose, he or she attends both to making a difference in lives and organizations and also to doing so with kindness and integrity. Effective leaders don't just talk about necessary change; they are able to orchestrate the steps to get there. Fullen writes, "Commitment to the environment and to the broader global community as part and parcel of the long-term success of the organization is moral purpose writ large."[15] James MacGregor Burns noted that, "At the highest stage of moral development persons are guided by near-universal ethical principles of justice such as equality of human rights and respect for individual dignity."[16] Larry has made unique contributions to others because of his ability to hear and understand the voices of those sometimes marginalized.

> One of the young women who was a student at Azusa and who was mentored by Vangie was Leslie Brown.[17] She was finishing college and she was pretty mixed up. She had a hard life, came to the Lord and was transformed, and Vangie did a lot of work with her. She graduated and moved back to Utah and got involved in

---

15. Fullen, *Leading in a Culture of Change*, 25.
16. Burns, *Leadership*, 42.
17. Not her real name.

prostitution and drugs in Salt Lake for several years. We lost touch. One Sunday while we were still in Glendora seven to eight years later, on Easter Sunday morning probably about 1976, we got a call at six am. I answered the phone, "Larry? " She was so stoned, it took me awhile to figure out who she was. She wanted to meet us. We arranged a place in Pasadena. We met her before service at ten am at a park. She showed up and she was unrecognizable. She was stoned and a hooker. She came over talked and cried. We established a connection with her for later in the afternoon. I made an appointment to pick her up down in a seedy part of Pasadena. I showed up at the address and a big guy answers the door. I rescued her from the place. They thought I was a client. She stayed with us to sober up, and we were able to get her connected with a street ministry in Honolulu. It took six months to get her healthy. She went over and stayed for three years and became a wonderful Christian. She met a guy in Northern California and got married. She's happy with two kids.

When I was waiting for a heart, Leslie sent me a letter. It was a love letter. She wrote, "I told God if you need a heart, if there is any way God could use mine I would gladly give it to you." She meant it. Several years ago in Portland at a convention she called me and we caught up and she's a healthy vibrant Christian. You never know what kind of influence we have on people.

I was on the faculty at WES/GFES from 1994 to today, a total of 19 years. I made peace with not being a primary influencer after I was fired from the Dean position, and I sensed I should become more of a mentor and it worked out that way. I especially wanted to serve those who might be overlooked among evangelicals. I mentored Felix Rosales. He was working at the seminary and we put together a conference at Tilikum (a local camp) in 1998, a three-day Hispanic theological conference, and 65 showed up. He developed all kinds of things out of that and the next year he had 120, and it began a movement for him. He's still working to educate Hispanic leaders.

I've supported and stood with the Native American peoples. I got acquainted with Richard Twiss in the late 90s and we developed a model similar to the one I did with Felix. Richard and I put a conference together in early 2000. We called a meeting on Native American studies at Tilikum and we put it together with Ray Levesque. We had 65–70 people for a three-day conference on Native-studies issues. Richard and I did a paper. We made connections and we kept up over the years.

During the Earth and Native American conference here in 2008–9, I really became closely connected to Randy Woodley and he started planning to come back here. At that conference I worked with Richard (Twiss) and Randy and Terry LeBlanc and Robert Francis. We had about 120 persons. That really formed a significant part of the foundation for Randy's contribution here in the Northwest after coming from Kentucky. He had a property called Eloheh (Harmony Way), which he developed as a Native American L'Abri type school and community. It was near Lexington and Wilmore, Kentucky. He was terrorized off the land—rednecks didn't want Indians setting up camp. Randy had called me and wanted to know if he came out here could he find a place and do some adjunct teaching. He moved out and found a place to rent in Newberg. His whole ministry that supported him fell apart when he left Kentucky. I helped get him started as an adjunct, and then he was hired on at the seminary.

Larry is a scholar who committed himself not only to academic excellence, but to compassionate engagement with the injustices of this world. He did not just write about a relational theology of love; he lived it.

Conclusion

In our postmodern environment extraordinary wizards are not nearly as impressive as ordinary men and women who are ethical and get the job done on behalf of others. People are not looking for a charismatic wonder but for an authentic human being whose walk and talk are one and the same thing. They are searching for persons whose life story communicates truth. Larry Shelton himself wrote, "What *is* effective is the interpersonal sharing of the transformational experience of our own faith."[18] Today words are not as powerful as lives.

Shelton says about effective leaders,

> I think in looking at the people that have been most effective and influential down through the centuries, they are those people who were not seeking to build kingdoms, but who sought to enrich Christ's love in people. The great leaders are not necessarily those leaders who have formed systems and cathedrals, but people who have sought to increase the sum of love in the world. I think it has to do with learning to incarnate in any structures that we have the

---

18. Shelton, *Cross and Covenant*, 2.

character of Christ—teaching, leading Bible studies, exemplifying in our own behavior a model of Jesus Christ.

Today's successful academic leaders are those who teach and study, lead with integrity, are dedicated to the mission they serve, and have an uncanny ability to transcend adversity. I believe Larry Shelton, the man behind the curtain of his successes, has these qualities and abilities and is an inspiration to scholars, pastors, and Christian leaders.

2

Finding a Home in Shelton's Vision of the Atonement

by Steve Sherwood

MY EXPERIENCE WITH LARRY Shelton's work, both through his role as my doctoral advisor and his book, *Cross and Covenant,* has been more pastoral than academic. While I found Shelton's work to be keenly insightful theologically, it was where that insight touched my own faith crisis and the struggles of those I interact with as a youth-ministry practitioner and professor that I feel most indebted to him. I begin with a bit of that story because I believe that my "atonement crisis" mirrors much of the push and pull of the atonement debates of the last decade or more, and I believe Shelton's help to me points to the larger role he could, should, and, I believe, ultimately will have for the church at large.

During the first 35 years of my life, all of which was spent within the textured world of evangelical Christianity, I would not have said I had even the slightest bit of tension or angst about the atonement. I certainly didn't feel as if there was an "atonement war" going on in my life or the worlds in which I moved. I don't know that I could even have articulated a distinct atonement theory that was foundational for my faith and ministry.

That changed fairly rapidly for me around the turn of the century. The precipitating cause of what became my theological crisis was a several-year stretch where I was asked to speak for a month at a time to several hundred adolescents a week at Young Life summer camps. It was on stage, night after night, for several weeks in a row each summer that I ran into trouble.

FINDING A HOME IN SHELTON'S VISION OF THE ATONEMENT

Young Life, in my 28 years of experience with the organization, first as a volunteer and then as a staff person, was a broadly evangelical ministry (I worked alongside Calvinists, Catholics, Anabaptists and more) with a keen focus on evangelizing adolescents and inviting them to personal response. In local ministries, approaches to evangelism reflected our organizational diversity. In our camp speaking, however, we tended to follow an approach that looked a lot like the Campus Crusade's *Four Spiritual Laws* or John Stott's *Basic Christianity*, a book that had impacted many in our leadership in the 70s and early 80s. Essentially, when we spoke at camp, we gave a message based around the penal substitutionary theory of atonement, or, as we called it "the simple Gospel."

So, at the heart of each week, I was on stage saying things like,

- God cannot look upon sin, cannot tolerate it, and therefore, cannot look upon you. He turns away from you in your sin.
- God's heart of love would reach out to you, but his heart of justice turns away. In fact, in his justice, God desires to punish and destroy you because of your sin.
- Just as God despises us in our sin, as Jesus hangs on the cross, taking on our sin, Jesus becomes repulsive to God. God turns away from his Son because of our sin.

On the surface, as the weeks of speaking went by, I was displaying the requisite public confidence and passion, but inwardly I was becoming less convinced that I fully believed these kinds of statements. Furthermore, I was less and less sure they made sense to the increasingly postmodern audience I was speaking to.

Yes, I believed God was deeply distressed by our sin and we were in need of the forgiveness that the cross and resurrection provided, but did God truly turn away from us? Was wrath the primary emotion of God the Father at the cross? If so, and Jesus responded in love at the cross, how did this not pit two members of the Trinity against one another, with one moving in righteous wrath and the other in self-giving love? Was the cross really about God's desire for revenge, a revenge God was willing to exact upon the Son, just so long as someone poured out blood to assuage God's anger?

Sometimes these questions were articulated by me in my own head, but often they came from young people in their teens and twenties for whom the "narrative" of penal substitutionary atonement (PSA) seemed jarringly divorced from the narrative of Jesus that they found in the Gospels. And, these questions were just the beginning. Many more would follow. Before I knew it, what began with my desire to clarify my talks had turned into tinkering with my theology and finally led to my questioning the viability of penal substitution as a framework for understanding atonement.

I also found that some of my friends, and others writing in the broader evangelical world, were asking the same questions. I was deeply encouraged by this and invigorated by the questions, but often left unsettled by the answers I seemed to find. For a good number of my friends, and seemingly, a fair number of others, a turning away from the legal, wrathful connotations of penal substitution meant turning away from the atonement altogether. During those years, the alternative to penal substitution I encountered most was the Moral Exemplar approach, which borrowed heavily from Rene Girard and his theories of mimetic violence. While I resonated with elements of this approach, it seemed pretty toothless in terms of dealing with the profound depths of human sin, our need for forgiveness, and the actual ways in which the biblical writers talked about the cross. Yes, Jesus is certainly our example, but is that all the cross is about?

I found myself betwixt and between. I could no longer find a theological place to stand within penal substitution, but I still believed there was a strong need to hold to the sentiment of "nothing but the blood of Jesus" that had formed my faith since my youth. I needed the cross to be more than an example of the depravity of human power structures and the depths of Jesus' self-giving love (though I think there's great truth in both of those statements). And it seemed to me that Scripture did not frame the cross exclusively in those terms.

I began finding a way out of the wilderness through a Fuller Seminary class with the late Ray Anderson, in which I was introduced to the work of T. F. Torrance. Shortly thereafter, I also had the honor of being taken on by Larry Shelton as a doctoral candidate. In one of our first conversations, he said, almost in passing, "The penal substitution folks think they own the concept of 'substitution.' Any view of the cross in which Jesus does for us what we cannot do for ourselves involves Jesus as our 'substitute.' I have trouble with the penal framing of the cross, but utterly cling to its substitutionary nature."

I was home. Or, at least, I now had a clear hope that there was a place out there to come home to.

Larry Shelton roots his atonement theology in the Old Testament concept of *covenant*. For Shelton, the concept of covenant permeates the narrative revealed in the text, even when specific covenant language is absent: "The specific covenants made between God and certain persons for particular purposes operate within the overall context of the general covenant fellowship between Yahweh and creation. We see the reality of covenant relationship even when the word covenant does not appear."[1] What do we know of God's irreducible essence? If Barth is correct that we can only know that of God which God has revealed in history, then at the core, from beginning to end, Shelton believes we see a God who moves in covenant faithfulness and initiative.

This foundational experience of a covenant-entering God provides a conceptual and experiential continuity from Old Testament to New often missing in Christian theology. Shelton does not see Jesus' institution of a "new covenant" as a replacement of the old, or an inauguration of a new *kind* of covenant: "The new covenant in Christ is related to those of the community of Israel; they share the same family tree."[2] His use of the phrase 'family tree' here is significant, for Shelton sees both the covenant and the ensuing Law (Torah) as fundamentally relational in nature.

Rightly conceived, then, Israel and its covenant laws create a true "community in relationship with God that is distinct from any culture before or since. To conceive of issues that affect this relationship, such as sin or salvation, in terms other than interpersonal ones distorts and impoverishes the richness of the covenant conception of righteousness. This is not to say that atonement does not deal with issues of civil law and lawbreaking, but that interpersonal covenant reconciliation is clearly the prevailing conceptualization."[3]

This rooting of atonement theology within the framework of relational covenantal reconciliation immediately resonated with me and I believe speaks well to a postmodern audience. Others have noted that one paradigmatic shift for postmoderns has been away from a sense in which sin is experienced as a matter of *right/wrong* or *guilt/innocence* and toward a sense of *being alienated and alone*. I find this significant. I believe it represents a shift away from a theoretical dealing with an abstract standard and towards an intuitive sense that *what is wrong* with us (sin) is fundamentally a relational issue. We experience sin as dysfunctional or estranged relationship with God, others, creation, self. Were Shelton's insistence that issues of

1. Shelton, *Cross and Covenant*, 38.
2. Ibid., 42.
3. Ibid., 47.

sin, forgiveness, and atonement are best understood through the relational lens of covenant correct, then this postmodern dis-ease is exactly what one would expect to find in a humanity in need of atonement. We would not primarily feel guilty: we would feel alone, and broken relationally. And, in fact, we do.

As I reflected upon my youth-ministry experiences, this seemed to be exactly what the postmodern youth I served articulated as their experience. When interacting with them about talks centered around alienation or relational rupture, they resonated absolutely and profoundly. As talks turned to forensic guilt before a righteous judge, connections frayed and ideas failed to make sense. Typically I, and other adults within Young Life, would write this off to "kids resisting in their hearts the truth," but I began to believe that there was something true and honest about their responses. They *experienced* sin relationally, both in their interpersonal human relationships and as alienation from God, much more viscerally than in a sense of having violated a legal code.

Additionally, the centrality of the covenant motif means there is no sense that God interacted in the Old Testament in one way with humanity via the nation of Israel only to shift gears in a new direction with the coming of Jesus. This dichotomy, often seen in Christian preaching and evangelism, comes when the relationship of Israel to God in the Old Testament is viewed first and fundamentally through the Deuteronomical system of law and sacrifice and not initially through the lens of covenant. Yes, there are obligations for both ethical conduct and ritualistic sacrifice throughout Torah, but we err when we see those as the determinants of God's relationship (or not) with the Israelites. Shelton asserts, "God says in Amos 3:2a, 'You only have I chosen of all the families of the earth.' His care and provision for them in the covenant community led them toward the covenant goal of *shalom* (keeping Torah). In this relationship of community fellowship with God, Israel experienced his care and provision. On the other hand, with relationship comes responsibility."[4] Or, as Leon Morris succinctly put it, "The Law had its place in the purposes of God, but that place was not the bringing of salvation (or inclusion in covenant relationship). God made that abundantly clear in his dealing with Abraham . . . the law was 430 years too late."[5]

---

4. Ibid., 45.
5. Morris, *The Atonement*, 36.

God does not give Israel the *Law* to provide for them a means (which God knows they will fail to utilize) to *enter into* relationship with God. Rather, the *Law* provides the framework of what *covenant relationship* looks like, a relationship God has already placed them in. Again, if Shelton's argument is accurate, another postmodern obstacle to faith is overcome. In conversation with young people who have not grown up with Christian (and, particularly PSA) presuppositions, I notice they find atonement theology wildly confusing. "So, in the Old Testament, God spends thousands of years demanding moral performance and responding in wrath when it's not provided, and then all of a sudden becomes loving and grace-giving when Jesus shows up? What did he do for those 400 years in between, attend some sort of divine anger-management class? You're saying God loves me infinitely, but also desires to destroy me, but God is willing not to destroy me as long as God can kill God's Son instead? Why would an infinitely wise God set up a system like this?!" In Shelton's covenantal framework, God moves toward us to initiate relationship (covenant), provides the law to give that relationship shape, mourns and is angered by the destruction of that relationship (by sin), and moves again to bring reconciliation. God is consistently and essentially relational in this covenant action.

This is what real relationships look like! Real marriages or parent/child relationships are not broken by the objective breaking of lists of rules, but by damage done (lack of trust, unfaithfulness, willful hurt) within the relationship. And reconciliation must take on a relational flavor. Merely taking out the trash after all, or repaying the financial debt, or vowing to do better next time, cannot bring reconciliation. The wronged, hurt party must move toward the wrongdoer to initiate reconciliation. Restitution, or changed behavior, is certainly helpful, but they, in and of themselves cannot trigger reconciliation. Only a grace-giving movement on the part of the wronged can facilitate healing.

But doesn't the pervasive nature of the sacrificial system, both in the number of prescribed sacrifices and their relentless repetition, season after season, year after year, century after century, suggest otherwise? Surely, they *do* point to a God withholding relationship, waiting to be appeased, no?

As I began to struggle with the logic of penal substitution, one of the significant arguments "for" PSA was, "the just requirement for retribution is hardwired into all of YHWH's interactions with Israel. The sacrificial system is proof of that." It seems true that if retributive appeasement is at the heart of sacrifice in the Old Testament, then it is clearly logical that this is what is at play in the cross. For me, it was Shelton's treatment of the mechanisms and theology of the sacrificial cultus in Israel that was most helpful in reframing my view of the atonement.

Certainly, Shelton is not alone in claiming that this view of how Israel in the OT viewed sacrifice is a misreading of the nature of God's relationship in the OT. NT Wright and the loosely connected others who make up the "New Perspective on Paul" have drawn needed attention to the likelihood that *covenantal nomism* characterized the Jewish view of their relationship with God vis-à-vis Torah. Shelton, however, is the first I encountered from the perspective that deals extensively with the very nature and mechanisms of sacrifice themselves to build his case.

In speaking to this issue of the nature of sacrifice in the Old Testament, Colin Gunton has noted, "When different cultures and religions do the same *kind* of thing—ritually slaughtering animals—they are not necessarily doing the *same* thing. The contexts affect, perhaps sometimes determine, the meaning."[6] In essence, just because other ancient cultures offered sacrifices to placate the gods or ameliorate their wrath, that is not necessarily what Israel was doing, or what God required. Just because, even today, we ache for revenge and retribution when we are wronged, it does not necessarily follow that God aches for retribution in anything like the same way. Shelton states, "While pagan religious sacrifices display a concern to propitiate, appease, or bribe to counteract a god's vengeance, Israel reinterpreted sacrificial practice in a countercultural way; the sacrifices were used in the context of covenant maintenance and renewal as a divinely appointed way of dealing with sin."[7]

Shelton provides an extensive look at the mechanics of sacrifice in the Deuteronomical codes. While all of this material is helpful, two points are of particular note here. First, let us explore the "laying on of hand(s)" by the priest on the animal to be sacrificed, and second, the relationship of propitiation and expiation, particularly as seen in the sprinkling of blood around the Holy of Holies on the Day of Atonement.

Shelton argues that inadequate attention has been given to the difference, in Israel's theology and practice, between the laying on of one hand vs. the laying on of two. "The laying on of *both* hands signifies the transference of something from one thing or person to another"[8]—for example, the

---

6. Gunton, *The Actuality of Atonement*, 121.
7. Shelton, *Cross and Covenant*, 63.
8. Ibid., 55.

placing of the sins of the people concretely upon the animal to be sacrificed. What is of utmost importance, however, is that as described in Leviticus 1–7, it is *not* the animal to be sacrificed that has two hands placed upon it. Two hands are placed by the priest upon the head of the *scapegoat*, the animal driven out from the community, but not killed. It is the scapegoat who receives the sins of the nation transferred upon it.

If the sacrificed animal is not being slaughtered, then, because it has become the object of God's wrath because of its now sinful state, what *is happening* here? Shelton argues that while transference of sin has happened with the scapegoat, the goat offered in sacrifice represents the people's *identification with* the offering of blood. "By identifying with the animal, the collective lives of the nation are symbolically offered up and incorporated into the holy so that they now have community with God."[9] "Because of the commitment of the offerer's life to what is holy (via identification with the sacrificed animal), God did not simply consider the offering *as if* it were the offerer; it *really was* the offerer."[10] Anyone who has ever learned to understand *justification* through the mnemonic device, "just *as if* I hadn't sinned" can begin to see the significance of this distinction.

Shelton drives this point home that the blood of the sacrifice represented an identification with the people offering their lives to God, rather than a transference where the sacrifice became the sin of the people, by looking at the use to which blood was put inside the Holy of Holies on the Day of Atonement. He maintains that the primary function of blood throughout the ceremony is to represent washing and cleansing, which would be impossible if the blood were now utterly contaminated by the collective sin of the people.

From the beginning, "the preparations for the ceremony emphasize the need for ritual cleanness,"[11] Shelton reminds us. The priest washes himself, puts on freshly washed linen garments, and provides personal sacrifices, all to ensure his personal purity. Then he sprinkles blood throughout the Holy of Holies, upon the Mercy Seat (Lev 16:14), upon the atonement cover (15:15) and finally on the horns of the altar and the altar itself to "cleanse and consecrate it from the 'uncleanness of the Israelites.'" (16:18–19). Shelton summarizes by stating, "Notice that the blood does not play the role of appeasing God, nor is it represented as some form of penalty. It

---

9. Ibid., 56.
10. Ibid.
11. Ibid., 61.

simply serves to symbolize the purification of sin from these places that are consecrated for God's use..."[12] Therefore, to view sacrifice in the Old Testament, and consequently at the cross, as the appeasement of God "represents a basic misunderstanding of the nature of sacrifices in the religious life of Israel . . . they are tokens of obedience, not *ex opere operato* bribes that automatically propitiate or appease him."[13]

While few will find it efficacious or appealing to engage a youth-ministry audience with a detailed analysis of the nuances of blood sacrifice in Leviticus, the lessons here can be easily absorbed and incorporated into our presentations of the Gospel. PSA proponents sweepingly summarize their understanding of the function of sacrifice in the OT with statements like, "Just as God required blood to turn away his wrath at sin in the Old Testament, God required blood for humanity's sin at the cross, and Jesus provides it." In a similar way, building upon Shelton's argument, a youth pastor might say, "Just as Israel's sin required God to provide a means for cleansing and expiation, Jesus' blood at the cross represents God's cleansing blood provided for all humanity."

This is just a cursory look at Shelton's atonement work, all of which is helpful to those doing ministry in a postmodern context. I have highlighted a few points where I have found him most helpful. His refusal to give sole proprietorship of the term "substitutionary" to proponents of PSA is the first key contribution, for in doing so he claims a way to hold to a "saved by the blood" nature of the cross that is neither tripped up by the concerns penal substitution raises nor eviscerated by a reductionist view that empties the cross of any real atoning function. He accomplishes this by setting all of the atoning action within a covenant-relational framework that both brings continuity to God's action throughout Scripture and resonates with a postmodern audience. Finally, his treatment of sacrifice demonstrates that, even here, the God of Scripture is a God of relational mercy and not one of legal wrath and retribution. Postmodern evangelicals often speak longingly for a "third way" between the extremes often presented to them. In the case of the atonement, few have offered a more viable, clear and cohesive third way than Dr. Shelton in *Cross and Covenant*.

I have experienced the efficacy of this approach in ministry. Whether in speaking to groups of young people or teaching/training folks for ministry, I have been able to share the core theology that Shelton lays out in *Cross*

---

12. Ibid., 62.
13. Ibid., 63.

and Covenant and have seen the "lights come on" for listeners. They will communicate, "Ah, *this* makes sense to me! There have always been parts of the way that I've heard the Gospel explained that didn't make sense either to my head or to my heart, and this all fits!" In Shelton's work, we have a God who takes sin seriously, who provides a robust description of genuine sacrifice, forgiveness and atonement, all framed within the steadfast covenant love of the God who is for us.

Whereas, previously, I had spoken to young people about a God who turns away from Jesus with the same revulsion God feels for us, I now speak of a God who enters in to cleanse and to heal. I speak of the Trinity's full engagement with Jesus at the cross. I speak of a God who, when establishing the guilt offering in Lev 5, doesn't demand blood, but says, "if the one bringing the offering is too poor to afford a lamb . . . they can bring two doves . . . and if they are too poor to afford two doves, they can bring a cup of flour and the priest will make atonement for them." I speak of a God who looks a lot like the father Jesus describes in Luke 15, one who runs to his son, embraces him, places his symbols of honor upon him (all of which bring shame upon the father) in order to be returned to covenant relationship with the one he loves. I speak these things, and, in my heart, I have no doubts or misgivings—and for that, I am indebted to Larry Shelton.

3

Participation and Dignity

IMPLICATIONS OF A COVENANT THEORY OF THE ATONEMENT FOR THE MISSION OF THE CHURCH

by David R. Wilson

Introduction

R. LARRY SHELTON'S RECENT book, *Cross and Covenant: Interpreting the Atonement for 21st Century Mission*, marks the zenith of more than 40 years of research and writing towards a biblically and theologically cohesive and an ecclesially and culturally engaged presentation of the gospel in contemporary context. His work offers more than simply another atonement theory to add to our compendia of soteriology. Its own exegetical and biblical-theological intent persists in its *implications* for ecclesiological mission and praxis. The daunting yet essential task of cross-cultural contextualization is at the forefront. Subverting longstanding claims regarding the juridical (i.e., penal) and moral exemplar theories of the atonement, Shelton asserts the supreme importance of a covenantal understanding of the atonement for shaping ecclesial identity, worship, proclamation and discipleship.

Intended as a continuation of Shelton's proposals, the present chapter asks, how does a covenantal *understanding* of the atonement[1] lend itself in form and substance to ministry in a cross-cultural landscape, especially concerning the contemporary currents of postmodernism? Some prefatory

---

1. Cf. Collins, "Understanding Atonement."

remarks are requisite for understanding such an attempt in the first place. The first section takes on the ticklish matter of contextualizing to a postmodern cross-cultural situation. (If there is a hint of what might really be called consensus among those who consider postmodern culture worth bothering with in the first place, it is that a thoughtful theological response and the application of this response to the ministry of the Church is vital to its identity and continuing mission.)[2] The second section unpacks the concept of "implications" themselves regarding theology in the light of its object, the Church. The two sections which follow introduce "participation" and "dignity" as sub-themes of a covenant theory of the atonement and as integrative and culturally relevant values for contextualizing the gospel in a postmodern culture. These themes are then looked at in the context of biblical studies for two important areas of evangelism-discipleship: incarnational ministry and biblical apologetics.

Rooting Around in the Things of Postmoderns

In an early scene in the movie *Notting Hill*, Spike, the slovenly flatmate of the lead character William Thacker, walks downstairs and into the kitchen—where William is standing—wearing William's scuba wetsuit and diving goggles. After a brief greeting lacking any explanation from Spike, William's bewilderment gets the best of him:

> WILLIAM: Just incidentally—why are you wearing that?
>
> SPIKE: Ahm—combination of factors really. No clean clothes . . .
>
> WILLIAM: There never will be, you know, unless you actually clean your clothes.
>
> SPIKE: Right. Vicious circle . . . I was like rooting around in your things, and found this, and I thought—cool. Kind of spacey.[3]

This humorous scene might be seen as a parable of the challenge of our situation. There seems to be a vicious circle in the attempts to contextualize

---

2. At this point in the discussion, critical analysis is central to any applications of theology to postmodern culture. As James Barr points out, much of the work being done is more reflective of popular trends than actual analysis of postmodern theory or culture, and is thus lacking in the most crucial of places. See Barr, *History and Ideology in the Old Testament*, 141–78.

3. See *Notting Hill*.

theology and the gospel in a postmodern world. Such attempts often begin with a set of assumptions that inform the questions asked. These questions then lead to the systematization of programmatic responses that are supposed to somehow speak to this new society that has shifted away from four centuries of modernist optimism, positivism, certainty, and the like, to a burgeoning postmodern skepticism, analysis of ideologies, and deconstruction of metanarratives of power and oppression. The process of systematization includes a (systematic if not objective) study of postmoderns—what they want, how they think. These findings are then studied and developed into a bulleted list of propositions that purport to help us relate (ourselves, information, theology, etc.) to this postmodern culture we've been studying.

To a postmodern reading the previous paragraph, the vicious circle probably became apparent after reading "attempts to contextualize . . . in a postmodern world." A modernist may have read the previous paragraph in its entirety and still be thinking, "Hmm, sounds like a good plan, but where's the vicious circle?" The problem here is with our starting point, and that our methodology is always at risk of precluding the very intent of our attempts to contextualize our engagement. In a world that is in the middle of a significant paradigm shift, the clothes of modernism (e.g., objectivist claims, foundationalism, propositionalism) are (or seem) dirty, or at least ill-fitting,[4] so we, in our attempts to fix the problem or bridge the gap, may have "rooted around" in the things of postmoderns (e.g., art, story, authenticity, inclusiveness, social justice), found something that fits, and put it on. But in the end, we have not cleaned our clothes, but rather have come out wearing a wetsuit,[5] which in fact only looks silly to the very community

---

4. This is not to say that all of modernism is irrelevant. It is, however, to say that the modernist epistemology and a devotion to objectivism leading to propositional truth claims requires more than a facelift for communication in a postmodern context. There are those who in fact maintain that postmodernism is a continuation of modernism or even the giving-up on modernism where ability to correct it was lacking. Cf. Barr, *History and Ideology*, 158–59. Barr shows that even some of the postmodern theorists themselves are not so confident in the postmodern project as many of its uncritical adherents. Barr cites Jürgen Habermas, Robert Carroll, and John O'Neill as critics of postmodernism and Richard Rorty and Terry Eagleton as postmodernist critics of postmodernism. Cf. McGrath, *Christian Theology*, 113.

5. An example of this might be churches that read somewhere that postmoderns are "into art," so they paste images of paintings into their presentation slides and hang pictures in the lobby, but keep their propositional preaching, modernistic technological pursuit of "quality" and "excellence," and foundationalist theological approaches to doctrine and ministry. None of these attempts can be judged as bad or wrong in and of

we aimed at reaching in the first place.⁶ When challenged that we'll not have clean clothes until we've cleaned them, we flounder in exasperation, saying, "yeah . . . vicious circle." If that is how we progress, then we are not any more contextualized in our approach and no more relevant than the proverbial wolf in sheep's clothing, with diminishing credibility in an already incredulous culture.

The paragraphs that follow represent an attempt both to empathize with and to empower communities of faith and their leaders and pastors to meaningfully reach a multi-generational setting that includes this nebulous culture we call "postmodern," often complicated even more by a sense of helplessness among those who minister. What is being put forth in this chapter is a call to the Church to minister incarnationally, to humble ourselves, empty ourselves, and enter into communities and cultures with the voice of hope that is the gospel. If we are to minister incarnationally, we must give attention not only to the content of the gospel message for a postmodern culture (or any culture), but to our method of understanding that culture (i.e. cultural exegesis) and our subsequent communication as well.

These are concerns which invoke the questions of participation and dignity discussed below. The call to contextualize theology makes certain assumptions about the requisites of the task. Thus, before we begin, it is of great import that we know and understand what it is we are attempting. We must examine, and often we must suspend our assumptions about even our method of understanding any given culture, and we must pay careful attention to the *telos* of our cultural exegesis. That is to say, that if the *telos* is genuine meaningful contextualization of the gospel, then the starting place for dialogue with the culture which draws our attention must be the culture itself. The very task must be critiqued by the culture towards which it is aimed.⁷

For example, if we were to state, "It is our goal is to *speak to* the postmodern culture with relevance," our very attempt is already characterized

---

themselves, but they should not be considered "postmodern."

6. For example, not only is there less corporate identity, cohesiveness, or solidarity among those who might be called or call themselves "postmoderns," but the framing of the understanding of postmodernism itself is far from conclusive among philosophers, theologians, or lay (and often unwitting) participants in or subscribers to postmodern trends of thought.

7. On the necessity of suspension of assumptions and the need to be critiqued by the presuppositions we may hold by being "members of a particular community" (Keller, *Reflections on Gender and Science*, 130), see ibid., 130–132, and Bohm, *On Dialogue*, 22–24.

not only by modernist jargon, but by modernist assumptions as well. The sentence cannot be reduced to being inherently modernist or postmodernist. What I am referring to regarding jargon and assumptions is that postmoderns in this sentence are the "goal" or project aim (i.e., being spoken to rather than engaged in dialogue) of those self-identified as "other than postmoderns." The implicit assumption of the sentence might be that postmoderns can be known by observation and then a plan can be strategically established and applied *to* them. In a postmodern culture, communication is more than speaking *on* something or *to* someone. The challenge is to not "speak to" anything, but rather to engage in discourse and dialogue, to share stories that give meaning to corporate and personal identity, and to acknowledge, despite the significant history of modernism and logical positivism, that subjective experience has value, albeit in a different way than empirical inquiry. What is being suggested here is not that any claims to objective empirical study nor that all of the modernist project must be (or even could be) rejected, but rather that response to this culture cannot be "from the outside." What is being called for is the ancient theological and missional[8] practice of incarnational ministry that is rooted in the biblical covenant and made real and effective by Christ's atonement.

Understanding Implications

In pressing for implications that move us from theory to praxis, we must regard well the earlier warning to enter into critical engagement with our presuppositions and assumptions. That is to say that there might be the temptation to oversimplify our understanding of implications themselves. For example, we might simply assume that the implications of theology flow completely from our desire to see the deep things of God brought face-to-face with the deep realities of life. The expectation is that implications positively change not only the response of active members of the body of Christ to the developing needs of a culture or society, but also usher in the newness that can be and always has been expected from the *kerygma* of faith in Christ. Thus, it is hoped that the diligent study of theology will bring an existential change and an eschatological hope through direct implications

---

8. On the biblical and early church models of missional and incarnational leadership and ministry, see Christopher J. H. Wright's excellent works (arguably the most articulate and thorough works on the missional church from a biblical theological perspective), *The Mission of God* and *The Mission of God's People*. Also see Hirsch, *The Forgotten Ways*.

or at least possibilities for developing meaningful working programs, structures, and strategies in the life of the Church and *thus*, the world. While the desire to move from the abstract to the applied is important, it cannot be approached uncritically in a postmodern context, lest our attempt once again leads to formulaic bulleted lists and programmatic offerings.

Thus, essential to our process is a critical evaluation of what we consider to be "implications" in the first place, and how we make applications of theology and a critical analysis of that engagement.[9] The implicative value of a theological framework must be evaluated not only by how it can be refined down to a list of "practical" steps of implementation, but by whether or not it lends itself to its own internal evaluation and the converse evaluation of the contemporary cultural frameworks, including but not limited to ideologies, in which the church finds itself embedded.[10] Churches and their leaders must get past the "I don't need theology, just give me something that works" mindset, particularly because one must be critically engaged with the context even to define what it means that something "works." In this sense, our culture should cause us to exegete our theological assumptions. The Church must ask not only "How does this theology *work* in terms of practical steps?" but also, "How is my question or concern for how theology *works* made clearer by and critiqued by the theology I'm studying and by the culture to which I am trying to relate it?" For example, one might say, "Such-and-such theology *works* (i.e., it is practical) because it offers three steps to growing our small groups or five principles for building a better worship service." To apply the second type of implication I am referring to would be to ask how this theology helps critique the assumptions that frame our understanding of what *works*. For example, does this theology help to reveal *why* small groups that are growing are a good thing, or what makes a worship team "good" or "better" in the first place. In the context of this chapter, one might ask, how does this theology help us to evaluate not only the effectiveness of our programs, but what qualifies as "effective."

This form of critical analysis is at the heart of the subversiveness of Shelton's theology of covenant atonement. Our ideologies and assumptions in the day-to-day life of faith are confronted by the presence of a God who invites and is known through our participation in mission with the church

---

9. On the challenge faced by pastors and students to move from theological reflection to application, see the comments by Ritschl in *Memory and Hope*, 2–4.

10. I write "partially or fully" here to imply the organic nature of culture; a society or group may find itself to be cross-pollinated or embedded simultaneously and even contradictorily in multiple cultural frameworks.

community as God's own dignitaries, ambassadors of the Kingdom of God. The immediate implication is that transactional models of the atonement that have shaped the church's proclamation and practice of disciple-making are displaced and controverted by the expectation that the work of Christ is effectual in restoring relationship with God, ushering in eternal life, the rule of God, and issuing forth expectations of faith-obedience that involve personal and corporate participation through worship and mission. The experience of dignity in servanthood in the context of covenant community of the restored people of God encourages and empowers creative expression of faith where obedience is neither reducible to legalism nor exploitable in the guise of progress.

Participation and Dignity

Henry Spaulding writes, "No one would argue that core doctrinal convictions are unrelated or unimportant for theology, but too much modern theology has been content to hammer out doctrine and never truly engage life."[11] Implicit in this statement is the call for theology that brings faith into action in the life of the Church. This is the aim of Shelton's covenantal theory of the atonement, in that it provides a theologically solid, biblically immersed, and logically coherent integrative motif that is not only conducive to, but actually expects the embodiment of faith. There are multiple themes that stem from a covenantal understanding of the Atonement that add dimension, shape, and texture for praxis in and through the community of faith—the Church. Two of these themes, "participation" and "dignity," provide the framework for this chapter.

Participation

G. K. Chesterton wrote in his classic *Orthodoxy*, "Tradition means giving votes to the most obscure of all classes, our ancestors. It is the democracy of the dead. Tradition refuses to submit to the small and arrogant oligarchy of those who merely happen to be walking about. All democrats object to [people] being disqualified by the accident of birth; tradition objects to their being disqualified by the accident of death."[12] One might observe a

---

11. Spaulding, "Practicing Holiness," 132.
12. Chesterton, *Orthodoxy*, 47–48.

more general principle than either tradition or democracy here, which is that both are representative of the desire for participation and both contain the idea that there is something inherently good, something dignified in not being disqualified from participating in the goings-on of life. There has been a proliferation of this theme of participation in the general sense of providing meaning and worth to personhood in recent secular and theological writings.[13] The hunger for participation in the current age is expressed by Paul Ray and Sherry Ruth Anderson in their book *Cultural Creatives*: "The kind of learning that Cultural Creatives like is *intimate, engaged* knowledge that is imbued with the rich, visceral, sensory stuff of life. The kind of action that especially appeals to them is what Margaret Mead called 'whole process,' where *they can be part of creating* something from the beginning."[14] This hunger can be seen in the increase in extreme sports and "reality" television. News stations allow viewers to "weigh in" with tweeting, texting, and tele-polling, and web sites, discussion boards, and blogs allow people to share their lives with people they will never meet around the globe.

Given this hunger for participation, there is good news: God desires our participation in his kingdom. In the atonement, Christ is not only our perfect substitute, but he identifies with humanity and invites and expects our participation. The rule of God is at hand and God *expects* our involvement. Michael Lodahl writes, "To say that God is a covenantal God is to suggest a divine interest in our cooperation, a divine commitment to partnership, a divine power that is empowering and affirming of the other. A biblical theology of covenant relationships would suggest that God . . . invites our participation, our cooperation, in the tasks of creation and redemption."[15]

Participation is not mere abstraction. Rather, it is active in the life of the Church in corporate worship, in social justice, in disciple-making, and in proclamation. In worship the atonement "calls for a recapitulating and participating response"[16] where not only praise is offered, but a commitment to Christlike living in subversion to the brokenness of our world. In social justice, the atonement calls for participation as active ambassadors (2

---

13. On the participation value in worship, see Sweet, *SoulTsunami*. On Trinitarian studies positing a Trinitarian model of ecclesiology emphasizing participation, see Fiddes, *Participating in God*.

14. Ray and Anderson, *The Cultural Creatives*, 9, italics mine.

15. Lodahl, *The Story of God*, 91.

16. Daniels and Michelson, "Passing the Peace," 17.

Cor. 5:20) acting with compassion and responsibility including participation in the stewardship of the whole creation that is groaning (Rom. 8:22). In disciple-making, the atonement calls for participation in intentionality of devotion to Christ and submission of self to the Word of God and in prayer.[17] In proclamation, our first apologetic is our identification with Christ as those who have been saved, redeemed, renewed, and reborn and are now called as God's dignitaries in and to the world.

In all of this we are invited to share or participate in the gospel (Phil 1:3–5),[18] made possible by Christ's action on our behalf where "'righteousness-identification' is both a declaration that the believer is acquitted (forensic) and an affirmation that the believer is really righteous by faith (incorporation or participation). The expectations of the covenant are fulfilled by Christ and the believer in him actually fulfills them and enters into proper relationship to God as well."[19] The participatory theme is not the adoption of culture, nor is it pluralistic syncretism nor is it relativism. It is the theme of redemption where we are known by God and know God, and our knowing changes our reality, our loyalty, our entire reorientation toward God's will.[20]

Dignity

Similar to participation, the resounding hunger for dignity in our age is ubiquitous. Issues of life and death are wrapped up in the language of "dignity" and the idea of dignity is associated with the ethical dilemma of "playing God."[21] But, as with participation, the search for dignity is not a creation of social psychology. Dignity is rooted in the God of creation who offers restoration of righteousness and calls for our involvement in the kingdom of God. The participation made possible in Christ is no less than participation in bringing the hope of God to others and indeed the whole creation.

---

17. On the participatory intentionality that flows from the covenant expectation of the atonement, see Willard, *The Divine Conspiracy*.

18. The words translated as "share," "partake," and "fellowship" are all from the same word or root in the Greek, *koinonia*, that is also translated as "participate." Thus, the sense of the word "share" here is that of one who participates in the Gospel, the incarnational activity of the believer is mixed in and provides the context for doing the "all things to all people" ministry Paul describes.

19. Shelton, "Justification by Faith in the Pauline Corpus," 118–19.

20. Cf. Spaulding, "Practicing Holiness," 135.

21. Wennberg, *Terminal Choices*.

To be justified, to become the righteousness of God (which N. T. Wright has exposited as the "covenant faithfulness" of God) [22] is to become dignified, to have purpose, and meaning and to be unified with those who are *in Christ* and called according to the same purpose[23] in becoming God's sent-out ones, modeled after Christ and living in incarnational servanthood and proclamation. The participation to which we are called is dignified, though it may only be experienced through identification with Christ and the cross. Richard John Neuhaus wrote, "The gospel of the Kingdom does not describe an alternative reality; it rather bestows meaning and dignity upon this reality that often seems so meaningless and unworthy."[24]

Thus, the search for dignity in contemporary culture should be acknowledged and engaged by the proclamation of the Gospel that declares the value of being known and loved by God. While there are many themes available, these two, participation and dignity, are culturally relevant and practical implications of a covenant understanding of the atonement in the life of believers and the ministry of the Church.

The Prodigal Son Revisited, Again: Covenant Participation in Incarnation

The concept of "wearing the right clothes," metaphorically speaking, to contextualize the message of God is not new. An important biblical example, the parable of the prodigal son,[25] has become a popular and useful parable for relaying the Christian message of a God who comes running to save with grace, mercy, and restored relationship.[26] Robin Collins, in his work on an incarnational theory of the atonement, points out that the juridical-penal substitution and ransom theories are far from the incarnational message of

---

22. Wright, "On Becoming the Righteousness of God," 207.

23. Cf. 2 Cor 5:20; Rom 8:28; 1 Cor 1:10; Eph 1:11; 2 Tim 1:9.

24. Neuhaus, *Freedom for Ministry*, 20.

25. This parable is an example of contextualization in both form and content: Its form (i.e., story, narrative) was culturally useful and relevant in terms of rabbinic teaching methods and understandability by all who gathered to listen; its content, even more important, carried the message of God's grace and mercy, over and against systems of shame and guilt.

26. Cf. Collins, "Understanding Atonement"; also see Chalke and Mann, *The Lost Message of Jesus*, 64–68. For three important expositions of this parable, see Thielicke, *The Waiting Father*; Bailey, "The Pursuing Father"; and Nouwen, *Return of the Prodigal Son*.

this parable. Likewise, Steve Chalke and Alan Mann show how contemporary theology has tended to focus on the sinfulness of the son, rather than the goodness God sees in the him. Each of these awarenesses is common to a covenantal view of the atonement and is in direct relationship to the *kenotic* activity, the incarnational (participatory) action of God in Christ, presented by this masterful parable. However, the context of the parable as well as the framing of it in the light of a covenantal theory of the atonement, tell us even more. Not only does the parable reveal God's grace and mercy in the Incarnation, but its context and framing declare the divine expectations for God's covenant people, God's redeemed community.

The parable which forms one part of a three-part parable, each part of which describes something treasured that is lost (a lost sheep, a lost coin, and a lost son), is set up by the first verse of Luke 15 where Jesus has been accused of hanging out with the wrong crowd. It would be easy to jump to the conclusion that what the Pharisees are challenging is Jesus' authority as the Messiah. However, the challenge is, first, at a more basic level. They are challenging his authority as a rabbi; "This man isn't even a *good Jew.* How can he possibly be anything beyond that?" This accusation is often set apart as its own focus of study in order to demonstrate God's compassion, manifested in God, the Son, Jesus. Jesus' response is certainly a defense in (at the very least) the rhetorical sense. But I would suggest, even more, that Jesus reveals the very core of the covenant good news, the Gospel, not only in its revelation of the Incarnation of God, the demonstration of the seeking grace of God, but also in direct implications for those who are found, for those who are good, righteous, justified.

Where the Pharisees and scribes are accusing Jesus of not even being a *good Jew*, Jesus redefines goodness in terms of the gospel. In our modern context shaped by centuries of developing systematic doctrine, the tendency is to look at this parable and say, "What does this parable teach about lost-ness?" or "What does this parable teach about salvation or justification?" Certainly, there is much there regarding these things that are certainly worthy of being preached. But the unasked questions that Jesus answers in response to the accusations grumbled against him are "What does God care for these miserable sinners who have none of the merits we have as expert keepers of the Law?" and "What does a *good Jew*, a covenant partner of Yahweh, look like?"

The way in which Jesus' response is framed or structured, specifically in the subtext (which would have been quite clear to the Pharisees) practically screams out against the misunderstanding of the God they claim to follow, while proclaiming in covenantal consistency the divine expectations[27] of God. What is implicit in the grumbling of the Pharisees is that they assumed they were in a place of enough righteousness not only to judge the sinners Jesus was drawing to himself, but to judge Jesus as well. Jesus knew what he was being accused of and in response he offered this parable in three sections. The first words of each section should not be overlooked, for they not only interpret the unspoken assumptions of his accusers, but they offer a subversive alternative. The first two sections begin with interrogatives setting the stage for the third.

In the first (Luke 15:4), Jesus begins, "Which one of you, having a hundred sheep . . . ?" In the context of Jesus being accused of not even being a *good Jew*, the crowd standing around would have heard, "Which one of you *good Jewish people* . . . ?" This is, of course, a rhetorical question to which the expected answer was, "Well any *good Jew* would do that." Indeed, even when Jesus declares, "I tell you that in the same way, there will be *more* joy in heaven over one sinner who repents, than over ninety-nine righteous persons who need no repentance," there were surely some who thought "okay, perhaps going after the rare but repentant tax collector may be worthwhile, if not too often. I do have my reputation to consider as a *good Jew*."

The second section takes the same approach and Jesus begins, "Or what woman, having ten silver coins . . . ?" in which would have been understood, "What *normal*—what *good Jewish*—woman wouldn't look for a lost coin?" Again, the concessions of the Pharisaical accusers might be heard, yet they were probably keen to be thinking even more of their reputations now. Twice now, Jesus has challenged their own concern for their reputations and has declared the value in heaven of repentant sinners, those the Pharisees considered unclean, unreachable, and certainly untouchable. Still, there was enough room for the Pharisees to turn the focus towards the sinners and say, "The *righteousness* we have is available, so, okay Jesus, if one of these sinners repents and follows the law as we do, that would be great." As Chalke and Mann describe it, "[if you were a sinner] . . . the Pharisees had a very simple message for you: Repent! Purify

---

27. For an exposition concerning "divine expectations," which incidentally was the original working title of Shelton's book, see *Cross and Covenant*, ch. 3.

yourself in order to make yourself socially and religiously acceptable. Until then, regard yourself as 'unclean' – a social and religious outcast!"[28]

The third section is the climactic finale. Jesus begins, not with a question, but with the statement, "There was a man who had two sons" (Luke 15:11). At this point, it would have been more than implicit that the person Jesus now introduced in this third part of the parable was meant to represent the archetypal *good Jew* ("There was a [*good* Jewish] man)." The interest (if not anger) would have been piqued as the dignity of those who already considered themselves *righteous* had now been twice challenged, but not nearly so much as was about to be exposited to them. In this third section, the disgraceful story—a nightmare to any *good Jew*—of a son trampling on the dignity of his father by asking for his inheritance early and then going out not only to squander it, but to do so in the most unclean of manners only to end up feeding the most unclean of animals—pigs—would expect an answer to the question, "*Now* what would a *righteous Jewish father* do?" And what is the response of this *good Jewish* father? He forsakes his dignity and runs to save the precious dignity of the son he so loves and cares for. The father empties himself. The father does not consider his own dignity something to be grasped or exploited.[29] Instead, in this parable revealing not only the character of God, but the divine expectation of God for those who are truly *righteous*, the father forsakes his own rightful dignity in order to restore relationship with his son whom he loves and cherishes more than a shepherd his lost sheep or a woman her lost coin.

Here Jesus does not demonstrate that reputation is unimportant, but rather, he redefines what a *good* reputation is, and indeed what a *righteous Jew* is. A *righteous* person is one who is in restored relationship with God, one who has been restored at the sacrificial cost of God's own dignity, not to mention the cost of the life of God's Son, and who acts in loving covenant faith-obedience to likewise love the outsider, the unlovable, the sinner. The message of the parable is inherently participatory in three important ways: (1) It demonstrates the character of God as love. God in this love will go and has gone to great lengths to restore right relationship that has been broken and damaged due to sin, "the assertion of our own will over God's in

---

28. Chalke and Mann, *The Lost Message of Jesus*, 87. On pages 116–22, Chalke and Mann exposit a brilliant revision of the traditional "turn away from" definitions of repentance to being a turning towards God, a reorientation of life where the covenant promises of God are experienced and enjoyed.

29. Cf. Phil 2:5–11.

a way that strangles our relationship with Him."³⁰ (2) It extends, invites, and expects participation of those who have been restored, declared righteous, justified, in the incarnational ministry of God in the world by enlarging the boundaries of inclusiveness in order to reach those who are lost; (3) It redefines lost-ness so that those who are far from God, even indignant prodigals, are not considered untouchable, unclean, unloved, *lost causes* but instead are, in reality, precious and priceless *lost treasures* whom God loves. To these, God calls the redeemed community, those who have been found, to go, seek out and love, as well.

A phrase attributed to Oliver Wendell Holmes that some people are "so heavenly minded they're no earthly good" is appropriate here. In the first two parables, the examples Jesus uses demonstrate a focus that still fits into the category of "heavenly good" in which God is the primary character doing the rejoicing. "Finding" those things that were lost, implying repentant sinners, was celebrated in heaven. But once concession has been made to the first two examples, the third example must have come like a punch in the stomach to Jesus' legalistic listeners as the demonstration of what a *righteous person* looks like was not in terms of seeking and finding an animal or an inanimate object—neither of which would be "unclean"—but in forsaking one's own dignity for the sake of a sinner, an outcast, an unclean person, and to do so at the cost of submitting oneself to the remolding of reputation and dignity.

Jesus both demonstrates the loving grace of God in seeking to restore relationship with sinners and issues a call to all who have been restored to participate as reconcilers in this Godly practice of incarnational ministry in which dignity is redefined by participation in God's covenant activity of salvation. The gospel is thus not that Jesus took on the penalty of death as a juridical substitution, but that God sought us out that we might accept his love for us and be restored to righteousness, becoming God's ambassadors or dignitaries that live in faith-obedience. The gospel is truly covenantal in that a life of faith-obedience is ushered forth as the privileged divine expectation of restored relationship in which purpose and fullness of life, and thus dignity, is found.

To apply these understandings means taking the next step beyond implication to application, a thing perhaps more challenging. This is an appropriate starting place for making application, that is, to ask what it is that is most challenging for us as individuals and as communities of faith. To

---

30. Shelton, "Sharing from My New Heart."

help facilitate the conversation, I would suggest a few possible questions on how we might engage in this kind of ministry: How do the structures of the church (be it a missional community, small-group model, house-church model, street model, etc.) foster this kind of ministry? How do they encumber this kind of ministry? Jesus' ministry before it ever "began" (in the way we tend to think of ministry as beginning) was incarnational. God stooped low, took on human form and humbled himself. Jesus didn't "study" sinners as an outsider but rather *went to them*, into their midst. The Apostle Paul said "To the weak I became weak, so that I might win the weak. I have become all things to all people, that I might by all means save some. I do it all for the sake of the gospel, so that I may share in its blessings." *Incarnation* is often thought of as strictly *going into* other cultures while often church ministries are aimed at *bringing* the lost *into* the church—that is, bringing them into the church rather than sending the church to them. What should be considered when doing this to protect the value of incarnational ministry? When is it better to "go into" rather than to "bring into"?[31]

Guts, Dialogue, and Authentic Faith

Readiness vs. Preparedness

Dallas Willard lamented that despite all the talk of discipleship in the church, little actual discipleship seems to take place, adding the question, "Should we not at least consider the possibility that this poor result is not in spite of what we teach and how we teach, but precisely because of it? Might that not lead to our discerning why the power of Jesus and his gospel has been cut off from ordinary human existence, leaving it adrift from the flow of his eternal kind of life?"[32] In addition, the challenge of disciple-making has been confounded not only by the challenge of postmodern pluralism and skepticism, but by the form of the message of the gospel based on assumptions that salvation may at bottom be reduced to a "get-into-heaven-when-you-die" kind of transaction, and by the damaging language and mode that has too often characterized evangelism and apologetics. While space here does not allow for the expounding of a full apologetic, Shelton's covenant atonement is foundational to a biblical understanding of apolo-

---

31. For more on incarnational ministry, see Kraft and Wisley, *Readings in Dynamic Indigeneity*; Lewis and Wilkins, *The Church of Irresistible Influence*.

32. Willard, *The Divine Conspiracy*, 40.

getics and disciple-making as we are exhorted by the message of 1 Peter 3:13–16.

While there remains some scholarly debate over the dating of the First Epistle of Peter, there is relative agreement that the context for Peter's writing was either anticipation of or the then-present persecution of Christians. His audience was primarily recently-converted Christians who had been truly changed, and were included and involved in the new community. Their new identity had set them apart, as strangers or aliens in the world, but the identity of the new community called them to covenant expectations that were made possible by Christ's atonement.[33] The story of covenant faith in the midst of the community called them to a place of courage and steadfastness in the face of suffering. In addition to reminding them of their covenant and new place in the community, Peter's use of the terms "aliens" and "strangers" evoked images of the story of faith, the narratives of exodus and wilderness, of slavery and emancipation, of exile and of hope, and ultimately of Christ whose own people rejected him and became foolishness to the Gentiles (John 1:11; 1 Cor 1:23). Salvation for Peter and Peter's audience was no mere "ticket into heaven," but rather a whole new way of living. They had been born again, and incorporated into new life as ambassadors whose current circumstances suggested their lives might be modeled after Christ not just in life, but also in suffering, persecution, death, and the hope of resurrection. This provides the background for understanding 1 Pet 3:13–16.

Peter's introduction to verses 15 and 16 begins with "Now who will harm you . . . but even if you do suffer . . ." If persecution is not a reality, the possibility of it certainly is, and he is preparing his readers/listeners for it. Next comes the classic verse of twentieth-century apologetics: "Always be ready (*hetoimos*) to make your defense (*apologia*) to anyone who demands from you an accounting for the hope that is in you" (3:15). The word Peter uses for "ready" here has special significance for Peter. In Luke's gospel, we find Peter faced with the same possibility of persecution. Jesus has just predicted that Peter will cave to the pressure and Peter rejects this possibility with his declaration of loyalty, "Lord, I am ready (*hetoimos*) to go with you, to prison, and to death!" (Luke 22:33). The kind of readiness Peter is declaring is courage, boldness—in plain terms, "guts." Peter has heard Jesus'

---

33. On the text that follows, I have utilized the following articles and commentaries in addition to my own study: Elliott, *A Home for the Homeless*; Volf, "Soft Difference"; Best, *1 Peter*; Brown, Fitzmyer, and Murphy, *The New Jerome Biblical Commentary*.

gospel of the kingdom and he believes. He has faith and he declares his readiness. This word is used by Jesus when he tells his disciples "You also must be *ready*, for the Son of Man is coming at an unexpected hour" (Luke 12:40). This readiness is not merely or even mostly intellectual preparation. It is a readiness to act according to what has been made real and effective in Christ's atonement, the possibility of standing ready in the face of tribulation and even judgment.

There is another word for being ready or prepared and Peter uses it in chapter 1 verse 13. "Therefore *prepare* (*anazonnumi*) your minds for action; discipline yourselves; set all your hope on the grace that Jesus Christ will bring you when he is revealed." The word *prepare* in this verse is Peter's call for those who follow Christ to be ready to learn, to have mental, intellectual readiness. But this is not the kind of readiness he uses in reference to the *apologia*. Peter writes to a new community of believers who were once "strangers" but are now members of the community, the household of faith. Peter reminds them of the Lord they have committed to follow, his life, death, and resurrection, and he calls them accountable in the context of the covenant community. He reminds them that persecution is not something about which they had no idea when they "signed up" to follow Christ. Rather, they knew that Jesus had modeled complete obedience to God in the face of death. Peter knows firsthand the challenge of Satan who was determined to sift the disciples "as wheat" (Luke 22:31).

Now, writing to this community of transformed believers and family members of Christ, he writes and urges them toward boldness, courage, and guts. While he exhorts them to intellectual readiness, their apologetic or *defense* is one of boldness in hope. They are urged to have an argument. However, the argument is not a proposition or a list of propositions, but a steadfast commitment to Christ in spite of all circumstances. This demonstration of hope is to be a testimony, a defense of the gospel. The message of the gospel and the hope of Christ is not a proposition, but the living reality of "Christ in you, the hope of glory" (Col 1:27).

The implication here is not that there is no place for a reasoned defense, but rather that the first context of apologetics is rooted in the real and present hope of God's rule, God's kingdom come near and made accessible through the atonement of Christ. Living out a life of obedience and commitment is not optional, but is both expected and empowered by Christ's perfect sacrifice, his conquering of the power of sin, and his resurrection from the dead, and his promise of return. This being said, the next question is how can we apply this to the varying context of successive generations of the household of faith, the church? What forms does boldness take? While reasoned and well-researched defenses of faith are both useful and effective in some situations, what will our response be to a culture that remains skeptical of absolute truth claims (no matter how good the research) and untrusting of institutions? The section above on incarnational ministry is one possible biblical step. The following section is another.

Participation: Dialogue vs. Monologue

Shelton has referenced practitioners and academics who have explored the power of story in sharing the gospel and in the worship and teaching of the church.[34] I will expand a bit on story-telling as a communal practice below. To these I would add one more confluent thread related to the message of the gospel: the power of discourse and dialogue. Two important sociological works were published in the last half-century that made acute observations of the dissolution of discourse in contemporary western society and interpretations of how this came to be from the slow erosion of the public square to the general "MacDonaldization of society."[35] Both reflections and implicative responses to the loss of dialogue and the consequences of this loss have proliferated in the last decade. While some of these tend toward the formulaic structuring of conversations in order to avoid conflict fostering relativism, others simply try to iterate the value of participation in meaningful conversations.

A central claim of Shelton's covenantal understanding of the atonement is that God is relational and that sin and righteousness are relational terms and that the atonement offers real restoration of relationship in place of our attempts to assert ourselves over and against God. This restoration is good news offering new life, a new way of being, a new direction, and a new cause. There is no more meaningful conversation with people than this one. It is true that this conversation has at its heart a proclamation, *the* proclamation that God is near, and God's rule is at hand, active, and available. But what does that proclamation mean? What form does it take? The covenantal understanding of the atonement places the message in the midst of the people in both proclamation and *dialogue*.

---

34. Shelton, *Cross and Covenant*, 2–3.

35. See Postman, *Amusing Ourselves to Death* and Ritzer, *The MacDonaldization of Society*.

The message is that God cares about you and wants to be in relationship with you. You have meaning and purpose and your participation is not only invited, but expected. Would it not seem that if this is true, that God wants us active in the kingdom, serving as ambassadors, the form of the message would reflect this? Unfortunately, dialogue has been left out of proclamation much of the time; proclamation has taken the form of monologue. With Jesus' preaching this was not the case, and indeed, the covenantal context itself suggests that God invites "narrative convergence" where God's story meets our story, calling us to lives of meaningfulness as that convergence is realized and God's grace is accepted. In the Gospels we see Jesus *interacting* with the crowds, *listening* to them express their needs and desires, *telling* stories of faith, and *asking questions* that invite participation and reveal their need for restoration in relationship to God. Jesus' proclamation included the sermonic, but the *kerygma* was not limited to it.

Ajith Fernando, who has spent decades in missionary work among the people of Sri Lanka, has faced the challenges of pluralism first hand. He describes two gospel messages offered on the same day. The first was a clear sermonic monologue expounding the message of Christ which he relates was not only ineffective, but exhausting. With the second, he took a different approach. He writes: "For my second talk, I adopted the dialogic approach. I asked questions of my audience and let them give their views on the topics I was covering. I also tried to present the gospel very clearly . . . Earlier they were not interested in what I had to say. Now they were willing to give me a hearing because I had drawn them into the communication process by asking them also to speak."[36]

When expressing this way of proclaiming the Gospel recently, I was challenged by a person who asked, "Doesn't focusing on the form and suggesting that dialogue is important dismiss the role of the Holy Spirit in evangelism?" My suggestion in response is that dialogue is not only biblical as seen in the modeling of Jesus' whole life and the preaching of the Apostles, and especially Paul, but it expands and tests our expectations and trust in the Holy Spirit by loosening *our* grip on the evangelistic-disciple-making process. To engage in dialogue seems risky in a world of pluralism where monologue allows us the semblance of control of the message. In

---

36. Fernando, *Jesus and the World Religions*, 28–38. He offers three suggestions of why and how dialogue and participatory preaching are helpful in contextualization of the gospel. Aptly, as several more recent writers have done, Fernando uses Paul's example "reasoning with the people" in the marketplace and with the Athenians at Mars Hill in Acts 17.

this way, monologue limits our view of the Spirit and implies that we are uncertain of how God would fare in the conversation if we allowed those we were engaging to enter in. As has been mentioned above, a key tactic to protect God from this shame has been to formulate a list of testable and certain doctrinal propositions and to ready ourselves to combat modernistic claims with modernistic claims of our own[37] under the name of apologetics. This is not to say that the study of the facts, history, and logical, reasoned defenses of the truth claims of Christianity have no place. It is to say that the dominance of these forms, especially within the confluence of enlightenment thinking and the loss of the public square in the last century, has edged out both narrative and discourse as valid and viable means of communicating the Gospel. Ironically, the contemporary works of both of theologians and social theorists suggest that postmoderns are starving for dialogue and participation in meaningful conversations and practices.

The question of implications of the practical kind is important here. While this chapter is aimed at laying the groundwork for application by providing implications, four items highlighted in the description of Jesus' proclamation (above) are significant and worth offering here. How is it that we might incorporate dialogue into proclamation-disciple-making? Above I wrote, "In the Gospels we see Jesus *interacting* with the crowds, *listening* to them express their needs and desires, *telling* stories of faith, and *asking questions* that invite participation and reveal their need for restoration in relationship to God." These italicized verbs help us to see into Jesus' method of proclamation of the reorientation of life towards God by accepting grace, forgiveness, and entering into covenant of faith-obedience with God.

(1) *Interact.* As we have seen in Jesus' telling of the parable of God's goodness in seeking out lost treasures incarnationally, so we must practice the messy art of seeking by interacting with the crowd. We must enter in incarnationally. As Paul interacted in the marketplace and had acute awareness of the spirituality and religiosity present in Athens, so we must interact with awareness in our contexts, be it in our home town or around the world at the "ends of the earth." We must pray and ask God for wisdom and discernment. But this must be in the context of interaction where we not only study the culture of a group or society, but we also engage in conversations with those whom God is so passionately seeking out. The forms this can take are many, from playing

---

37. See Grenz and Franke, *Beyond Foundationalism.*

soccer in the street with a ball made of twine in Mexico, to having a cup of tea on the Curry Mile in Manchester. Incarnation involves entering in. This doesn't just happen by observation, either. We must engage in actual relationship with people in the culture. This tends to be a more normal expectation (though often no easier) for those going to do missionary work in countries foreign to their own. It is seemingly taken for granted in localized church ministries where it is easier to assume we know a culture because it is *near* us. But proximity in no way requires interaction or engagement.

(2) *Listen*. Jesus listened to people. Jesus countered arguments he had listened to. Jesus sat in the synagogue listening as a boy. Jesus listened to the claims of the Scribes and the Pharisees. His parables were often in response to their accusations or claims that revealed their own ideologies and need for grace. He listened to the requests of the people who came to him for healing. Jesus listened, and he wasn't ashamed to be caught listening to or "hanging out" with the "wrong" kind of people. When was it that evangelism became predominantly about speaking? The act of listening extends respect to those we engage. It validates their personhood and suggests openness to relationship. It models leadership through submission. It subverts our tendency to judge or assume and offers insight into the person we're declaring the gospel to. We must pray and act to become better listeners. In listening we humble ourselves and become learners. We make ourselves available to the hurts and needs of real people in need of grace. Listening does not imply either strength or weakness, because it is about neither. It is about valuing, treasuring the lost. It is about waiting and watching for the prodigal's return so we can run out to meet her on the road. It is about patience and trust in God's power to work in a person's life and it offers us insight into the lives of those to whom we are engaging.

(3) *Tell Stories*. I grew up going to church and Sunday school. My lessons were always stories. Noah's Ark. The Exodus. The Prodigal Son. The Early Missionary Journeys of Paul. The teachers retold the stories of faith, and we learned much from them. In the children's sermons, flannel-graph boards were used until the felt had holes in it and everyday objects were turned into messages of faith. During the worship services I would be a part of the children's musicals where we acted

out stories. Each week during the service a person would give a "testimony" where they told their story of God's work in their lives. The shaping of my faith came from stories. It is odd in retrospect to look back and realize that when I reached junior high and high school, I was trained to evangelize (distinct from disciple-making) not by telling stories, but by listing claims and presenting "laws" of salvation and faith. Certainly understanding our faith and what it is we believe is important. The implications drawn here are based on claims that the way we understand the atonement is pivotal to shaping our faith and message. But when did we outgrow stories? Leonard Sweet has pointed out that many adults are most attentive in a worship service during a children's sermon. This is no insult to the intellect, but rather a compliment to the image-rich, participatory, and meaningful stories that are used in the typical children's sermon. We must pray and discern how our stories, our testimonies, and supremely, the narratives of scripture can be read and re-read as proclamations of faith.

The use of narrative invites participation. Storytelling is not limited to tales or fables, but is the communal process of participating in life together. It is a rhetorical form whereby truth is communicated in non-propositional form. The use of narrative is invitational in that it expects an audience. That the audience is invisible in that it is a future, not a present, audience makes the story no less truthful nor less communal.[38]

Storytelling is a participatory act even when the story is being read, for what meaning does the story hold apart from the shared meanings of the listeners. Even more significant is that there are often if not always unshared meanings that speak imaginatively into old stories or that find ancient original meaning with new implications for a current age. In all, the flexibility of the story renders it not only useful for teaching, but practical for imparting understanding in the community of faith according to the faith family's story. An age of propositionalism has ushered us into a place where story has been so picked apart, all that remains are the fragments of meanings expected by an expert. Indeed, our stories call us accountable and ask questions of us. They ask us to evaluate our lives in the context they provide. This is a central and covenantal role of stories in the biblical tradition.[39] And

---

38. Cf. Barton and Halliburton, "Story and Liturgy," 80–81.

39. On function of the biblical narrative and narratives as communal covenantal

we should listen to others whose stories tell of a pilgrimage not yet finished.

(4) *Ask Questions.* First of all, it's important to know there are different kinds of questions, but they all invite participation. Rhetorical questions suggest that something is amiss or might be understood in a different way than is often supposed. They invite reasoning, discourse, thought. There are experiential questions that ask how people are affected by something or how they feel about something. Creedal questions ask what someone believes. Accountability questions ask people how their lives are aligned with their commitments and values. Scriptural questions ask about knowledge or analysis. Small-group training guides often offer taxonomies of questions such as "open" questions that allow any answer, "yes or no" questions, or "springboard" questions that ask someone to respond to something someone else has said. Each invites engagement and participation. Question-asking is often left to youth or children's ministry or is controlled by the context of a small-group situation, but Jesus also asked questions in the midst of crowds, often countering claims made against him. The effectiveness of questions is not only biblical. Indeed, recent research has made strong cases that invitation to participate increases learning, fosters relationships, and demonstrates a willingness to engage in dialogue, not just monologue.[40] And asking questions can demonstrate our genuine interest in persons and their experiences, religious background, personalities, interests, and stories. While rabbinic method[41] may have provided the cultural context for Jesus' question-asking, he was no less an expert asker and we must pray and learn to ask questions that help us to engage incarnationally, listen intently, and relate stories of faith that reveal the awesomeness of God.

---

accountability, see Brueggemann, *Theology of the Old Testament*, 22–27 and idem, *The Prophetic Imagination*. On the social functioning of literature and other stories in asking questions, see Coles, *The Call of Stories*, 78–88 and passim.

40. Brown, "Daring Greatly."

41. On the communal nature and form of rabbinic interpretation and the dignity of participation in the hermeneutical process, see Visotzky, *The Genesis of Ethics*, 6–8.

Dignity: Theatre vs. Coliseum

We have seen that "apologetic" takes a variety of forms and that it is not limited to the realm of rhetoric. Narrative and dialogue apologetic can be seen in the rhetorical but invitational question-asking of God, such as "Where were you when I laid the earth's foundation" (Job 38:4), and of Jesus, such as "Is there anyone among you who. . ." (Matt 7:9) or "If you love those who love you . . ." (Luke 6:32), or the parabolic "The Kingdom of God may be compared to . . ." (Matt 13:24). Testimonial apologetic involves personal story and narrative convergence such as Paul's Damascus Road conversion (Acts 9: 22). There remains an apologetic of praxis that is bound to covenantal atonement in expectations of lives of holiness that are crucial for credibility in an incredulous culture of postmodernism. Such apologetics are called for by Jesus. He evokes no less than all-out commitment and expects it unreservedly: "Go and sell everything you own" (Mark 10:21); "I was hungry and you gave me food . . ." (Matt 25:35ff); "And whoever gives even a cup of cold water to one of these little ones . . ." (Matt 10:42).

This praxis apologetic is twofold: (1) It is based on the humble willingness of Christians to submit themselves to the Bible in their communities and to lives of justice and holiness in the world. (2) It is witnessed in the willingness of Christians to sacrifice, to serve, and to face suffering and persecution with resolve, not in antagonism, but in hope of the present and coming Kingdom of God. These two are both represented in the call of Jesus to be his witnesses. In contrast, Jesus referred to as *hypocrites* those who were religious in word but not deed. By the end of the first century, the word "hypocrites" would still connote the theatre where actors would mask their true identities and character on the stage. In contrast, the word "witnesses" or "martyrs" would strengthen to mean those who laid their lives down for their faith. Their apologetic extended beyond their words. The call of covenantal atonement embraces and produces each of these forms of apologetic where the faith of Christians is not a proposition, but truly a new birth, a new life, a testimony in both belief and praxis. Contemporary praxis in some parts of the world still takes the form of enduring physical and life-threatening persecution, which has created a continuing refugee crisis. But contemporary praxis may also be seen in our actions as witnesses towards the concern for ecology in a covenantal model,[42] our willingness

---

42. See McGrath, *The Reenchantment of Nature*. Also see Hall, *The Steward* and Meeks, "Introduction," i-xi.

to move outside the walls of the church in action towards those who live in poverty, or our willingness to take the risk of engaging in friendships and taking the time to become "safe spiritual friends" to those who consider the church as anything but safe or helpful.[43]

Conclusion

The covenantal context of the atonement is not only profoundly biblical and foundational for an understanding of the gospel that breathes new life and hope into the present as well as the future, but it offers timeliness for ministering to a culture brimming with doubt and skepticism and challenged by pluralism. Covenantal atonement is at the heart of the New Testament call and experience of faith and renewal that is locatable, real, and tangible, in the community of faith, the church.[44] Jesus Christ is at the center offering forgiveness of sin and the declaration of righteousness inviting participation under the rule of God that speaks eternity into the present and provides the substance for hope that is at the heart of Christian apologetics even in face of persecution. Covenant is intrinsically relational; the atonement restoration of righteousness comes with expectations of Christ-centered faith-obedience lived with intentionality in incarnational mission.

This mission is not only message, but medium as well; that is, it is the story of faith that converges with the story of lost treasures, lost daughters, and sons' being restored to relationship with God. The story invites and empowers participation, as did Jesus' parables where dialogue opened the way for persons to practice the faith they had, where the vastness that is the rule, the kingdom of God could not be narrowed down or nailed down by a list of propositions. The message was far more invasive, offering not merely a bandage, but rather a life-sustaining, life-renewing transplant. But the life is new and the restoration is real, requiring ongoing submission to the loving care and authoritative purview of the Holy Spirit. And this whole story is called accountable to the God of faith in the Bible that in relationship is constantly subverting our ideologies and speaking new life out of old narratives. And, the covenantal understanding of the atonement issues forth the dignity that comes from finding meaningfulness in being God's ambassadors, proclaiming the good news of restoration and the invitation to participate in the story of God.

43. Cf. McLaren, *More Ready Than You Realize* and idem, *Finding Faith*.
44. Cf. Brueggemann, *The Bible Makes Sense*, 19.

4

Creation's Cry against Shallow Shalom

The Uneasy Relationship between Covenant Theology and Creation Theology in the Conflict between True and False Prophets

by Steve Delamarter

Introduction

One of the central concerns in Larry Shelton's teaching and writing in recent years has been the subject of covenant. One could, I think, characterize his perspective on biblical theology as stemming from the conviction that covenant is the central context for understanding biblical theology. As first a student of Shelton's and later as a colleague with him at Seattle Pacific University and at George Fox Evangelical Seminary, I extend my hearty respect and congratulations to him on the occasion of his retirement from teaching. Further, I would like to offer a few comments on the interplay between covenant theology and creation theology in the Old Testament.

Covenant and Story

Over the course of centuries, Israel developed a body of convictions about itself in relation to its God and in relation to what the Israelites believed was God's work in the world. These convictions took their particular shape in the form of a collective memory of all the ways in which God had called them, blessed them, and formed them into a covenant community across time. And their memory included not just a memory of how God had acted toward them, but also of all the ways in which they had acted towards God.

Israel came to remember this history as one in which God had acted with unilateral commitment toward them to bless them and to secure their place in the world. The measure of this grace could be demonstrated in their remarkable growth from a small and insecure handful of wandering nomads into a formidable people, now living on and in possession of a land previously occupied by others. And this status in the world had not come about as a result of their human intentions and labors. Their God had, they remembered, directed their forefathers to come to this place. And even before they had themselves begun to act in a manner consistent with the modes of conduct to which their God would eventually call them, their God had in various ways blessed them with growth and prosperity in spite of their reckless and wanton behavior. And when, through a series of desperate circumstances, they ended up slaves in Egypt, it was not because they had a dynamic and courageous leader or because the people themselves were ready to follow a leader courageously that they were delivered from these circumstances. It was, they remembered, because their God had, "with a mighty hand and an outstretched arm," brought them up from that place, and had done so with demonstrations of power that showed their God to be sovereign over other deities and even the forces of nature.

This same God, they came to remember, had brought them by the hundreds of thousands through the harshest conditions in the desert to meet with them at Mount Sinai. It was there that God and Israel had formalized their relationship. God had said, "I will be your God and you will be my people." Almost from the beginning, though, Israel had strained against their obligations in the covenant. But God, they remembered, had remained faithful to the covenant even in the face of their rebellion. In mercy, God had led them on into the land that they now possessed. And their memory of the conquest itself was that it was not accomplished through the usual exploits of a strong military. Instead, they believed, God himself had fought the battles for them, requiring only faithful obedience on their part to the initiatives and commands of their God. In their recollection of the story, this was the distinctive characteristic of the conquest generation: with one notable exception (by a man called Achan), they had obeyed God and followed God's leadership and, as a result, received the land. It had come to them as fulfillment of promises to the Patriarchs, as a covenant gift from a God determined to give them a place, and as a demonstration of the power of obedience in covenant relationship.

Ultimately, their memory of the early generations in the land was that this was not an easy time of which Israel could be proud. Instead, it was a dizzying cycle, driven time and again by Israel's propensity to "do evil in the eyes of the LORD." The consequences of these choices were, they remembered, as inevitable as their apostasy, leading time and again to conquest by outsiders and suffering at their hands. Nevertheless, in mercy God had raised up judges to deliver them. Eventually, God had even allowed them to establish the institution of kingship, even though this institution could be understood as a rejection of God's direct leadership in their midst. And, ultimately their memory was that for most of their kings this is exactly what it was: a rejection of the rule of the purposes of God and license for the kings to accumulate wealth and power to secure their place in the world by their own means and strategies, most of which had led to disaster. In spite of this memory of the failure of the kings to do right, Israel clung to one other memory: that God had made a covenant with the second of their kings. This David was a king extraordinary in that he was a man after God's own heart, and though he had his failings, Israel remembered that God had made covenant with David and promised him that "one of your descendants would be on the throne forever and ever; I will be to him a father and he will be to me a son."

The memory of Israel's most holy sites came to be bound up with David. It is he who captured Jerusalem and established it as the place God had always intended it to be, namely "that city over which I will cause my name to dwell." And the pinnacle of Jerusalem, Mount Zion, came to be known as God's holy hill, beside which David would build a palace for himself and for his descendants, and upon which David's son, Solomon, would build a temple in which God would dwell in their midst. Israel came to remember this as the culmination of all the ways in which God had walked with and been present to them throughout their history. The tent of meeting in the desert and the tabernacle set up by David prefigured Zion and Temple and solidified the memory of Israel's history as one of God's continuous presence with them and of the security that resulted from that presence.

Covenant and Collective Memory

Now you might imagine that what you have just read is the history of Israel. But this is not actually what it is. What we have recited above is the *memory* of Israel's covenant history as it came to be told in the final, canonical form of the Old Testament.

But, you ask, could it have been told otherwise? The answer to this is emphatically, "yes." The Old Testament makes it clear that at virtually every moment in Israel's history, the meaning of the events taking place in that moment was contested. In fact, it is more drastic than that. The memory of Israel's history that ends up in the Old Testament represents what was a minority perspective at just about all of the crucial moments in Israel's history, sometimes held only by a lone prophet with, perhaps, a few followers.

For instance, the canonical book of Amos informs us of that prophet's perspective on the meaning of social and political events in Israel in the mid-eighth century BCE. But the book also makes it clear that, at that time, Amos' perspective was probably rejected by just about everyone in the North who heard it! Amaziah, priest of Bethel, probably represents the dominant perspective. He makes this position clear in the charges he laid against Amos in a letter to King Jeroboam II: "Amos has conspired against you in the very center of the house of Israel; the land is not able to bear all his words" (Amos 7:10). And he makes clear the utter incompatibility between the dominant perspective and Amos' perspective when he tells Amos: "O seer, go, flee away to the land of Judah, earn your bread there, and prophesy there; but never again prophesy at Bethel, for it is the king's sanctuary, and it is a temple of the kingdom."

How do we explain the fact that a book appears in the Old Testament with a message that, at the time of its delivery, was judged by most everyone who heard it to be antithetical to correct thinking? Clearly something changed between the time that Amaziah told Amos to leave the Northern Kingdom and the time that the Old Testament collection of the Minor Prophets was assembled. What happened? In Amos' case, the answer seems fairly obvious: 722 BCE happened, the military destruction and dismantling of the Northern Kingdom of Israel. This process of initial rejection followed eventually by acceptance of a prophet's words happened not only to Amos. Their books tell us that the identical pattern happened to Isaiah of Jerusalem and to the prophet Jeremiah. Apparently national trauma has a way of changing a people's collective memory of their past.

This is, in fact, a central thesis of Arthur G. Neal's work on collective memory and national trauma.[1] In the same way that individuals respond to personal trauma with intense reactions such as recurrent nightmares, eating disorders, and psychological numbing, trauma can also be experienced by an entire culture and have profound effects on it. The challenge of assimilating the meaning of a personal injury fades almost into nothing when compared to the challenge of assimilating the effects of a national tragedy: "Here conditions of trauma grow out of an injury, a wound, or an assault on *social* life as it is known and understood. Something terrible, deplorable, or abnormal has happened, and social life has lost its predictability. Initial responses to a traumatic event are shock, disbelief, and incredulity. Chaos prevails, and people become uncertain about what they should or ought to believe. Individuals lose confidence in their ability to see the interrelatedness of events, and disturbing questions are raised about the linkage of personal lives with historical circumstances."[2]

We might imagine that very few people in Israel would have known or cared about the invectives of a prophet from the Southern Kingdom. Easily enough, the situation could be ignored. But this indifference cannot be sustained in the face of national trauma. "An extraordinary event becomes a national trauma under circumstances in which the social system is disrupted to such a magnitude that it commands the attention of all major subgroups of the population . . . The social fabric is under attack, and people pay attention because the consequences appear to be so great that they cannot be ignored."[3]

The upside to national trauma, if we can put it that way, is that it can cause people's perspectives to go from being fixed and unassailable to being open and flexible. Neal points out, "A national trauma frequently has liberating effects on a social system. Older ways of doing things are called into question, and new opportunities for change and innovation surface. The very fact that a disruptive event has occurred opens up the possibility that the social system will be perceived as defective in some way or another. In the confrontation with the danger implied in a crisis event, new opportunities for innovation and change emerge."[4]

1. Neal, *Major Events*; Browne and Neal, *Ordinary Reactions*; Neal, *Extraordinary Events*.
2. Neal, *Extraordinary Events*, 4, emphasis mine.
3. Ibid., 10.
4. Ibid., 18.

Apparently it took the traumatic events of 722 BCE (the destruction of the Northern Kingdom at the hands of the Assyrians), 701 BCE (the near destruction of the Southern Kingdom at the hands of the Assyrians) and 586 BCE (the full destruction and exile of the Southern Kingdom at the hands of the Babylonians) to force a reassessment of what had happened and, more importantly, why it had happened and what it all meant. It seems in these seasons of flux—brought about by the traumas of military devastation—that the words of the prophets commended themselves to the community again. And this time they listened and heard in the words of the prophets a message from God that had escaped their attention before.

Thus, it is most interesting to realize that much of the perspective of the Old Testament comes to us not as Israel's *first* reading of her history, but as her *second* reading of her history, and that it took nothing short of national calamities to force Israel away from that first reading and towards a second reading, away from the rejection of the prophets and into the embrace of the prophets. And though we don't have space here to go into all the reasons why we know this to be the case, what is true of many of the prophetic books is likely also true of the books of Joshua through 2 Kings (known collectively to scholars as the Deuteronomistic History). This gigantic, six-volume retrospective was written some time after the last of the events recorded in it: "in the thirty-seventh year of the exile of King Jehoiachin of Judah," (2 Kings 25:27), i.e., around 560 BCE and in the shadow of the events of 586. It is highly unlikely that the memory of Israel's history that is found in Joshua to 2 Kings would have been received as persuasive before 586 BCE. It seems much too unflattering to have been acceptable to the sensibilities of pre-calamity Israel.

The Canon's Memory of the Rejected First Reading

This brings us to our next set of questions: What was going on when Israel was trying to sort out its first reading of its history? Who was disagreeing with the prophets, and why? And on what basis did they disagree? Or, what might a pre-586 account of Israel's history have looked like and how would it have differed from the one we have in the Deuteronomistic History? Would it, for instance, have been as harsh in its criticism of the failure of the entire panel of kings of Israel and Judah as was the Deuteronomistic History? Would it have critiqued the exploitation of the marginalized poor and powerless, as Isaiah and Jeremiah did? Would it have judged the religious institutions of Israel to suffer a profound disconnect from the character and core values of their God, as did Amos? The fact is, we do not have a pre-586 version of Israel's history, except to the extent that one may find vestiges of it in the final form of the Deuteronomistic History. But one still wonders, were there competing visions of Israel's present moments throughout this period of time? Did people disagree? How did people argue with one another about the meaning of the moment while they were still in it?

Is there any evidence yet available in the Old Testament that gives us glimpses into the pre-calamity disputes about what God was up to in Israel's world? Most certainly there is. Many of the prophetic books remember these disputes vividly. They remember and record what was said and how it was argued. That is, they preserve the voice and perspective of the majority culture at the time when their own perspective was not yet accepted and had not yet become the "canonical" version of the events.

The book of Amos remembers the perspectives of those who contended with Amos. It was not just Hananiah, the priest of Bethel, whom we mentioned above, who bitterly renounced Amos' proclamation (7:10–13). Just before the end, all sorts of people who were destined to die by the sword were telling one another, "Evil shall not overtake or meet us" (9:10). And a culture completely given to an elaborate system of religiosity involving festivals, solemn assemblies, burnt offerings, grain offerings, offerings of well-being, musical compositions, and performances were apparently clueless about what God actually thought about their religiosity: "I hate, I despise your festivals . . ." (5:21–24).

The book of Micah remembers people objecting to Micah's message: "'Do not preach'—thus they preach—'one should not preach of such things; disgrace will not overtake us.'" (2:6). And elsewhere it remembers the people saying, "Surely the LORD is with us! No harm shall come upon us" (3:11). And the book of Hosea remembers the people claiming, "My God, we—Israel—know you!" (8:2).

The book of Jeremiah remembers people saying that, "No evil will come upon us, and we shall not see sword or famine" (5:12) and people telling one another, "It shall be well with you" and "No calamity shall come upon you" (23:17), and others saying that God was promising, "I will give you true peace in this place" (14:13). It remembers that just before the end, people were telling God with confidence, "You, O LORD, are in the midst of us, and we are called by your name." It remembers the oracles of Hananiah, a well-known prophet of God, who was claiming that, "Within two years I will bring back to this place all the vessels of the LORD's house, which King Nebuchadnezzar of Babylon took away from this place and carried to Babylon. I will also bring back to this place King Jeconiah son of Jehoiakim of Judah, and all the exiles from Judah who went to Babylon, says the LORD, for I will break the yoke of the king of Babylon" (28:3–4).

The book of Jeremiah remembers that, not long before the Babylonians came and razed it to the ground, people were boasting about the presence of the house of God in their midst, "This is the temple of the LORD, the temple of the LORD, the temple of the LORD" (7:4), and that they believed that they could simply run inside and say, "We are safe" (7:10). The book of Jeremiah remembers that people were so convinced of the utter inviolability of Jerusalem that they would retaliate against Jeremiah saying, "This man deserves the sentence of death because he has prophesied against this city" (26:11). And the book remembers that the people of that time had utter confidence not only that they possessed the word of God, but that it had profoundly shaped them: "We are wise, and the law of the LORD is with us" (8:8).

Likewise, the book of Ezekiel marvels at the memory of "the prophets of Israel who prophesied [just before 586] concerning Jerusalem and saw visions of peace for it, when there was no peace" (13:16) and who were delivering oracles saying, "Says the LORD" (13:6 and 7), even though it was obviously not the case. And it remembers that just after their land was overrun by the events of 586, the people in the devastated areas were still telling one another, "Abraham was only one man, yet he got possession of the land; but we are many; the land is surely given us to possess" (33:24). We begin to see a pattern.

The Theological Foundations of Type-II False Prophets

When we listen to the statements of those who opposed the prophets and who articulated the majority position about what God was up to in their time, we are perhaps most surprised by how "biblical" they sound. Were we to combine these voices into one position, it is actually rather fascinating how coherent that position is.

The opponents of the prophets say time and again that God will not allow evil, sword or famine to overtake Israel (Jer 5:12, 14:13, 23:17; cp. Mic 2:6); they believe, instead, that peace is on the horizon (6:14, 14:13, 23:17; cp. Ezek 13:10 and 16), in fact, they demand it from God (Jer 14:20) because He is in their midst (14:9; cp. Mic 3:11). They do not believe that God would give them over into the hand of the Babylonians (Jer 27:9, 14, 37:19) and consider it treasonous that Jeremiah would say so; the devastating incursions against them from the Babylonians are temporary, they believe, and will all be reversed shortly (Jer 27:16, 28:1ff, 29:9). They cite God's promises to Abraham as proof that they will maintain possession of the land (Ezek 33:24) and claim to know God in a special way (Hos 8:2). They revel in the fact that the very temple of the LORD is in their midst (Jer 7:4, 14:9) and believe this to be a sign of God's presence and their security. They find it utterly impossible that God would reject Judah or allow anything to happen to Jerusalem (Jer 26:11) or Mt. Zion (Jer 14:19, cp. Amos 7:10–14), in part because a Davidic king sits on the throne (cp. Mic 4:9). They rejoice that they are the recipients of the Torah of God and believe that it has made them wise (Jer 8:8–9). Even though they have sinned against God, they look to God to be their savior and deliverer (Jer 14:13–15). They understand themselves to be called by the name of the LORD (Jer 14:9, cp. Isa 48:1–2) and blessed by him with prophets in their midst, even in exile (Jer 29:8ff).

These are not the ideas of so-called type-I false prophets, those who advocate going after some other god. These are the ideas of the other category of false prophet mentioned in the Old Testament—what we call type-II false prophets—the type described in Deuteronomy 18:20 as one "who presumes to speak in my name a word that I have not commanded the prophet to speak." These false prophets do not speak in the name of Marduk, god of the Babylonians, or in the name of Chemosh, god of the Moabites. They speak in the name of the Lord and they appeal to the central tenets of Israel's theological traditions.

In the voices of the type-II false prophets we hear appeals to the Abrahamic Covenant, in which God promises to give them land and descendants. We hear them appeal to the stories of the exodus from Egypt and the conquest of the promised land, as proofs of the validity of the promises to Abraham. We hear them appeal to the Mosaic Covenant as proof that God is indeed their God and they are indeed his people. We hear their conviction that God has elected Israel for special relationship and has been present with them throughout their history. We hear their passion about those places in Israel that have been sanctified for special purposes and which are imbued with the presence of God: Jerusalem, Mount Zion, and the Temple. We hear their expressions of confidence that God is Israel's savior and warrior and that God will fight their battles for them. We hear them say that the very name of the Lord has been invested in them and that this has created a vested interest in their welfare on the part of the deity. We hear them rejoice in the torah as covenant gift and as the mechanism by which God has blessed Israel with special knowledge and insight about God.

Again, we recognize these ideas. They are essential components of Israel's theological tradition. So how is it that these ideas are coming out of the mouths of false prophets? What is it that has gone wrong here?

Ideological Criticism and Theological Argumentation in the Old Testament

In order to understand this phenomenon, it will be helpful to introduce an explanatory model put forward by Michael Calvin McGee[5] in a sub-field of rhetorical criticism having to do with the analysis of ideology in rhetoric. Here's why. It is not just that our memory of the past is shaped in community; the same is true for our thinking within the present. What ideas do we find persuasive in the present and what is it about the expression of those ideas that seizes our attention? We might think that it is because we have come independently to certain conclusions, which we then discover are shared by others. And, in certain cases, this may be the way it actually works. But for most of us, our convictions are *shared* convictions. That is, they are ideas and beliefs that have been formed in community. But sometimes the core ideas of a community can degenerate into mere ideology. How does this work?

When ideas are first being cultivated within a community, we have to articulate them, explain them, unpack them, and argue them until enough people accept them that they become the property of the community. But once the ideas are accepted and occupy the status of *common* conceptions, we find that we no longer need to explain, argue, or unpack anything. These commonly held ideas can be reduced almost to slogans, because everyone has been indoctrinated into full acceptance of the argument. McGee calls these condensed forms of an ideology an *ideograph*. He observes that,

---

5. McGee's influential piece on this subject is "The 'Ideograph.'" His later article, "Text, Context, Fragmentation" deals with the larger field of rhetorical criticism and its recent developments. An article by McKerrow, "Critical Rhetoric," provides a helpful review of the field as well.

"Each member of the community is socialized, conditioned, to the vocabulary of ideographs as a prerequisite for 'belonging' to the society."[6] McGee points to terms like "law," "liberty," "freedom," or "equality," as examples of ideographs in the modern American context. When these ideas become so commonplace that their authority is no longer discussed or explained but merely assumed, then it is no longer the ideas themselves that are under discussion; it is all about the *use* of the idea to prove other points. McGee would say that political discourse—the public discussion about the common fate or common good or common meanings—is rife with the use of ideographs: ". . . ideology in practice is a political language, preserved in rhetorical documents, with the capacity to dictate decision and control public belief and behavior."[7] And the intention of employing ideographs is to gain assent; the ideograph is a power term, that is, it has power to evoke assent without actually bringing any substance to the conversation. All one has to do is employ the slogan, the ideograph, as a warrant for some other idea and because the ideograph is unquestioned, people will be more likely to assent to the point being made even if they haven't thought through the substance of the idea. In fact, according to McGee, "The society will inflict penalties on those who use ideographs in heretical ways and on those who refuse to respond appropriately to claims on their behavior warranted through the agency of ideographs."[8]

McGee explains: "An ideograph is an ordinary-language term found in political discourse. It is a high-order abstraction representing collective commitment to a particular but equivocal and ill-defined normative goal. It warrants the use of power, excuses behavior and belief which might otherwise be perceived as eccentric or antisocial, and guides behavior and belief into channels easily recognized by a community as acceptable and laudable."[9]

Thus we can see the distinctive location and function of ideology in the life of a community. Ideology has to be distinguished from ideas. Ideas are formulated by the community to define the structure of their belief systems and their systems of practice. And as a normal part of their socialization within the community, people are steeped in the ideas in such a way as to orient them to the truths of the community. But the dissemination of

6. McGee, "The 'Ideograph,'" 15.
7. Ibid., 5.
8. Ibid., 15–16.
9. Ibid., 15.

these truths can degenerate into the reduction of the ideas into mere slogans or ideographs with the agenda to force assent to these shallow forms of the idea. Once this is accomplished, the ideographs function as meaning in the service of power. They become a mechanism by which assent can be assured, if not demanded. And they become efficient means of compelling people to adopt other ideas for which the ideographs serve as unquestioned warrants. Sociologists of rhetoric are convinced that this use of language is a tool crafted and exploited with the primary purpose to protect the vested interests of entrenched power structures and the privileged members who occupy them.

I offer here the models of McGee and the sociologists of rhetoric for our consideration because I believe they may illuminate the nature of the argument between true and false prophets in the Old Testament. It would appear that the type-II false prophets appeal to Israel's theological traditions, but often merely as ideographs, vacuous slogans meant to elicit agreement with a position, but without any real dialogue over the issues that make up the substance of the ideas in the first place.

Covenant Theologies as Expressions of Salvation Theology

There can be no doubt that the bulk of Israel's theological tradition has to do with what we would call collectively *salvation theology*, or *salvation theologies*. Under this heading we refer to all those stories that tell of God's gracious and saving work on Israel's behalf: calling, promising, saving, delivering, blessing, preserving, and defending. These would include many of the themes in the stories of the Abrahamic covenant, the Exodus and conquest stories, the Sinai and Mosaic covenant, and those stories in which God functions as Israel's Holy Warrior. But this category would also include the ongoing belief that God had made covenant with David and his descendants as Kings of Judah, and the belief in God's sanctification of the holy spaces of Jerusalem, Mount Zion, and the Temple itself. And it would also include the notion that the name of the Lord was invested in his people, that the Torah had been given as a covenant gift, and that God was Israel's healer. The details about each of these elements of Israel's theological tradition are somewhat different, but they all have in common an emphasis on God's saving actions on their behalf.

To hear the type-II false prophets tell it, you would probably get the impression that these ideas and stories of salvation comprise the totality of Israel's theological tradition. Virtually every recorded utterance of the type-II false prophets in the Old Testament is grounded in salvation theologies of one sort or another. But, in fact, there are two other major elements within Israel's theological tradition. The first is the set of ideas that center on the character and core values of God, and the second is what we will call broadly "creation theology." And though the number of their expressions is not so abundant as are the variations on salvation theology, these theological notions are so potent that they alone are the theological ideas that possess the power to override or cancel the validity of salvation theology—at least, in the estimation of the canonical prophets.

The Reduction of Covenant Theology to Ideographs by Type-II False Prophets

Our critique of the theological argumentation of type-II false prophets, then, is two-fold. First, they have reduced covenant and other forms of salvation theology to mere ideographs. Second, they have isolated salvation theologies from the larger theological context. Specifically, they would pass off salvation theologies as the whole of the theological tradition, instead of leaving them in tension with theologies of the character and core values of God and with creation theologies.

What do we mean when we say that the type-II false prophets have reduced covenant and other forms of salvation theology to mere ideographs? Israel's theological tradition is not a set of simple slogans or formulas, and it was not formulated in terms of straightforward propositions. The most potent of Israel's theological notions are embedded in stories rich with detail, stunning in their complexity, and filled, at times, with seeming contradictions and irony. They lend themselves to diverse conclusions. They simply cannot be reduced to mere slogans.

Take, for instance, the question of whether the promises of God to Israel are conditioned on their righteous behavior or whether they are sureties regardless of the performance of compliant behaviors. It would be rather difficult to prove the conditional nature of relationship to God from the stories of the patriarchs and matriarchs. The first iteration of the promises to Abraham, recorded in Genesis 12:1-3, is perfectly ambiguous on this point: "Go . . . and I will . . ." Is this conditional language, or is it merely descriptive? In the following episode, Abraham is blessed with abundant goods even though he lies to the Pharoah and endangers Sarah by passing her off as his sister (Gen 12:10–13:2)! Again, in chapter 17, God reiterates the intentions behind the covenant, but again it is not clear whether this is set forth as a conditional or as a description: "'I will establish my covenant between me and you, and your offspring after you throughout their generations, for an everlasting covenant, to be God to you and to your offspring after you. And I will give to you, and to your offspring after you, the land where you are now an alien, all the land of Canaan, for a perpetual holding; and I will be their God.' God said to Abraham, 'As for you, you shall keep my covenant, you and your offspring after you throughout their generations'" (Gen 17:7–9).

A few chapters later, after the incident of the near-sacrifice of Isaac, God speaks in a way that seems to indicate that Abraham's actions somehow influence the certainty of the promise: "By myself I have sworn, says the LORD: Because you have done this, and have not withheld your son, your only son, I will indeed bless you, and I will make your offspring as numerous as the stars of heaven and as the sand that is on the seashore" (Gen 22:16–17). But, Jacob, acting as though he were holding tryouts for his deity, has the audacity to make his allegiance to the LORD contingent on the LORD's care for him! "If God will be with me, and will keep me in this way that I go, and will give me bread to eat and clothing to wear, so that I come again to my father's house in peace, then the LORD shall be my God" (Gen 28:20–21).

Overall, when we finish a reading of the patriarchal narratives, we conclude that the point of the narrator is that God loved and blessed the patriarchs and matriarchs *in spite of* their unrighteousness. In some mysterious way, God's actions for good trumped the greedy and self-serving actions of people. As Joseph puts it, "You meant it for evil; but God meant it for good" (Gen 50:20). The blessings of God were certainly not contingent on the righteous choices of his people.

But the stories in Deuteronomy suggest a very different conclusion: "If you will only obey the LORD your God, by diligently observing all his commandments that I am commanding you today, the LORD your God will set you high above all the nations of the earth . . . But if you will not obey the LORD your God by diligently observing all his commandments and decrees, which I am commanding you today, then all these curses shall come upon you and overtake you . . . (Deut 28:1–68). Nothing could be clearer in the deuteronomic perspective. Life is a choice: choose obedience and gain life; choose disobedience and choose death.

Our point here is that the stories out of which theological conclusions were gleaned by ancient Israel are stories rich in detail, complexity, ambiguity, and even in irony. They cannot be reduced to a simple formula like "Abraham was only one man, yet he got possession of the land; but we are many; the land is surely given us to possess" (Ezek 33:24).[10] But this is just the sort of argument that the prophets' opponents were making.

The Isolation of Salvation Theologies from the Larger Theological Context by Type-II False Prophets

Israel's canonical prophets contended that their disputants—the type-II false prophets and the people at large—had reduced Israel's rich traditions into simple and self-serving ideographs. And this reduction was accomplished in large part by disconnecting salvation theologies (in their various forms) from the two other primary components of Israel's theological tradition: the theology of the character and core values of God, and the theology of creation. As we will see, the canonical prophets argued as though the validity of Israel's theological tradition was tied to maintaining the tensions that stand between these three broad theological categories: salvation, character and core values of God, and creation theology. When the false prophets tried to ground a theological position solely on an appeal to some form or forms of salvation theology, the canonical prophets challenged the validity of their position by an appeal to one or the other, or both, of the other theological ideas.

The Use of the Theology of the Character and Core Values of God to Combat a Warped Salvation Theology

Following are just a few examples of the way in which the canonical prophets used the theology of the character and core values of God to trump, so to speak, arguments based solely on salvation theologies.

---

10. Isaiah 51:1–2 makes it clear that this argument, though rejected in the day of the prophet Ezekiel for reasons we will describe below, is, under different circumstances, a potentially valid application of the tradition: "Listen to me, you that pursue righteousness, you that seek the LORD. Look to the rock from which you were hewn, and to the quarry from which you were dug. Look to Abraham your father and to Sarah who bore you; for he was but one when I called him, but I blessed him and made him many." The point here is that blessing in relationship with God is not a simple formula.

It was a treasonable offense in the eyes of some to speak of the destruction of Jerusalem, Zion or Temple. Salvation theology argued that these sacred spaces had come to Israel as covenant gifts from God and, as such, were inviolate. Isaiah's indictment of Jerusalem, however, reminds the people that this sacred space was not merely an expression of covenant grace; their very existence was to be a monument to God's core values:

> How the faithful city has become a whore! She that was full of justice, righteousness lodged in her—but now murderers! Your silver has become dross, your wine is mixed with water. Your princes are rebels and companions of thieves. Everyone loves a bribe and runs after gifts. They do not defend the orphan, and the widow's cause does not come before them. Therefore says the Sovereign, the LORD of hosts, the Mighty One of Israel: Ah, I will pour out my wrath on my enemies, and avenge myself on my foes! I will turn my hand against you; I will smelt away your dross as with lye and remove all your alloy. And I will restore your judges as at the first, and your counselors as at the beginning. Afterward you shall be called the city of righteousness, the faithful city. Zion shall be redeemed by justice, and those in her who repent, by righteousness (Isa 1:21–27).

Jeremiah held the same conviction regarding the Temple. Its enduring substance and stability derived not from some promise made in the history of salvation, but from the willingness of its inhabitants to live out the core values of God: "Amend your ways and your doings, and let me dwell with you in this place. Do not trust in these deceptive words: "This is the temple of the LORD, the temple of the LORD, the temple of the LORD." For if you truly amend your ways and your doings, if you truly act justly one with another, if you do not oppress the alien, the orphan, and the widow, or shed innocent blood in this place, and if you do not go after other gods to your own hurt, then I will dwell with you in this place, in the land that I gave of old to your ancestors forever and ever" (Jer 7:3–7).

Ezekiel heard the people in post-586 Judah using salvation history to assure themselves of a return to blessing. They said, "Abraham was only one man, yet he got possession of the land; but we are many; the land is surely given us to possess" (Ezek 33:24). One hears in Ezekiel's response an expression of horror that God's people could embrace a set of beliefs that contained such confidence in the benefits of salvation history alongside such a complete lack of passion for God's vision for covenant community. "Thus says the Lord GOD: You eat flesh with the blood, and lift up your eyes to your idols, and shed blood; shall you then possess the land? You depend on your swords, you commit abominations, and each of you defiles his neighbor's wife; shall you then possess the land? Say this to them, Thus says the Lord GOD: As I live, surely those who are in the waste places shall fall by the sword" (Ezek 33:25–27). Here was a profound disconnect. And, in the end, Ezekiel did not see how one could expect the blessings of salvation history without a commitment to the character and core values of God.

When they would boast in the blessings brought on by salvation, Jeremiah reminded the people of God's commitments to mercy, justice and righteousness: "Do not let the wise boast in their wisdom, do not let the mighty boast in their might, do not let the wealthy boast in their wealth; but let those who boast boast in this, that they understand and know me, that I am the LORD; I act with steadfast love, justice, and righteousness in the earth, for in these things I delight, says the LORD" (Jer 9:23–24)

Within Israel's long history and relationship with God developed elaborate and venerable traditions of thanksgiving and worship. But, according to Amos, these meant nothing to God without a commensurate commitment to justice and righteousness: "I hate, I despise your festivals, and I take no delight in your solemn assemblies. Even though you offer me your burnt offerings and grain offerings, I will not accept them; and the offerings of well-being of your fatted animals I will not look upon. Take away from me the noise of your songs; I will not listen to the melody of your harps. But let justice roll down like waters, and righteousness like an ever-flowing stream" (Amos 5:21–24).

Micah is of the same opinion: "'Will the LORD be pleased with thousands of rams, with ten thousands of rivers of oil? Shall I give my firstborn for my transgression, the fruit of my body for the sin of my soul?' He has told you, O mortal, what is good; and what does the LORD require of you but to do justice, and to love kindness, and to walk humbly with your God?" (Mic 6:7–8).

If the people of God believe that the covenants and promises of salvation history guarantee, *in themselves*, a place of security, peace, and blessing, then the canonical prophets were there to tell them that these meant nothing if disconnected from the character and core values of their God. To put it another way, the purpose of the covenants and acts of salvation had always been to produce a people in whom the character and core values of God would reign supreme and be lived out before a watching world. God's acts of salvation were rendered devoid of meaning by a people who cared nothing about the outcomes they were intended to produce.

The Use of Creation Theology to Combat a Warped Salvation Theology

If salvation theology must be held in tension with the theology of the character and core values of God, then the same is true of creation theology. The canonical prophets appeal to creation theology time and again to shock the people of Israel out of a theological position grounded solely on salvation theology.

Jeremiah listened with skepticism to the oracle of salvation delivered by the prophet Hananiah: "Within two years I will bring back to this place all the vessels of the LORD's house, which King Nebuchadnezzar of Babylon took away from this place and carried to Babylon. I will also bring back to this place King Jeconiah son of Jehoiakim of Judah, and all the exiles from Judah who went to Babylon, says the LORD, for I will break the yoke of the king of Babylon" (Jer 28:3–4).

Jeremiah argued at one point that this sort of oracle was out of keeping with the history of prophecy he had come to know, one in which prophets were more prone to deliver oracles of "war, famine, and pestilence" (Jer 28:8). But at a deeper level, Jeremiah was convinced that, in the current situation, God's role as author of salvation had been superseded by God's role as creator. The promises of salvation history had been rendered null and void by the failure of king, priest, and people to take on the character and core values of God. Therefore, God was engaged in an act of re-creation: "It is I who by my great power and my outstretched arm have made the earth, with the people and animals that are on the earth, and I give it to whomever I please. Now I have given all these lands into the hand of King Nebuchadnezzar of Babylon, my servant, and I have given him even the wild animals of the field to serve him" (Jer 27:5–11).

Jeremiah's mention of the wild animals is not a throw-away line. Creation theology is very knowledgeable of the hierarchy of creation, with the earth as foundation, vegetation as the source of food for animal life (divided into domesticated and wild animals) and human life. By saying that God was giving even the wild animals to Nebuchadnezzar, Jeremiah was asserting that the totality of the created order was being given to him.

CREATION'S CRY AGAINST SHALLOW SHALOM 71

The theology of the book of Jonah is wrenched into place by the same forces driving the theologies of salvation, character and core values of God, and creation. The writer of the book of Jonah—who is the true prophet behind the book—makes it very clear that Jonah is a type-II false prophet. Jonah knows right theology intellectually, but has no passion for it himself. When he sees the mercy of God extended in forgiveness to the Ninevites, he is furious: "But this was very displeasing to Jonah, and he became angry. He prayed to the LORD and said, 'O LORD! Is not this what I said while I was still in my own country? That is why I fled to Tarshish at the beginning; for I knew that you are a gracious God and merciful, slow to anger, and abounding in steadfast love, and ready to relent from punishing. And now, O LORD, please take my life from me, for it is better for me to die than to live.'" (Jonah 4:1–3).

These phrases, "gracious God and merciful, slow to anger, and abounding in steadfast love, and ready to relent from punishing" are directly from the mouth of God describing himself to Moses on Mount Sinai (Exod 34:1–6). They represent the key text in the Bible on the theology of the character of God as merciful.

And when Jonah becomes suicidal over the loss of a piece of vegetation that provided him shade, then the stage is set for the creator to put a question to the (false) prophet: "You are concerned about the bush, for which you did not labor and which you did not grow; it came into being in a night and perished in a night. And should I not be concerned about Nineveh, that great city, in which there are more than a hundred and twenty thousand persons who do not know their right hand from their left, and also many animals?" (Jonah 4:10–11).

It is creation theology that enables us to make sense of this final question. Jonah, lacking any commitment to take on God's heart for mercy, suffers a warped view of the world. In the end, he cares more about the lowest orders of creation (vegetation) than he does for those higher in the system, the humans and animals of Nineveh.

When the people of God fail to take on the heart of God, then God the creator becomes willing to engage in acts of re-creation. And these can be very hard for people, involving as they do acts of what we might call "dis-creation." Listen to the tension between theological themes in the oracle of judgment delivered by the prophet Ezekiel:

> The word of the LORD came to me: Mortal, when a land sins against me by acting faithlessly, and I stretch out my hand against

it, and break its staff of bread and send famine upon it, and cut off from it human beings and animals [creation in reverse], even if Noah, Daniel, and Job, these three, were in it, they would save only their own lives by their righteousness, [salvation through righteousness] says the Lord GOD. If I send wild animals through the land to ravage it [creation in reverse], so that it is made desolate, and no one may pass through because of the animals; even if these three men were in it, as I live, says the Lord GOD, they would save neither sons nor daughters; they alone would be saved, but the land would be desolate. Or if I bring a sword upon that land and say, "Let a sword pass through the land," and I cut off human beings and animals from it [holy war in reverse]; though these three men were in it, as I live, says the Lord GOD, they would save neither sons nor daughters, but they alone would be saved. Or if I send a pestilence into that land, and pour out my wrath upon it with blood, to cut off humans and animals from it [creation in reverse]; even if Noah, Daniel, and Job were in it, as I live, says the Lord GOD, they would save neither son nor daughter; they would save only their own lives by their righteousness. For thus says the Lord GOD: How much more when I send upon Jerusalem my four deadly acts of judgment, sword, famine, wild animals, and pestilence, to cut off humans and animals from it! (Ezek 14:12–23).

This is an outright attack on the notion that Jerusalem is inviolate. It is not that the promises of God have failed. It is more a matter that when the people of God fail to take on the character and core values of God, then the promises of salvation theology are rendered void and the forces of creation are set in motion in reverse, to dismantle and to destroy.

These biblical texts bear witness to the healthy tension in which the theology of salvation stands in relation to the wider scope of biblical theology. As important as salvation theology is, and as central as salvation is to the message of the Bible, it is frightfully easy for the people of God to twist the promises of covenant and salvation into something they were never intended to be. A theological system grounded solely on salvation theology is likely—perhaps guaranteed—to degenerate into something quite twisted and self-serving when it is passed off as the whole of theology. It must be held in tension with the theological themes of the character and core values of God, as well as in tension with creation theology.

Creation theology, in particular, has the function to shock and to challenge any system in which humans would make their own comfort the highest good and the central activity of God. Creation makes it clear that

God is up to things far above and beyond such parochial limits. It de-centers human comfort as the measure of all good. It underscores the freedom of God and the utter centrality of mercy, justice and righteousness as the goals of His saving work. In so doing, it directs the people of God toward mercy, justice, and righteousness as their own calling.

5

Did Jesus or Custer Die for Our Sins?
Exploring the Mission of Covenant among Non-Western Indigenous Cultures

Randy S. Woodley

Dr. Larry Shelton has become a good friend, close confidant and colleague. His interest in and promotion of North American Native theology has been clearly demonstrated over the past decade. Larry has attended most of our NAIITS (North American Institute for Indigenous Theological Studies) Symposia; created several important opportunities for dialogue; and somehow found a way to wrangle me into full-time academic work. I owe Larry a lot. I appreciate his keen theological mind, his irreverence for orthodoxy simply for orthodoxy's sake, and his Southern mountain humor. Larry always brings out the good ol' boy in me even when this ol' boy ain't so good. For Larry's friendship and the honor he has shown me, and our Indigenous work, I will always be grateful. A scholar, friend, and humorist—but above all—Larry is a real human being.

In 1969 Vine Deloria, Jr.'s famous book, *Custer Died for your Sins*, named after a bumper- sticker slogan, had just come out. At the time, as an 8th-grade Native American boy and wannabe activist, I read the book with great enthusiasm. It was easy for me to understand how such an evil man as George Armstrong Custer could be held up like Jesus as atonement for the whole nation of American White folks. After all the damage they had done to the Indigenous peoples of this land, my people, their sins were many. Later, when I was taught the ways of Christianity from a conservative Western worldview, it was easy for me to substitute Jesus, who practiced no evil, for Custer and conform to a simple "payment," transactionally oriented understanding of atonement. Unfortunately, both constructions I had in mind were in error. In his book *Cross and Covenant*, Larry Shelton lays waste to classic substitutionary atonement theories through a unique understanding of covenant that comes close to what might be considered Indigenous thinking. By doing so, he frees Indigenous North American Christians, and others, to understand naturally what Christ has done for us and all humanity.

For some White Americans, the imagery of Custer paying for the sins of White people may be offensive. But through Native American eyes, according to how God's love is portrayed in the Scriptures, it seems equally offensive to hold up Jesus, as representing penal substitutionary atonement or other related atonement theories. When the relationality of the trinity is explored, the love of God is realized as a great force with which to be reckoned, and Larry Shelton's understanding of relational covenant is such a model.

Peace and Covenant

The closest thing I know in Native American culture to the type of relational covenant, in the way Shelton portrays it, is a treaty, which usually includes both parties smoking what has formerly been referred to as a *Peace Pipe*. The term *Peace Pipe*, though, is a misnomer. The White man always saw the pipe used at these treaty ceremonies and through typical misinformation and poor assumptions, began to think of the pipe mainly in terms of Peace, thus, forever it seems, referencing it as a "Peace Pipe." In fact, the use of the pipe for most tribes is much more sacred than assumed by the White Men who made treaties with Native Americans. A more accurate description would be to call it a "Covenant Pipe."

Because the pipe is such a sacred object, it was most often used only in the most sacred ceremonies, the making of a covenant being one of those times. The pipe was used specifically during these times because it meant that two people, or people groups, who were likely at odds with one another for whatever reasons, were now becoming one. The covenant was indeed a marriage of sorts, which bound the two entities together from the time of the ceremony forever in intimate relationship. The sacredness of such a powerful and revered symbol as the pipe assured the fact that no lies would be told to one another and that everyone's intentions would be pure.

The problem, of course, while making treaties between the United States and most Indian nations was that the Indigenous people were the only ones taking the covenant seriously. Most of the treaties forged between Indigenous Americans and the U.S. were forced under martial restraint, never intended to be kept or never intended to be enforced. With such a "tainted" history and superficial understanding of treaty, it is easy to recognize how Western Americans could miss understanding our relationship with the Creator in such covenantal and relational terms. Nonetheless, there is much we can learn theologically by doing so.

When two warring Indian nations came together in treaty, gifts were always exchanged. These gifts served as tokens of the relational covenant. The gifts were not trivial. Often, they were the best possessions a person held, including horses, pipes, and they may have even included inter-marriage and/or family adoptions. Such exchanges demonstrated the seriousness of the covenant and familial relationality. Notably, the commitment was not simply to serve as a means to end a war. No, treaty or covenant between most Indigenous American peoples meant, not just an absence of conflict, but instead, a whole new proactive time of peace and prosperity. The idea was that by working together, much more good could be done for all communities or entities involved. The construct very much resembles the ancient Jewish understanding of shalom, when a sensible and relational harmony that was broken was to be restored.

> Traditionally, Native Americans understood our role on earth as those who restore harmony in very practical ways. Our indigenous ceremonies often require, not only symbolic acts but also practical restitution and full restoration. A vivid example of practical shalommaking is the ancient Cherokee cementation ceremony that occurred annually each fall. At that time anyone with grievance against a fellow Cherokee was required to participate in the ceremony.
>
> The basic components of the ceremony included a fire and prayers that were spoken by the holy person. Then, the families and friends on each side of the rift would face each other with the lead persons (those with whom the division originated) at the

head of the line. Each would give an account of the offense. Then the persons would go to the fire to pray for the strength to forgive. The two would then strip naked and exchange clothes. Following this action they spoke words of forgiveness and vowed never to bring the issue up again. The pipe was passed back and forth down the line for everyone to smoke. Finally, gifts were exchanged and a feast was put on by both parties for the whole community. The result was both ceremonial and practical.[1]

Worth exploring, for the purposes of this chapter, was the public nature of covenant among Native Americans in ceremonies such as the one referenced above. Not only were all family members present, but the whole community came out to observe the ceremony and then they were hosted with a feast given by the restored families. For harmony or shalom to be restored, there must be some kind of a public record kept. Such records, symbolized by whatever was culturally appropriate, helped to ensure that if the animosity that once existed was ever brought up again, future generations would be able to tell the story of how the covenant was once made and it could avoid future misunderstandings and offenses. In the Indigenous ceremony of covenant, the whole community was often included in the restoration. The resultant symbols from such a covenant safeguarded the issue from becoming a festering point in later generations. I have heard stories of 200-year-old covenants between tribes told in both public and private settings.

As mentioned earlier, shalom seen simply as "peace" is an anemic understanding of a meta-narrative type of theological construct in the Scriptures. In fact, sometimes shalom even comes through creative, actionable conflict. For example, where injustice prevails, living out shalom covenant may dictate that the structure perpetuating the injustice be transformed through direct action. Certainly, wherever the weak are marginalized, or the poor, the disempowered, and the "ethnic other" are neglected, living out shalom covenant demands that someone challenge the oppressive system and lift up those who are being oppressed.

Sin and Covenant

Wherever shalom is broken, sin is present and it demands Christ's restoration, particularly if it be found in those who bear Christ's name. As one

1. Woodley, *Shalom and the Community of Creation*, 23.

writer puts it, "God is for shalom and, therefore, against sin. In fact, we may safely describe evil as any spoiling of shalom, whether physically (e.g., by disease), morally, spiritually, or otherwise."[2] Sin, in a very real sense, can be defined as the absence of shalom. Sin without hope is the absence of a shalom-based, relational covenant.

As a result of the practicality of a relational shalom covenant, sin is neither ignored nor relegated to the private, more personal areas of life. Shalom makers clearly need to be active in the world, influencing society towards the vision of the Trinitarian community on earth, reflecting God's desire for everyone to dwell in the divine shalom covenant. Sin is brokenness in harmony and it is an alienating force that works against God's vision for community. A relational shalom covenant does not assert unattainable utopian dreams without prescribing the means to a "peaceable kingdom" (Isa. 9:7; Rom. 14:17). Usually the terms are very clear, but not particularly legislative, and they are practical.

In such a construct of sin as held by some Native Americans, a penal substitutionary atonement has little meaning or place. Sin, to many Indigenous people, is not immutable nor is it related to guilt. A sin, to many traditional Native American understandings, is a mistake. We are neither forced to sin, nor is there some kind of idea of inherited guilt, nor do we need to continue making mistakes. Among Indigenous North Americans, there is no perfection for which one must strive. A good life comes by realizing we are limited and fallible human beings, and that realization is of the highest order of spirituality. Human beings seem to be the only part of creation that has difficulty remaining in its proper place in creation. Given this propensity to drift into anthropocentrism, indigenous peoples have many stories and ceremonies to remind us of our humanness.

The Interconnectedness of All Creation and Covenant

Larry Shelton originally hails from Cherokee country, so it is appropriate to share two stories from my own tribal traditions that shed light on shalom relational covenant. The first story deals with God's covenant and the gift of land to all creation. The second story sets humanity in right relationship with God and creation, especially revealing the interconnectedness of all creation.

2. Plantinga, *Not the Way It's Supposed to Be*, 14.

Grandmother Turtle and How the Earth Was Made

When the earth was first made, it was covered all over with water except for one small island. This island was the top of a high mountain. This was Blue Mountain, in the Cherokee country. For the Cherokees, the Ani-Kituwa, the Ani-Yvwiya, this is where it all begins.

Everyone lived together on this mountaintop island. The human beings and the animals all got along fine. In those days they could understand one another's speech, for this was before the humans broke the harmony. The animals were also much bigger in those days. In fact, the animals of today are but shadows of those who once were. It was a good place to live. Sure, the island was small, but it was what everyone knew and was used to. All were content, until there came to be more of them than the small bit of land could support.

As they noticed they were getting crowded, a general council of all the people (both humans and animals) was called. The question was asked, "What can we do?" The only answer given was, "We can pray. All we can do is pray and ask the Grandfather Above to please give us some more land."

So all the people prayed, and Creator/Apportioner answered, "Oh my precious children, there is nothing I enjoy so much as giving good gifts to my children. But if I do everything for you without asking you to help in any way, how will you ever learn any responsibility? I really want to teach you some responsibility. Here's what I will do: If one of you will swim to the bottom of the ocean and bring up some mud, just a little bit of mud, I will take that mud, that little bit of mud, and make a whole great land of it."

All the people (animals and humans) began to look at one another. Someone asked, "Who will go? Who will get the mud?"

A slow, deep voice answered, "I will go. I will get the mud." It was Grandma Turtle.

"Grandma Turtle, you can't go!" They said. "You're too old and slow. We don't know what it's like down there. We don't know how deep it is."

"I'll go," quacked Duck.

"Now that's more like it," they said. "You're a good swimmer, Duck. You can go; you can do it."

Duck paddled out onto the ocean and dived, but he popped right back up to the surface. Duck dived again and again and again, but the same thing happened each time. Well, you know how ducks are. They dive well, but they float much better. Duck paddled back to shore, shook the water off his tail and said, "I can't dive that deep. I float too well."

The question was asked again, "Who will go? Who will get the mud?"

Grandma Turtle said, "I will go. I will get the mud."

"Grandma Turtle," they said, "we settled that before! You can't go. You're too old. Who will go? Who will get the mud? Hey Otter, how about you?"

"What?" Otter said.

"How about you going to get the mud?"

"Mud? What mud?"

"The mud we need so Creator/Apportioner can make more land!"

"Oh, sure," said Otter, and he slid off into the water and was gone a good long while. When he came back, he had a fish in his mouth, but no mud. Without a word to anyone, Otter climbed up onto the beach and began munching on the fish.

Everyone was watching him, but Otter paid them no mind, just kept eating his fish. "Hey Otter!" someone yelled.

"What?" Otter said.

"Where's the mud?"

"Mud? What mud?" Otter asked. "Ohhh the mud! Well, I left here to go and get it. Then I got started playing. Then I caught this fish. Then I forgot all about the ummm, ummmm, whatever it was I was supposed to get."

Oh my! They were nearly at their wits' end. "Who will go?" they all asked. "Who will get the mud?"

Grandma Turtle said, "I will go. I will get the mud." No one even paid her any mind.

"Who will go? Who will get the mud?"

"I will go," said Beaver. "I will get the mud. I don't play, and I do not eat fish."

Resolutely, Beaver swam out into the ocean. He took a deep, deep breath and dived. Wow, Beaver was gone a long time. Some of the people watching and waiting were holding their breath in sympathy, but none seemed able to hold it that long. Finally, Beaver popped to the surface gasping for air. He swam to shore and climbed onto the beach shaking his head. "It's too deep!" Beaver said. "I don't know how deep it is. I never reached the bottom."

Everyone was in despair. Beaver was the last best hope. How would they ever get mud? Maybe there would never be anything but the little mountaintop island. "Who will go?" they asked. "Who will get the mud?"

A slow deep voice answered, "I will go. I will get the mud."
"You can't go, Grandma Turtle, you're too..."
"I WILL GO! I WILL GET THE MUD!"

There were no other volunteers, so they let Grandma Turtle go. She slowly paddled her way out onto the surface of the ocean. As everyone watched, she took a slow, deep breath, then another and another and another. She took three more breaths and disappeared beneath the water.

They waited a long time. Grandma Turtle was gone much longer than Duck or Otter or even Beaver had been. She was gone all that day and the next and the next and the next. They posted a sentry up on the very top of the mountain. Finally, on the seventh day, the sentry called out, "I think I see something coming up. Yes, yes, something is rising in the water. Could it be? Could it be? Yes! It's Grandma Turtle!"

Sure enough, Grandma Turtle rose to the surface of the ocean, and there she lay, not moving, with her legs, her tail, her head all hanging down... Grandma Turtle was dead.

Quietly, reverently, Duck, Otter and Beaver swam out and drew Grandma Turtle's body to the shore. They pulled her up on the beach, as all the people (humans and animals) gathered sadly around, and what's this? There, under her front feet, they found... mud.

Someone took the mud, that little bit of mud from under Grandma Turtle's front feet, rolled it into a ball and lifted it up toward the sky. The Grandfather took that mud, that little bit of mud and cast it out, making this whole, great land that many nations call Turtle Island.[3]

The Origin of Disease and Medicine

In the old days all the animals, birds, fish and plants could all talk, and everyone lived together in peace and friendship under the delight of the Creator. But after a while the people began to spread over the whole earth. The animals, birds, fish and plants found themselves beginning to be cramped for room. This was bad enough, but then Humans began to slaughter the animals needlessly, becoming wasteful. The humans no longer thanked the Creator for supplying food, nor did they thank the animals for feeding their families by the giving of their lives. Every traditional Cherokee knows that it is considered polite to thank the Creator and also thank the animal when it furnishes its own life so people may eat and sustain their lives for another day. So in order to protect themselves from the evil

---

3. As told by Richard Francis.

that had come upon them from the once grateful Cherokee, the animals resolved to hold a council to discuss their common survival.

The Council was first led by the bears. The Great White Bear asked, "how do the people kill us?" "With bows and arrows" someone replied. "Then we must make bows and arrows," declared the leader. But soon the bears found they could not shoot straight with their claws, and they needed their claws to dig for grubs and such. After much debate, the animals decided to bring diseases upon the Cherokee people. The Cherokee people began getting sick and dying from these diseases. After many Cherokees had died they pleaded with the animals, "Please, we will become grateful and kill only that which we will eat." But the animals would not take back the diseases they had created to kill the Cherokee.

At the same time, the plants were watching all of these things. They watched as the Cherokee children and old people got sick. Then the strong warriors and even the women began to die. The plants decided to hold a council. In the council they agreed to provide medicine for the Cherokee. Each night, as the Cherokees would sleep, the plants would come to them in their dreams and show them how to use the plants to heal the diseases that the animals had brought upon them.

The Cherokees recovered and agreed always to kill only what they absolutely needed. They also agreed to say a prayer of thanks to any animal that they killed, and to any plant that would be harvested for food or medicine. The Creator was happy with the Cherokees once again because harmony was restored among all that he had created.

The first story illustrates, among other things, that all of creation needs help occasionally and those who have the most lived experience among us will likely know best how to relate to God and the land. It is also a good story for understanding shalom relational covenant. Harmony can only be restored if we all do our part. The second story begins with all creation, including all human beings, living in harmony with one another and the Creator. The problem in the story arises when the humans overcrowd the rest of creation, disrupting harmony and becoming ungrateful. Ingratitude both precedes and follows greed. In this case, it was greed for land. The humans believed they should have more resources than everyone else, causing there to be a great imbalance to the world. Christians would describe this greed as sin. Native Americans generally refer to it as imbalance or broken harmony.

With these two stories in mind, recall the Genesis 1–3 narratives. Everything is good, in balance, in harmony or in a natural implied state of shalom relational covenant. God has gifted all creation with life and those lives are to be lived in relationship with God and all other creation. Then, similar to the Cherokee story of the Origins of Disease and Medicine, human beings break the harmony through abusing their relationship to creation in a way God has forbade by eating what they should not have eaten. As a result, there is a problem with the land and all creation. The Genesis story reveals that human beings must live outside of the harmonious Garden of Eden and make the long journey to another promised place in order to learn how to live in harmony with all creation once again.

I surmise that the story of the Creator making a covenant with all creation, including human beings, is the real focus of all similar covenants in Scripture. Many of God's covenants in Scripture, whether with Abraham (Gen 17:7); David (Psalm 89:3–4); Israel (Exod 6:4–5); the church (Acts 2:39), or others, can be implied to have all of creation in mind when seen in light of the grand covenants of Scripture.

In Genesis 9:8–17 God said to Noah,

> Then God told Noah and his sons, "I hereby confirm my covenant with you and your descendants, and with all the animals that were on the boat with you—the birds, the livestock, and all the wild animals—every living creature on earth. Yes, I am confirming my covenant with you. Never again will floodwaters kill all living creatures; never again will a flood destroy the earth." Then God said, "I am giving you a sign of my covenant with you and with all living creatures, for all generations to come. I have placed my rainbow in the clouds. It is the sign of my covenant with you and with all the earth. When I send clouds over the earth, the rainbow will appear in the clouds, and I will remember my covenant with you and with all living creatures. Never again will the floodwaters destroy all life. When I see the rainbow in the clouds, I will remember the eternal covenant between God and every living creature on earth." Then God said to Noah, "Yes, this rainbow is the sign of the covenant I am confirming with all the creatures on earth."

Notice that the covenant is with all creation, which points to the implied interconnectedness of humans with other creatures and with the land. This implied interconnectedness begins to be shown in the Genesis 1 account of creation but it is directly expressed in Genesis 2:18–20, "Then the Lord God said, 'It is not good for the man to be alone. I will make a helper who is just right for him.' So the Lord God formed from the ground all the wild animals and all the birds of the sky. He brought them to the man to see what he would call them, and the man chose a name for each one. He gave names to all the livestock, all the birds of the sky, and all the wild animals. But still there was no helper just right for him." (NLT)

It was the important task of Adam to get to know the animals of the Garden of Eden well enough to give them names. In most Indigenous societies, this means the namer will have an intimate familiarity with the animal, including its patterns and purpose in creation. God's concern for all creation, even in the covenants where creation is not specifically mentioned, is implied because God is concerned about all creation, not just humanity. The fact that many of the covenants are anthropocentric speaks much more about humanity's view of our self-importance over other creatures than it does about God's lack of concern for the importance of all creation. Fortunately, there is enough mentioned of all creation throughout the Scriptures to form an understanding of relational covenant with all creation.

In the New Testament, Paul in Romans 8:19–23 implies that the restoration of creation, including land, and the restoration of humanity are inseparable.

> For all creation is waiting eagerly for that future day when God will reveal who his children really are. Against its will, all creation was subjected to God's curse. But with eager hope, the creation looks forward to the day when it will join God's children in glorious freedom from death and decay. For we know that all creation has been groaning as in the pains of childbirth right up to the present time. And we believers also groan, even though we have the Holy Spirit within us as a foretaste of future glory, for we long for our bodies to be released from sin and suffering. We, too, wait with eager hope for the day when God will give us our full rights as his adopted children, including the new bodies he has promised us.

The summation of Paul's understanding of Christ's role in covenant and how it relates to our interconnectedness of all creation is found in the first chapter of Colossians.

> Christ is the visible image of the invisible God. He existed before anything was created and is supreme over all creation, for through him God created everything in the heavenly realms and on earth. He made the things we can see and the things we can't see—such as thrones, kingdoms, rulers, and authorities in the unseen world. Everything was created through him and for him. He existed

before anything else, and he holds all creation together. Christ is also the head of the church, which is his body. He is the beginning, supreme over all who rise from the dead. So he is first in everything. For God in all his fullness was pleased to live in Christ, and through him God reconciled everything to himself. He made peace with everything in heaven and on earth by means of Christ's blood on the cross (Colossians 1:15–20, NLT).

In the storyline of God's covenant with God's creation, the Cosmic Christ, Creator of all things, becomes the created and he makes a sacrifice, both in the Incarnation and in the Crucifixion, as an act of love. We, and all creation, as benefactors of the gift of creation and the gift of continuous healing from our mistakes, now are covenanted to learn to live in shalom relational covenant with the land, all her creatures and with our Creator, Christ. The transaction occurring on the cross is not a transaction at all, but rather a gift of love for which we should live in gratitude with all creation. Eventually, our salvation will be linked, as it is right now, to all the rest of creation for eternity.

Indigenous peoples have little place for such Western constructs as a penal substitutionary atonement, but if they did, it would make much more sense for Custer to die for the sins of White people than for Jesus to do so. Fortunately, Custer dying as a sacrifice for us makes little sense, since he has no power to change things. Such an exchange lacks the relational component necessary to bring the community together in loving, familial relationship and in shalom covenant. Such an exchange lacks the notion of the interconnectedness of all things necessary in covenant love.

6

The Salvation of a "Sinister Kid"[1]
by Robert W. Wall

Introduction

THIS ESSAY BEGAN ITS life as a pastor's response to a practical problem. We all observe that certain biblical texts are routinely taken out of context as the pretext for their misuse as proof texts. Folks sometimes impose their peculiar understanding or personal experiences onto Scripture to wring out an agreement that is simply not there. There are those infamous "texts of terror," for example, that legitimize the silencing and even abusive treatment of others—of women, of people of color, of the economic poor and politically powerless. Then there are those more benign "texts of compromise" that lend succor to Christians who want their cake and eat it too. I have observed this passage, Romans 7:14–25, used as a "text of compromise."

But who can blame people for doing so?! The longer I live with this passage, the more I want God's permission to skip it—just go *from Romans 6:23 to Romans 8:1 without missing a beat. What would we actually lose with the eclipse of Romans 7?* Reading it has always included much hand-wringing and puzzlement, so much so that I suspect its famous wail, "wretched man that I am," is the exegete's lament finding herself at wits' end trying to figure out what this text means! In any case, that's the task for this chapter:

---

1. This chapter, which I dedicate to the life and legacy of my friend and colleague, Professor Larry Shelton, is adapted from my 2012 Paul T. Walls Lecture, "The Salvation of a 'Sinister Kid,'" delivered on May 2, 2012, at Seattle Pacific University. For the lyrics to the Black Keys' song "Sinister Kid," some of which are referenced here, please see http://www.songlyrics.com/the-black-keys/sinister-kid-lyrics/.

to figure out why Paul adds Romans 7 to an argument that would do very well without it.

Let me admit that the history of this passage's use by the church has produced an array of applications at odds with its plain sense,[2] even if many respond to gospel truths, precious and plain. Some readers feel the pain of its first-person character, who seems to speak knowingly of those dark moments of the soul most of us experience, when our conversion to Christ doesn't remove the persistent tendency to sin and fail him. And, of course, interpreters both ancient and modern have found it natural to think that Paul is describing himself in the first person, whether as a new Christian or pious Pharisee, trying in vain to meet the religious expectations of the Jewish law.

But there are good reasons for thinking that the first person of this passage is neither Paul nor even a Christian. In the first place, the big-ticket idea of Romans 5–8 is that the believer is no longer an old self but a new one, freed from sin's power and raised with Christ to live a Spirit-filled life. Moreover, Paul's prior story in Acts makes it clear that he never experiences what Romans 7 describes—a point he repeatedly makes in his letters where he describes himself as having a clear conscience, blameless under the law (cf. 2 Cor 1:12; 4:2; Phil 3:6).

But if not Paul, then who is its celebrated character and what difference does it make to us 20 centuries later? So not to make you wait in suspense for my answer, let me say this at the outset: Paul writes in the first person as a rhetorical device to impersonate the old self, Adam's child, whose futile attempt to use Scripture without the Spirit results in sin's triumph and a deep sense of spiritual failure contrary to life with the risen Christ.[3]

Before we press on to an examination of Romans 1–8 to make this point more clear, let me mention something most Wesleyans don't know. We stand, if a bit awkwardly, in the Arminian theological heritage, named after the Dutch theologian, James Arminius. It was his dissertation on Romans 7:14–25, published shortly after his death by his children, that triggered the famous Remonstrance of 1610, a protest movement within Protestantism over the practical effects of the Reformation's doctrine of justification by faith alone. Arminius didn't think the Reformers understood

---

2. Achtemeier says that an interpreter of this passage faces the problem of a history of interpretation that "has distorted Paul's intention in these verses" (*Romans*, 124).

3. Aristotle calls its use in an argument "ethos" when a speaker attempts to persuade an audience not by barrage of facts and charts, or by a crude appeal to emotion, but by crafting a personal connection an audience make with the central character of his speech.

or applied the doctrine rightly. He was right, of course(!), and Wesleyans continue his protest even to this day.

In the dedicatory of Arminius's dissertation, his children make two observations that indicate how their father, our theological mentor, approached and applied Romans 7 to the doctrine of justification. It begins with a quotation from Paul's magnificent epiphany text, Titus 2:11–12, which asserts, "The grace of God has appeared, bringing salvation to all people. Grace educates us so that we can live sensible, ethical, and godly lives right now by rejecting ungodly lives and the desires of this world" (CEB).[4] This text is stipulated by Arminius as an interpretive rule that guides our every interpretation of Scripture: Scripture's use as a means of grace by the Spirit's inspiration must have the holy effect of training us to reject sin and live godly lives.

In this regard, Arminius makes a second observation that underwrites his protest of Protestantism. Arminius argues that the effect of the Reformers' reading of Romans 7 does not train Christians to live a holy life; it actually has the opposite result. Luther and Calvin had identified the I-character as a genuine Christian, whose sin has been pardoned by God but whose sin nature still gets the best of him. This spiritual conflict and the misery it produces is the central feature of the Christian's life. And many today identify with that tortured boy with the broken halo: that's me, that's me, the devil won't let me be. Christians are, Luther said, *simul justus et peccator*: "justified while simultaneously a sinner." Forgiven but unchanged.[5]

The real offense for Arminius, as it was a century later for Wesley, is this practical compromise of Scripture's *covenantal* way of salvation. The biblical idea of salvation, he argued, is never monergistic—something that God alone does, detached from an invincibly fallen humanity who cannot possibly choose for God. For Wesley, as for Arminius, salvation, its experience, and its benefit, is a new creation of God's grace powerfully and progressively worked out within the bounds of a deeply affecting relationship with the risen One. Salvation is cooperative and always participatory. As Paul reminds Titus and us, the grace of God has appeared to educate us about salvation so that we might choose to live godly lives. This, I will

---

4. All Bible translations by Robert W. Wall unless noted.

5. But what does this say of God's grace? Is the practical effect of its epiphany into human existence so puny that sin triumphs after all? Has God stacked the deck against even Christians who can do nothing else but continue to sin and fail God? Is God's grace that justifies the sinner reduced to a declaration of our innocence that imputes righteousness but leaves nothing else for us to do? Does God do all of salvation's heavy lifting?

argue, is the theological rubric Wesley wraps around Romans 7, and it stands at the heart of a Methodist's Scripture way of salvation.

Larry Shelton has dedicated a substantial percentage of his intellectual and pastoral energies in building a similar response to this same problem.[6] But his attention has not been Romans 7 but Romans 6 as glossed by his understanding of the Christology of Romans 3 and Pneumatology of Romans 8 in constructing a covenantal (or relational) understanding of what we Wesleyans call "full salvation." Accordingly, Shelton rejects a strictly forensic conception of justification in favor of a participatory model in which a transformed relationship with a relationship-building God is predicated on Christ's healing sacrifice on the Cross ("covenant renewal") but then also his continuing priestly ministry to the reconciled community, mediated by his life-giving Spirit, which restores its loving communion with the triune God.

The purpose of this essay is to try and fit Romans 7 into this larger revision of a Scripture way of salvation in a way that continues Shelton's work, and the legacy of Wesley and Arminius. I do so in conversation with Paul and a cut from *Brothers*, a recent album by my favorite rock group, The Black Keys. It's called "Sinister Kid" and narrates the desperate downward spin of a kid trapped in sin and inevitable death. In part, this is to pick up yet another theme of Shelton's work, which he drilled into me as his young colleague at Seattle Pacific University: the ideas we retrieve from Scripture and our Wesleyan tradition to teach our students must be translated in a way that speaks into their contemporary culture. Many of my Christian students identify with the "sinister kid" of this rock riff. Some think of themselves as "kids with broken halos," whom "the devil won't let (them) be." An answer to this question is what concentrates this study: How does God's saving grace get these kids off their spiritual shide?

Reading Romans 7 in Context of Romans

Romans is the first letter we receive with the NT and Romans should be the first letter we read. Its priority is not only symbolized by its placement among the NT letters, but by the church's traditional use of it to introduce Bible readers to God's gospel according to St. Paul. In fact, many historians

---

6. See in particular Shelton, "Sanctification in Romans 6"; idem, *Cross and Covenant*, especially his participatory idea of the community's covenant obligation to God (i.e., "divine expectations"); and idem, "Covenant Atonement as a Wesleyan Integrating Motif."

now suspect that Paul wrote Romans to set out his gospel message for those who like us had never before heard him preach it in person. For good reason, Wesley writes in his preface to Cranmer's *Homilies*, "He who desires to more perfectly understand the great doctrines of Christianity ought diligently to read the Holy Scriptures, especially St. Paul's Epistles to the Romans and the Galatians."[7] Wesleyans approach Romans as the means of grace by which the inspiring Spirit educates us in "the great doctrines of Christianity."

But our angle to any of Paul's NT letters must also align with his apostolic witness. And his witness did not take shape in a theological or historical vacuum, nor should we read it as such. Paul was a Pharisee by training and inclination; his witness to God's gospel was formed within the womb of Judaism and in response to the problem Jews grappled with under Roman rule: God had not yet come in power to fulfill Scripture's promise of a restored Israel. For this reason Paul says in the opening sentence of Romans that the good news he announces is "promised beforehand through God's prophets in the holy Scriptures" (1:2). It should come as no surprise, then, that Paul would quote one of God's prophets in Romans 1:17 to supply the epigraph of his entire letter. If Romans expounds Paul's witness to God's gospel, it is in his sanctified commentary on God's promise made beforehand through the prophet Habakkuk in Holy Scripture that "the righteous will live because of faith." It is that the promise Paul witnesses has now been fulfilled because of Messiah Jesus.[8]

---

7. Even if I would add only when we reread Paul by the light of 1 John! First John, not Romans, is the trump card for Wesley.

8. There are good reasons why Paul should recruit Hab 2:4 to provide the canonical setting for hearing his gospel. This prophecy climaxes a difficult conversation between God and the prophet that bears a striking family resemblance to the difficult conversation between Paul and Jewish opponents of his Gentile mission. In its opening oracle, Habakkuk complains that treacherous Gentiles are being used to execute God's judgment against Israel. How can a holy God expect Israel to repent by using unholy Chaldeans (cf. Hab 1:13 LXX)? In response, God tells Habakkuk to await the appointed time (2:3 LXX), when the "righteous will live because of *my* (i.e., God's) faithfulness." Romans, especially 9–11, responds to Paul's claim that pagan converts are grafted into the covenant community to make Jews jealous. Some Jews heard Paul saying that that Israel is being threatened by Gentiles. But in Paul's time-zone, Israel's complaint targets those Gentiles who are being initiated into the body of Christ without first being initiated into Judaism. The claim is made that Paul's unauthorized mission to the Gentiles is swallowing up God's biblical promises to historic Israel according to the Scripture (cf. Hab 1:13 LXX and Rom 4:5). It is as if Paul makes God out to be unfaithful! But Paul's response, finally worked out in Romans 9–11, is that God's response to Habakkuk's Israel

Read within its OT setting, God's promise to the prophet climaxes a difficult conversation. Habakkuk had complained of the Lord's use of treacherous Gentiles to humiliate Israel into repentance. How can God realistically expect Israel to repent, the prophet asks, if its hand is forced by the violent actions of unholy Chaldeans (cf. Hab 1:13, LXX)?[9] How fair is that? God's sharp response to the prophet is recorded in Habakkuk 2:3–4: "wait for an appointed time"—a *kairos* event, God says, when the "righteous will live because of *my* (i.e., God's) faithfulness" (Hab 2:3–4, LXX; cf. Rom 3:26). Well, that wait is over, Paul says in Romans 3:26; the Messiah's Cross is a faithful God's appointed *kairos* when the promise God made to Habakkuk is fulfilled for all who believe.

It is Paul's elaboration in two grand movements of this fulfilled prophecy that we must wrap around Romans 7 to make plain sense of it. So let me set these two movements before you in a series of fast-paced observations to provide the context for this text.

1. Most recent interpreters of Romans agree that the letter's main body consists of two integral parts: 1:18–5:11 and 5:12—8:39. I take it that each part offers a distinctive Pauline commentary of Hab 2:4 that "the righteous will live because of faith." Each has its own theological interests, its own working vocabulary and attendant practical concerns. Yet to read one part without the other or to read one as if it merely repeated the other leads to a gross misunderstanding of Paul's apostolic interpretation of God's life-giving promise to Habakkuk.

2. We should note that Paul shapes his two interpretations of Hab 2:4 in a similar way, which makes clear the flowchart of his gospel. Each part of the letter's main body begins with a message from the grim reaper about the human condition. Paul opens in 1:18–32 with an expansive

---

is also God's response to his Jewish opponents: at an appointed time, "the righteous will live because of faith." Repeatedly in his letter, Paul announces that God's appointed time is now because of Jesus, when God makes good on the promise made to Habakkuk that the righteous will live because of God's faithfulness. Notice that Paul has strategically edited his prophetic epigraph so that its reference to God's faithfulness is removed: "the righteous will live because of *my* faithfulness (*pistis*)" (Hab 2:4 LXX) par. "the righteous will live because of *my* (= God's) faith (*pistis*)" (Rom 1:17). The effect of doing so not only suspends the identity of that one whose saving faith makes the righteous live; Paul has also raised a puzzlement: *whose* saving faith makes the righteous live? And it is this implied question that his gospel targets.

9. This is similar to the complaint of Jewish opponents of Paul's Gentile mission, according to Romans 9–11.

catalogue of various religious, moral and political evils of human culture that deny the Creator's existence. God condemns such criminal behavior to death in 1:32: clearly, these are folks who suppress the gospel truth in unrighteous and are not among those who will live because of faith. This same assessment is repeated at the beginning of his second track in 5:12–21, where Paul recalls the biblical story of Adam whose sinful rebellion against God defines the human condition: Adam's children all sin and they all die; they too are not among the righteous who will live.

3. If Paul begins each commentary with bad news, he concludes each with good news. In concluding the first track in 5:1–11, he affirms that those who trust Christ are justified by his blood; they are declared righteous by God and live at peace with God. And who can forget the stunning doxology that concludes the second track in chapter 8: "I am convinced that neither death, nor life, nor anything else in all creation will be able to separate us from the love of God in Christ Jesus our Lord." Paul's gospel ends with God's yes. The righteous *will live* because of faith.

4. Working within this frame, then, Paul's initial interpretation of God's promise to Habakkuk in *Romans 2–4* drills down on the relationship between "the righteous" and "faith," two catchwords that are repeated and related over and over again in the letter's first section. Let me make four observations about the relationship between the two.

   A. Paul's story of salvation is covenantal (see Shelton). God's promise of life concerns the restoration of a broken relationship between God and God's people. The mending of their relationship is largely a matter of God's faithfulness to this covenant—what Paul calls "the righteousness of God." Perhaps no text illustrates this better than the pivotal proof-text of the Protestant Reformation, Romans 3:21–26.[10] No other biblical passage brings faith and righteousness into closer proximity than this one. Here Paul announces a seismic shift in salvation's history: "but now," he writes, at the appointed time, the faithfulness of God is revealed when God accepts the Messiah's faithfulness on the Cross as sacrifice for sin that puts to

---

10. "Righteous/righteousness/justified" is used seven times and "faith/believe" is used four times in just seven verses.

right all who believe in him. What has become of our boasting? It is excluded, Paul says. For God pardons the sinner's guilt not because of the quality of our spiritual résumés, but because a faithful God cooperates with a faithful messiah to atone for the sins of all who place their faith in them--what I call a coalition of the faithful. And the acquitted will live because of this coalition of the faithful.

B. Abraham is pitched by Paul in Romans 4 as Scripture's exemplar of this justification by the faithful. His story is cued by Genesis 15:6, which says that Abraham trusted God would make good on the extraordinary promises God had made to him and Sarah, and God credited them with righteousness as a result. To give credit is the practice of a business accountant who pays a fair salary for the work done. The work done is by the crucified Jesus; and the wage God pays is to declare that those who trust him are members of the community covenanted with God to receive the blessings of the life promised them.

C. We should observe that Paul is careful to define Abraham's faith in God in radical rather than simplistic terms. Abraham trusts God without wavering, fully convinced that God will keep the promises made to him and Sarah. They trust a God who will make good on an improbable future: God promised them a son that Sarah was unable to conceive to begin a family that would settle a land they did not yet occupy. The faith that saves is a faith that is as hard as nails in the complete confidence that God will keep the promise of life.

D. Most Protestants don't make it out of Romans 1–4; and why should they?! What spectacular good news that God's promise to Habakkuk has already been fulfilled on God's decision and declaration. What a safe haven to trust in God's moral rectitude rather than our own. To depend on heaven's Chief Justice who fairly condemns sinners to death, but who now fairly acquits sinners of their guilt and declares them righteous because of faith—that is, a faithful God's embrace of a faithful Messiah's work for all who have faith in them and in them alone.

5. But Paul is not nearly finished retrieving the full gospel from Hab 2:4. He lays down a second track in *Romans 5–8* that elaborates the kind

of life the righteous will live according to God's promise. The apostle's gospel not only announces that sinners are pardoned and placed in right relationship with God because of faith; their acquittal also enables them to participate with the risen Christ as instruments of God's righteousness.

A. The crucial verse in this second part of Romans is 6:1. Here Paul puts into play a very different conception of righteousness—no longer a righted relationship but now a right practice. One of Paul's more attentive parishioners has raised a most excellent question: "Pastor Paul," she asks, "If Christ has already inaugurated the reign of grace and eternal life is ours for the asking, why can't we just keep on sinning so that God's grace has something to forgive?" That is, if the entire debt accumulated by our past sins has already been paid off by Jesus, why not extend the grace period into the present?

B. The force of this question is felt by the compelling contrast Paul draws up between Adam and Christ found in 5:12-21 where Paul shows that the reign of death, inaugurated by the first Adam's sin, has been replaced by a reign of grace inaugurated by the second Adam, Jesus. Eternal life is the result, which might imply—or so the question of 6:1 suggests—that those in Christ can live like hell with the assurance that they still get heaven when they die.[11]

C. Paul's famous retort (various translations, some more salty than others): "Goodness no, dude." That way of thinking is dead wrong. Paul's stunning elaboration of his retort in Romans 6 is one of the most powerful essays on grace found in Scripture. We no longer

---

11. Paul begins his commentary on God's promise of life with a discussion of God's victory over death. He does so by contrasting two Adams. The first Adam of Eden brokers sin into the world and with it a dominion of death that extends to everybody: all have sinned and have failed God. Life in the likeness of this first Adam is a life outside of Christ; it is living in place where the grace of God is not fully experienced. On the other hand, the second Adam of the cross brokers justification and life for everybody. Whilst the disobedience of the first Adam brings condemnation into creation, the obedience of the second Adam makes many righteous, leading to eternal life. As J. Levison nicely puts it, Paul's comparison of the first and second Adams turns his readers toward God's promise of a new creation "by reaching back to Adam made from dust while simultaneously lunging into the future toward the second Adam from heaven" (*Filled with the Spirit*, 315).

LIVE in sin; but we share in the results of Jesus' BODILY death and resurrection; our old selves are toast, we are raised with Christ to live resurrection. Not only is our résumé of persistent sinning crucified with him on the cross, we are set free from sin's powerful grip to live as instruments of God's righteousness—i.e., in the likeness of God's moral rectitude (v. 7).

And so here Paul describes in a series of matter-of-fact statements what we will call the resurrection life. This is the kind of life that God promises those justified by faith. Christians are not only pardoned from sin's guilt and repositioned in right relationship with God; Christians are liberated from sin's power to participate with the risen Jesus in Easter. We no longer practice death but are transformed by God's grace to walk in newness of resurrection life.

D. Yes, Paul adds a footnote in 6:12–13 that resurrection life is qualified by our mortality this side of the Second Coming. And so those who participate with Christ in his resurrection are still citizens of a fallen creation whose groans await its full redemption. But unlike our old self, our new self is no longer enslaved to master-sin. We don't "got to" sin; we "get to" sin no more. Remember epiphany: Grace appears to train us to reject sinning and to live Easter.

E. I love 6:22 because it so neatly summarizes God's promise of life. It's an earthshaking verse, and Wesleyans in particular should preach and parade it: *But now, the good fruit of having been freed from sin and enslaved to God is sanctification, the end of which is eternal life.* In Paul's letters, *nuni de*, "but now," announces seismic shifts in salvation's history—what I call a "gospel tsu-nuni" (cf. 3:21–22). This gospel tsu-nuni captures the soul of God's promise of life to the righteous: But now, since the justified have been freed from sin's grip (6:6–7); but now, since the justified have been enslaved to a faithful, loving God (6:18), they get holiness, and the holy get eternal life with God (cf. 2:7). Where is *simul justus et peccator* in this picture? Nowhere, my sisters and brothers! In this picture, the justified are not sinners but the sanctified.

6. *Romans 7*. With this confirmation of fulfilled promise, we come to our text and back to the question I raised at the beginning of this chapter: why not jump to 8:1 and skip all the fuss and foment of Romans 7?

What insight do we gain into Paul's gospel by including Romans 7? Let's see.

A. We first should allow that Romans 7:1 picks up a topic that has concerned Paul all along: what role does Jewish law, the biblical Torah, perform during the reign of grace? This question would have been personally important to Paul, a Pharisee now following Jesus. And it probably also responds to concerns registered by the letter's first readers in Rome. Many were converts from Judaism who now opposed Paul's Torah-free mission to the Gentiles. According to Paul's Judaism, the Torah, which includes the first five books of the Bible, was the principal mechanism that not only formed the community's public identity, but stage-managed its covenant relationship with God.[12] Simply put, the Torah functioned as the principal mechanism of life with God for Jews, especially for Bible-believing Pharisees like Paul.

B. In fact, according to 7:12 the biblical law is received as holy, just and good, and is even recognized by the wretched character Paul impersonates in Romans 7 as spiritual (14) and good (16); law is a holy object in which we take delight (22), echoing the Psalmist's sentiments. Paul even claims in 8:4 that the requirements of the Torah are realized in the Christian's resurrection life. What Paul claims is new about our life with Christ is not its content, which is inscribed by the law code and narrative of Torah. Paul is NOT engaged in Torah-bashing; the issue on the table is whether it can properly function as a mechanism of resurrection life during the reign of grace inaugurated by the Messiah. Can Scripture by itself produce the manner of life it reveals?

Paul answers by drawing an expansive contrast the old written code and God's Spirit, a contrast introduced in 7:6 and then expanded in 7:7–8:17. Sharply put, the wretched man of Romans 7 illustrates the failure of the Holy Bible, when used without the

---

12. Paul's defense of the inherent divine qualities of law may well address an anti-Torah supersessionism in the Roman church, unlike in the Galatian churches where some were advancing a Torah-observant Christianity. Different first audiences require different approaches to the question of Torah. Within canonical setting, the conversation between the two offers a more balanced assessment of the enduring importance of God's law (esp. in messianic form, e.g., Sermon on Mount) as stipulating covenant-keeping practices for the faith community.

Holy Spirit, to function as the mechanism of resurrection life during the reign of grace.

C. Paul initially channels Adam in 7:7–12. We know he is impersonating Adam because of the loud echoes we hear from Eden where Adam coveted God's capacity to discern good and evil, was deceived by the serpent into eating the fruit forbidden by God's command, where he sinned and so he died. Paul continues Adam's story begun in Romans 5, where Adam plays the role of Christ's anti-type, the very epitome of humanity's old self enslaved to sin, destined to die, in desperate need of saving grace brokered by heaven's second Adam.[13]

---

13. The conception of law in Romans is that it is GOD'S law—a revelation of God's will—and therefore must be perfect, eternally valid, and efficacious, and used as such. As a Pharisee, Paul will naturally link law with Torah. So, the relevant question is how then should Torah be used in Christian existence? But, with respect to 3:31, the issue is more limited it seems to me. That is, Paul is not yet ready to deal with the status of sin, which Torah helps to define, in Christian existence. This he will do magnificently in 5:12—6:23. Rather, I think his point here is to agree that Torah discloses God's plans for creation/Israel/nations, most especially God's promise made to Abraham and Sarah (Rom 4), which God faithfully brings to realization in Christ. In all of this, the quotation of Hab 2:4b from LXX in 1:17 is subtext—in my reading (agreeing with the sense of Hays' reading of Romans), Romans is a commentary/midrash on Hab 2:4b. But in the LXX, the promise that the "righteous will live" is predicated on "my (i.e., God's) faithfulness." That is, Torah reveals God's plans for creation, which a faithful God has brought to realization with Christ. But God has done so in a way that establishes Torah as word of God—that is, as a promise of blessing (eternal life) that is conditioned on a life of moral rectitude. Protestants tend to emphasize only a positional or juridical righteousness. That is, God has made/declared those who believe in Christ "righteous," and on this basis they "will live" with God forever. Righteous is a legal standing, not a lifestyle. However, this offends the Jewish sensibility of divine wrath according to which God will judge everyone impartially on the basis of their good works (= moral rectitude). Eternal life is awarded on the basis of good works. Scripture does not disagree in any part with this conclusion. So in some sense faith also must establish Torah's definition of the righteous life in this practical and not only in a positional sense. Rom 6:20–22, in concluding Paul's dense and expansive response to the student's question in 6:1 (via his reiteration of it in 6:15), returned to the conception of divine judgment raised in 2:5–11: eternal life is granted by a faithful, just God on the basis of good works—the works of sanctification. But now Paul is able to say faith is actually an obedient act by which the believer participates in Jesus' obedience on the Cross, which results in resurrection/Easter/newness of life. Even though qualified by our mortality (6:12–13a), believers have a new capacity to live holy lives. We can sin, but we don't have to (6:13b–14)! In fact, the dramatic claim is finally made that the fruit of our new works that God accepts for eternal life. I think Paul is walking the very same fine line, using the very same dialectic that Wesley does. Sanctification by grace through faith alone—but which does not over-emphasize faith and

D. So the question asked in 7:13, whether God's law, which intended good ends, causes us to die, it is Adam who asks it and it is for Adam's children, outside of Christ, that Paul again responds, "Goodness no, dude." But in elaborating his response, Paul changes the verbal tense from Eden's past to Seattle's present to impersonate Adam's child who seeks after God's pleasure without Christ and so without the Spirit of new life.

And sin will not let this kid alone: "I got a tortured mind and my blade is sharp, A bad combination in the dark." Paul does not think of sin as a feeling or intuition, but a real power, a driving force, a felt compulsion that drives the sinister kid headlong toward death. And he is powerless to resist averting sin's deadly result: he continues to do things he knows he shouldn't. He is enslaved to sin's power, which seizes opportunities to create havoc. Sin is Eden's serpent that entraps and entices the old self to covet and die. So sinister is sin that it even corrupts those holy things that God has sanctified for good ends. Whether Jewish law or the Christian Bible: without the holy Spirit, it simply will not work as a mechanism of resurrection life.

E. The key word of this speech is 7:24's *talaipōros*, which means miserable or wretched. Paul uses this rare word to attract our attention. It combines a word that means "to cultivate" with an adjective that means "misery"—i.e., a cultivated state of wretchedness, what Veblen calls a "trained incapacity."[14] The effect of using the bibli-

---

rather emphasizes its effect, its result: a holy life in compliance with God's will, revealed in Torah. The problem of Protestantism, with its roots in a kind of Augustinian reading of Scripture's narrative of salvation, is its over-determined conception of saving faith. Of course, this trades on the deep logic and profound theocentrism of Scripture's Pauline canon. I actually think that this is a misreading of Paul, which the Catholic Epistles help correct. Evangelical and liberal Protestants both emphasize the Torah ends with Christ. That Christian existence in some sense voids Torah and its definition of the holy life. Its focus is on faith alone. But Wesley (and I think a profoundly Jewish Paul) would never argue that Torah is ruled out of Christian existence; rather it is "established"; it is made efficacious because of grace that comes to those who are baptized with Christ in his death and resurrection.

14. I'm quite taken by Thorstein Veblen's notion of "trained incapacities" (introduced in Veblen's *Instinct of Workmanship*), by which he observes that people are so trained and shaped by a particular intellectual or disciplinary regimen that they are "blind" or incapable of seeing what others see from their different angles. It's not that we see things differently, but our training actually incapacitates us from thinking or understanding

cal law without the Spirit is to train a spiritual incapacity. Look, people, sin is powerful and it will defeat even our sacred texts by turning them a self-help manual, a system of proof texts, of lifeless tradition that cultivates a joyless futility and spiritual frustration. Sin transforms Scripture, if used outside of Christ and so without the Spirit's company, into a catechesis of the wretched Word.

F. 8:1–4, then, and not 7:7–25 is Paul's personal testimony. This is where he cashes out the dramatic change that comes with the reign of grace: with Jesus the believer gets the Spirit, and with the Spirit she receives the gift of a new and improved mechanism of life by which a community's identity and covenant-keeping practices are more effectively formed. The extensive catalog of contrasts between the incapacity of the old self to experience God's pleasure in Romans 7 and the believer's Spirit-filled life in Romans 8:1–11 leads Paul to make his climactic assertion in 8:12–17: that God's adopted children (i.e., "the righteous") are led by God's Spirit and so did not receive (aorist indicative) a spirit of slavery that produces fear but the divine spirit of adoption that funds and forms our human spirits to assure us that we are forgiven and our relationship with God restored.[15]

---

different points of view. Bias is an intellectual habit. In any case, I think that's what's going on in Romans 7. The effect of using a mechanism of covenant-keeping without the Spirit's company = disaster. Of course, we can apply this to the church. But I don't think Paul understands the "I" as a believer in this sharply dualistic passage. Nor do I think applying it to Christian existence simply because we experience something like this gets us to where Paul is taking us in Romans. Resurrection life is impossible without the Spirit. Abba is a profoundly intimate confession of God without which our use of Scripture produces wretchedness, insoluble conflicts, frustrations. In any case, I'll try and make Wesley's point about justification in light of what I take Paul's point is Romans is. I read Romans as a midrash on the prophetic epigraph from Hab 2:4—i.e., how are Christians to understand God's promise to Habakkuk that "the righteous will live because of faith." If his first interpretative track in Romans 1–4 seeks to elaborate on the relationship between "the righteous" and "because of faith," then Romans 5–8 seeks to elaborate on the nature of God's promise of life to the righteous. And it is resurrection life in the present ("walk in newness of life") that concerns Paul the most. Romans 7 fits into that second interpretive track. Somehow. Whatever is being lamented, it isn't resurrection life!

15. But the most important point made here regards the nature and mechanism of the life that God has promised the righteous according to Hab 2:4. At ground level, the life of God's children in contrast to Adam regards affections and direction.

(1) 8:2: the source of life is the Spirit—the Spirit of life (genitive of source)
(2) 8:5: those who live (*ontes*) by the Spirit set their minds on spiritual things

G. Not only does Spirit-filling enable the Christian to practice covenant-keeping; it ends our fears and allows us to approach God with intimate acquaintance, even addressing God as "Abba." The Spirit's inward testimony assures the hearts of those who belong to Christ that the promise God made to Habakkuk has been realized: the righteous will *indeed* live with the risen Christ because of faith.

A Wesleyan Reading of Romans 7

A Wesleyan theological reading of Romans 7 begins with this observation: John Wesley is less interested to make sense of what a biblical passage plainly says and more interested to search out its theological meaning in response to a practical problem. A useful interpretation is one that elaborates what he calls the Scripture way of salvation, which plots the advance of God's grace from original sin, to justification by faith, resulting in present, inward salvation—or holiness, which Wesley calls "religion itself."

Throughout his life, Wesley preached this same threefold narrative of salvation, using various typologies to do so but always with the same beginning, middle, and end. At every moment along salvation's way, he envisions a corresponding advance of God's grace always in the company of the indwelling Spirit who mediates and monitors the distribution of grace in different ways and by different degrees according to a person's spiritual maturity and circumstance. There is no moment along salvation's progress that we do not experience God's victory over sin, depending on our faithful response to it. There is no moment along the way that the appearance of grace does not require a response without which grace cannot empower newness of life by the Spirit.

---

(3) 8:6: to set mind on the Spirit produces life and shalom—i.e., virtue.

(4) 8:8–9: those who live (*ontes*) in the flesh cannot please God, but you are not in the flesh since the Spirit lives (*oikeo*) in you

(5) 8:10: the righteous will die because of sin (mortal bodies), but the righteous also have the Spirit, which is (new) life

(6) 8:11: Spirit is the agent of new life—God gives life through Spirit who lives (oike) in the righteous.

(7) 8:12–13: you will die if you live according to the flesh; you will live if by the Spirit you put to death "body works" (i.e., 1:18–32; 5:12–21).

Original sin / prevenient grace / repent

Justification / forgiving grace / faith

Present, inward salvation / sanctifying grace / works of mercy / piety

Christian perfection

FIGURE 01

For Wesley, all of life depends on grace, and grace is always at work in every person, pulling each of us toward a life of holiness and happiness.[16] Grace is powerful but not coercive; grace is always at hand but always dependent upon our reception of it since God's Spirit refuses to distribute it without our permission to do so. As Wesley puts it, "No one sins because he has not grace, but because he does not use the grace which he hath."

Wesley's canonical sermon, "The Spirit of Bondage and Adoption," is important for many reasons, but here its importance is because it provides us with a remarkable example of how Wesleyans should read Romans 7 theologically. The first thing of note about this sermon is that it is one of six that Wesley preaches to clarify the substantial revisions he made in his doctrine of justification by faith alone following his profound religious experience in 1738 that turned his world upside down. He famously wrote about it in his Journal: "In the evening I went very unwillingly to a society in Aldersgate Street, where one was reading Luther's preface to the Epistle to the Romans. About a quarter before nine, while the leader was describing the change which God works in the heart through faith in Christ, I felt my heart strangely warmed. I felt I *did* trust in Christ alone for salvation; and an assurance was given me that He had taken away *my* sins, even *mine*, and saved *me* from the law of sin and death." Hear the echoes of Romans 7? We'll come back to the sermon in a bit.

---

16. Wesley, then, is not any kind of Pelagian if by this one means that humans have the innate ability not to sin without aid of divine grace. Wesley rather believes that grace frees us from the power of "must sinning" so that we can freely choose not to sin. Prevenient grace is that portion that comes before our salvation, preparing our mind and heart for our conversion by making the decision of faith possible.

Wesley had gladly received his gospel of justification from the Protestant Reformation. But his experience at Aldersgate and also the practical concern he shared with Arminius that some Protestants recruited the wretched man of Romans 7 to provide cover for a thin doctrine of justification—a belief that God declares one's sins pardoned but without providing the power to change one's life—prompted Wesley to revise his doctrine of justification by faith. Moreover, he moved the *gravitas* of salvation's narrative from justification to new birth—a changed nature—which prompted him to look forward to sanctification rather than backward to justification as the crucial moment of salvation's progress.

This shift of interest from the justified sinner to the sanctified believer transformed how Wesley viewed the practice of *repentance*. According to the doctrine of justification Wesley inherited from the Reformers, repentance followed justification by faith as the ongoing practice of the Christian who is simultaneously justified and yet sinful. Remember Luther's slogan: *simul justus et peccator*. Accordingly, Christians, even though justified by grace, must continue to repent daily of their sins. Wesley observes, however, that such a practice makes the believer complacent, even reversing Paul's response to his imaginary parishioner: why not keep sinning so that grace may abound? To which some Protestants might respond: well sure, why not?! I'll just repent to square things with God.

Wesley rather takes the offensive by emphasizing the believer must respond to God's sanctifying grace, which diminishes the threat of sin over time and with it the religious importance of believer's repentance. As a result, Wesley moves the initial act of repentance to a moment *prior* to justification by faith when the *unbeliever* repents of sin in response to God's prevenient grace and is able to freely respond to God's justifying grace and rest assured of God's pardon from sin.

Wesley was routinely horrified by how passive people are toward sin. Folks might even agree with Romans 6:23 that the wages of sin is death but never experience its menace, its devastation to the soul, its self-destructive effect on human relationships that Paul describes in Romans 7. For Wesley, the real result of sinful behavior is the hard evidence that sinners need salvation, their souls need healing, their lives need a change of direction. Sin is no theological abstraction, an irrelevant fuss and bother that God has already defeated on the cross. Wesley teaches us that sin is a present and real danger, an unmitigated malevolent force that corrodes every nook and cranny of human existence. Sin is so powerful that even sacred objects, the Jewish Torah, the Christian Bible, cannot defeat it when used on its own. God's offer of salvation is deliverance from sin's sinister power, which results when one repents and turns toward God's loving embrace in faith.

But a sinner's repentance raises a practical matter for Wesley. How can Adam's child, trapped in a state of original sin, come to know that the wages of sin is deadly and that he badly needs pardon from sin's guilt and release from sin's power? How is the sinister kid made aware of this when no thought is ever given of her peril, because her spiritual senses have been trained so that she is incapable of sensing the Spirit's presence or the offer of God's grace it brokers? As Wesley puts the problem, "none will come to the Physician but they that are sick *and sensible* of it."

The practical problem is how the sick become aware of it. Wesley addresses this problem in his sermon, "The Spirit of Bondage and Adoption." He calls the experience an awakening, when grace "touches the heart of him that lay asleep in darkness and in the shadow of death. He is terribly shaken out of his sleep, and awakes into a consciousness of his danger. They see themselves naked of all poor pretense and their wretched excuses for sinning against God." Wesley recognizes that Paul impersonates an awakening experience in Romans 7, and to an advance of God's prevenient grace, when the sinner, Adam's child, becomes convinced of sin's guilt and self-destructive power but finds himself helpless to deliver him from the terror of death. At last he cries out in thanksgiving for Christ's deliverance. Adam's child has been led by prevenient grace onto the porch of repentance and to the door of faith that justifies sinners.

Wesley's radical re-reading of the contrast spread across Romans 7–8 between the wretched non-Christian and the Spirit-led Christian does not follow Paul, who sets out the contrast in 7:6 as between the biblical law code and life-giving Spirit. Rather Wesley interprets Paul's contrast as a vivid description of contrasting experiences of the indwelling Spirit, indexed by 8:15–17. On the one hand, even those outside of Christ experience the Spirit's mediation of God's prevenient grace, which they experience as the "spirit of bondage and fear." It is this operation of the Spirit that awakens the non-believer from spiritual slumber to the awful threat of sin, that allows him to feel the misery of sin's sinister power; that makes him fear heaven's loss; it is the Spirit who convinces him that the wages of sin is death. We are never without grace and so never without God's Spirit who brokers grace by degrees and at every step along salvation's way. And it is this same Holy Spirit, first experienced as a terrifying presence, who then is experienced as a spirit of adoption, leading the awakened sinner to repent and, assured of her forgiveness, to confess God as Abba.

Hear again the fourth stanza of Charles' anthem of our *Methodist* Remonstrance: "Long my imprisoned spirit lay/Fast bound in sin and nature's night; Thine eye diffused a quickening ray, I woke, the dungeon flamed with light; My chains fell off, *my heart was free*, I rose, went forth, and followed Thee."[17] I know we should end there with Wesley's hymn; but let's return to Romans 7 one last time for a final comment. In his sermons, Wesley enlists all kinds of providences to awaken sinners of their spiritual peril—personal tragedies, natural disasters, Christian testimonies, even the reading of the preface to Luther's commentary on Romans! But the primary trigger remained for him biblical preaching. Had Paul been writing Romans for a congregation filled with Protestants rather than Jews, he probably would have used the Christian Bible instead of the Jewish Torah to make his point. Let me reimagine it with Wesleyan tenor for our use today: the use of the Bible without the Holy Spirit—*sola scriptura*—to realize God's promise of resurrection life will only end in a miserable failure. Sin would win out. But Wesley's Scripture way of salvation would score this same point by arguing that the non-believer's hearing of a clear exposition of Scripture is an auxiliary of the Spirit to mediate God's prevenient grace so to awaken and terrify a sinister kid of his need for salvation, and so draw him into the swift flow of grace, straight into the arms of his Maker, whose name is love.

Romans 7:13—8:2 (Wall Trans.)

7:13. Did what is good for me, then, become death? Goodness no!! In order for sin to be clearly shown to be sin, worked itself out in me as death through what is good (*agathos*) in order that sin would become even more evident through the commandment.

7:14. For this reason we know Scripture is spiritual; I, however, I am fleshly (6:19; 7:5), sold into slavery under sin: 15. I don't understand what I'm doing; in fact, I don't do what I want but rather what I hate. 16. Yet even if I do what I don't want, I agree that Scripture is right (*kalos*).

7:17. But now it is no longer I doing it; instead, it is sin that dwells within me. 18. For I know nothing dwells within me—that

---

17. Wesley, "And Can It Be?"

is, in my flesh—that is good (*agathos*). The desire to do what is right (*kalos*) is in me; I just can't do it! 19. I don't do good (*agathos*) even though I want to; rather, I do the very evil I don't want to do! 20. But if I do what I don't want, it is no longer me doing it but sin that dwells in me.

7:21. You see, I encounter Scripture when I want to do the right thing (*kalos*); but evil is right there with me. 22. I thoroughly delight in the law of God in the inner self, 23 but I see a different law within me that wages war with the law of my mind and holds me prisoner by the law of sin within me. 24. I am a miserable person! Who will rescue me from this body of death? 25a. I thank God through Jesus Christ our Lord! (7:25b. So then, I serve the law of God with my mind but the law of sin with my flesh. 8:1. So now, there is no death sentence in Christ Jesus, 2 for the law of the life-giving Spirit has freed you from the law of sin and death.)

7

The Kerygmatic Covenant

A UNIFYING CENTER FOR THE NEW TESTAMENT?

Literary and Historical Considerations

by Eugene E. Lemcio

I. Introduction

IT IS AN HONOR to join my colleagues in celebrating the contribution Larry Shelton has made to the study of covenant.[1] My original intent for this chapter had been to show how "The Unifying Kerygma of the New Testament" that I had identified within nineteen of its twenty-seven documents[2] could be viewed as the equivalent to the prologue of the type of covenant configuration appearing in such places as Exod 20:2–17 and Deut 5:6–21 in whose context *brith* and *diathēkē* occur (Deut 5:2–3).[3] My next

---

1. This has been given its most developed expression in Shelton's *Cross and Covenant*.

2. Lemcio, "The Unifying Kerygma [parts 1 and 2]" 3–17, 3–11. These were combined and expanded in an appendix to Lemcio, *The Past of Jesus*, 115–31 (endnotes: 158–62), with a chart displaying the data (130–31). It is reproduced with permission at the end of this chapter, although I have revised its title accordingly.

3. In the modern period, attention to covenant form was given renewed impetus with Mendenhall, *Law and Covenant*. See also Kenneth Kitchen's analysis of the pros and cons of Mendenhall's and others' treatment of this theme in "The Fall and Rise." Because the tradition-history of such forms had long been fixed by the time that NT writers appealed to these Scriptures, I am not engaging tradition-historical issues.

goal was to argue that the widespread, essentially literary pattern could be shown to be historically widespread as well.

However, the more I worked with both the relevant OT and NT texts, the more I realized that the pattern occurring in the latter was not, strictly speaking, merely equivalent to the succinct declaration of that which God had done to deliver Israel from bondage in Egypt (Exod 20:2 and Deut 5:6). Rather, the nineteen NT writers had included two more elements of the covenantal structure in question: the required response to God and the promised benefits (displayed more fully below in Table One). In other words, in both the OT and NT instances, we have a version of the theological-ethical phenomenon that scholars often call the *indicative* (that which God has done), providing the basis upon which the divine *imperative* of what the people should do—and could expect—is declared. This led me to wonder whether a renaming was in order—hence the title of this essay.

TABLE 1: The Sinaitic Covenant and a "Kerygmatic" Covenant of the NT

Components	SINAITIC "COVENANT" (Deut 5:2–21, 29, 33. Cf. Exod 20:2–17)	A "KERYGMATIC" COVENANT OF THE NT (See Table 2)
"Historical" Prologue	1. God	1. God
	2. delivered	2. sent/raised
	3. Israel	3. Jesus
Response	4. Ten Commandments	4. Response (various)
	5. in response to God	5. to God
Blessings	6. Resultant blessings	6. brings blessings (various).

Finally, I also came to recognize that, besides the addition of the Christological element, the audiences in each instance were different: to the people of God exclusively (in the OT) and to God's people and/or to Gentiles in the NT. In the case of the OT, the proclamation of God's rescue and requirement for the people's response is aimed at those who had been already brought in relation to him (i.e., it is not an announcement designed for initiation, but as the basis for maintaining that relationship).[4] So far

---

4. See the discussion in Shelton, *Cross and Covenant*, 38–40 (and throughout) and

as the NT is concerned, the kerygmatic covenant targets those (both Jews and Gentiles) whom its speakers regarded as in need of God's initiating salvation.[5]

II. THE ARGUMENT REVISITED

Terminology

The term "kerygma" does not occur in Deuteronomy 6. Nor does "covenant" appear in any of the passages cited from the nineteen documents of the NT (even though the passages themselves reflect the covenantal structure of that OT text). However, in several of the nineteen, the recital is introduced by a statement that what follows is "kerygma," "gospel," or "message/word" (*logos* or *hrēma*).[6] Therefore, I have created a (perhaps unhappy) hybrid expression: "Kerygmatic Covenant."

That the nineteen instances are a unifying factor is, of course, a judgment call. Reasonable people will differ regarding *quantity* (as to how many instances are required for unity) and with respect to *quality* (a question of significance). So far as *centrality* is concerned, one can hardly argue against something identified as "kerygma," "gospel," or "word/message." Perhaps the word "proto-" should also have been utilized to reflect the fact of the form's skeletal nature—to which systems (both nervous and vascular) and musculature had to be added. Furthermore, "proto-" or even "pre-" would call attention to the *informal* characteristics of this "form:" although the six categories are always present, the sequence varies—as does the content of items 4 and 6. Perhaps this reflects sensitivity to the needs of various audiences or circumstances; or it may signal something as practical as the desire to vary style (a matter of aesthetics).[7] Although this is not a function

---

my Excursus (Section V., Covenant Partners), where I elaborate this very important (but much neglected) point, which Shelton makes early on.

5. This shift warrants a separate, fuller treatment of its own.

6. Rom 10:8–9; 2 Cor 5:19–20; 1 Thess 1:5; 1 Tim 3:16, 4:9; 2 Tim 2:8–9, 11, 15; Titus 3:9; 1 Pet 1:25.

7. Räisänen, in *Beyond New Testament Theology*, 260–61 sees little difference between my position and that taken by Dunn in *Unity and Diversity*, 30–31. Perhaps this is because he did not take into account my point that this formulation was both formal and adaptable, internal rather than external (i.e., supplied by an interpreter), concrete rather than abstract, and native rather than artificial. See Lemcio, *The Past of Jesus*, 117–119, 127. A more attentive view is expressed by Segalla, "La Testimonianza Dei Libri," 304–19. Besides mine, five others' works are evaluated: those of C. H. Dodd, W. Thüsing, J. Noël

of terminology *per se*, it is the case in OT and NT that the emphasis is consistently theocentric/patricentric—God being both the initiator of the drama and the recipient of the response.

III. HISTORICAL CONSIDERATIONS

Having taken into account the covenantal features of my earlier kerygmatic studies, I should like in this section to sketch several aspects of the historical question that were not part of the original articles (dealing as they did with the final literary forms of the NT canon): the time spread, geographical distribution, traditions represented, and "apostolic" associations of this material. To the extent possible, I begin with the hardest data available (that which is evident from the documents themselves), moving to the softer and implied evidence of Church tradition and scholarly inference. My contention is that the data enable one to infer that, although the individual *documents* of the NT may not have universally circulated at first, the six-fold, kerygmatic-covenantal pattern behind them did.

A. Time

Recognizing that scholars differ in their educated speculation (for, as all observe, none of the documents is dated), I cite, for the sake of illustration, the "moderately critical" dating of Bart Ehrman[8] to show that this kerygmatic covenant (whose display in Table 2 at the end of this chapter should be the regular point of reference) appears in traditions and documents spanning a seventy-year period, given the probability of the cited gospel traditions' origination with Jesus: 30–100 CE, the latter requiring some defense.

Principally through the work of three Cambridge scholars (P. Gardner-Smith, C. H. Dodd, and J. A. T. Robinson), it is easier to argue that St. John

---

Aletti, V. Fusco, and R. Penna.

8. Ehrman, *The New Testament*, xxx–xxxi. Oddly, Ehrman does not include Acts in his list. For a sample of the range of possibilities other scholars have promoted, see the displays and discussion by Robinson in *Redating the New Testament*, 5–7. His own tabulations (covering the period 40–68 CE) appear on 352–53. Although citing Robinson in no way commits me to adopting his position about a dating of all of the canonical documents prior to the fall of Jerusalem (70 CE), I do side with those who admit that this maverick view has not been decisively challenged. It must also regularly be acknowledged that scholars provide only their best, educated guesses on the matter of dating NT literature and the traditions they incorporate.

drew upon independent gospel traditions—or slanted common ones in his particular direction.⁹ As my own contribution to their argument, I cite the two strikingly similar logia independently rendered at Mark 9:37 and John 12:44, respectively:¹⁰ "Whoever receives one of these children in my name receives me. And whoever (4) receives me does not receive me but (1, 5) the one who (2) sent (3) me" ([the benefit being (6) God]). Although John will otherwise be John, at this point he parallels the synoptic tradition. "Jesus cried out and said, 'The one who believes in me does not (4) believe in me, but in the (1, 5) one who (2) sent (3) me'" ([the benefit being (6) God]).¹¹

A somewhat less exclusive, but nevertheless theocentric, stress occurs at Matt 10:40: "Whoever receives you (pl.) receives me; and whoever receives me (4) receives the (1, 5) one who (2) sent (3) me" ([the benefit likewise being (6) God]). Were one to apply a version of the notorious and contested "criterion of dissimilarity" here, these sayings would satisfy its demands for historical probability: the absence of an explicit post-Easter christology or the presence of an overt theo- or patricentricity.

B. Geographical Distribution

During this period of time, the pattern in question shows up in traditions and documents that originated from or reached most of the eastern Mediterranean. Geographically, we may speak of it as "universal" during the latter half of the first century CE. In other words, this recital and response occurred wherever the Church (about which there is any evidence) was to be found.

---

9. Gardner-Smith, *St. John and the Synoptic Gospels*; Dodd, *Historical Tradition*; and Robinson, *The Priority of John*.

10. I am using *Novum Testamentum Graece*.

11. Although there is no alternative manuscript evidence at this point, long ago an original member of the NIV's governing panel told me that (out of concern that the ordinary reader might perceive a contradiction at this point) they had inserted "only" after the second "me." Ironically, though motivated by the project's commitment to biblical inerrancy, they had eliminated this connection between the Synoptic and Johannine traditions.

Palestine

Here may be set the dominical logia: in Judea and Galilee (Matt 10:40, Mark 9:37, John 12:44).

Asia Minor: The Roman Province & Interior

In the province of Asia itself, the following may be assigned with confidence: Colossae (Colossians), Ephesus (Ephesians, 1 Timothy, 1 John (?), Revelation), Smyrna, Pergamum, Thyatira, Sardis, Philadelphia, Laodicea (all from Revelation). 1 Peter was written as a circular letter to Pontus, Galatia (where, of course, one would have found Galatians), Cappadocia, and Bithynia. A version of Ephesians apparently functioned as a circular letter throughout the province of Asia.[12]

Europe

To the Greek mainland, Paul wrote to Thessalonica, Philippi, and Corinth. Rome received at least a letter from him; and, if the third-century testimony of Clement of Alexandria and Origen is to be believed, Mark wrote his gospel in Rome.[13] Very early on, this document transcended its particular setting to be appropriated elsewhere by Matthew and Luke. Should Hebrews be located in Italy?

C. Ecclesiastical Traditions

The six-member announcement-response in Tables 1 and 2 was circulated during these times and in these places by the Church as it developed within two major traditions, acknowledged by St. Paul in Gal 2:7-8.

---

12. I have argued that Ephesus acted as a magnet and centrifuge for apostolic persons and the literature which they had produced or influenced: "Ephesus and the New Testament Canon," 210-34.

13. For texts, translations, and discussion, see Taylor, *The Gospel According to St. Mark*, 5-7 and Guelich, *Mark 1-8:26*, xxix-xxxi.

Jewish Christian: Aramaic-Speaking and Greek-Speaking

Although all of our material comes by way of authors writing in Greek, two varieties may be clearly discerned from internal evidence: Mark and John (in logia where Semitic words and phrases are followed by Greek translations[14]) and Acts 6:1 (which explicitly cites the parallel streams, using language as the distinguishing mark).

Gentile Christian

The groupings here are more subtle and contested — in part because of some congregations containing converted Jews and God-fearing Gentiles as well as Gentiles unfamiliar with Judaism: Pauline (2 Corinthians, Galatians, Philippians, 1 Thessalonians); post-Pauline (?): Ephesians, Colossians, 1–2 Timothy, Titus;[15] and non-Pauline: 1 Peter, 1 John, Revelation).

D. Apostles and Apostolic Associates

Jesus and notable figures are involved or inferred as promulgators of the kerygmatic covenant. A companion of Paul's authored Luke-Acts, which mentions Peter, Paul, Mark, and Timothy. Paul cites Titus in Gal 2:3. The Apostle to the Gentiles is responsible for Romans, 2 Corinthians, Galatians, Philippians, 1 Thessalonians. There is the "Paul" of Colossians and Ephesians and the "Paul" of 1–2 Timothy and Titus. The individual receivers of this correspondence are "Timothy" and "Titus." Presumably, the readers of "Mark" and "Hebrews" knew the authors (15:21; 13:19, 20–23, respectively). 1 Peter attributes authorship to the most prominent leader of the Jerusalem Church. There is John (Revelation), who may or may not be the same as the Beloved Disciple (John) or the author of 1 John.

IV. CONCLUSION

The historical discussion above indicates that, whenever one samples these Christian documents of the first century (or slightly later), wherever one

---

14. E.g. Mark 5:41; 14:36; 15:34 and John 1:38, 41–42.

15. Even those who do not maintain full Pauline authorship acknowledge the presence of Pauline traditions and sentiments in these letters. For the latter three, see the summary of evidence and arguments in Wall, *1 and 2 Timothy and Titus*, 4–7.

looks, whichever tradition one consults, whomever of the authors one interrogates, s/he encounters the kerygmatic covenant of divine saving activity in Christ upon which subsequent covenantal formulation and further reflection depend. It is the continuing legacy of the covenants associated with Sinai—and perhaps the unifying center around which a NT theology (and even a full, theocentric biblical theology?) might revolve?[16]

Finally, I take the risk of being accused of engaging in apologetics in raising the subjects of unity and centrality. The penchant for preferring early multiple and diverse Christianities (that were later displaced by a dominant orthodoxy intolerant of many and various alternatives) cannot be sustained if the above is historically probable.

V. EXCURSUS: Covenant Partners (An Elaboration)

In Exod 24:1-8 (without equivalent in Deuteronomy), the covenant bond between God and God's people is formalized ritually by Moses' slaughter of oxen, half of whose blood he throws against an altar—the other half being sprinkled upon the people: the blood *of* ["associated with"?] the covenant (vv. 7-8). It is important to note here that the covenant ceremony appears twelve chapters after the report of the initial saving event (12:33-51). In other words, Israel did not become the people of God upon the sacrifice of oxen and the application of their blood in both directions. Thus, this covenant is not an initiatory event *per se*. The people, according to 20:2, had already been saved. And the fuller story that it summarizes (the opening narrative of 2:24-25) informs the reader that God had remembered promises made to Abraham, their ancestor in the faith (as expressed in Gen 15:6). In other words, through him, they had been elected (so goes that story told earlier) to be those by whom all nations would be blessed (Gen 12:1-3). And that promise could not be fulfilled in a state of political and economic oppression in a country not their own. To belabor this foundational point, the covenant ceremony recounted in Exod 24:1-8 is for insiders.

---

16. Michael Bird cites my kerygma studies and argues that covenant ought to be the organizing category for NT and biblical theology. See "New Testament Theology Reloaded" 265–91, esp. 282 n. 6 and 284–291. I make the point about the need for NT scholars to give theology *per se* its due because, even when one looks at certain NT christologies, they are God-derived: "the Son *of God*" and "the Christ *of God*." Then, of course, there is "the Word *of God*" and "the Kingdom *of God*." God is the beginning and end of the Christian story.

The same goes for the sacrifice of lambs for the Passover celebration (Exod 12:1–36). Their shed blood did not achieve forgiveness so that the participants could become the people of God. It provided *protection* for their first-born sons from the Destroying Angel sent throughout Egypt. As a result, Israel (*already* collectively God's firstborn son [4:22]) experienced *liberation*. Furthermore, the same is true for the Day of Atonement (Leviticus 16). A *live* goat bearing Israel's sins into the desert provided *restoration* for God's people, not their initiation. A similar dynamic occurs in the synoptic Gospels. *Prior* to Jesus' pronouncement at the Last Supper of the wine as his blood of the [New] Covenant (Mark 14:24), the disciples had been called, authorized, and sent on a mission resembling his (chs. 1 and 3). The covenant ritual at Passover formalized a relationship with Jesus that had *previously* been established—the account of which can be duly regarded as the beginning and middle of Mark's expanded, narrated "kerygma." However, this partnership becomes expanded by the inclusion (the initiation?) of "the many."

TABLE 2. The Unifying Kerygmatic Covenant of the New Testament

GOSPELS				ACTS	
Matt 10:40–41	Mark 9:37	Luke 1:68–75	John 5:24	5:30–32 (Peter – Jews)	17:27–31 (Paul – pagans)
(1) who	(1) who	(1) Lord God	(1) who	(1) God	(1) God
(2) sent	(2) sent	(2) raised up	(2) sent	(2) raised	(2) raised
(3) me	(3) me	(3) horn	(3) me	(3) Jesus	(3) him
(4) receives	(4) receives	(4) serve	(4) believes	(4) trust	(4) turn to/ seek God
(5) him	(5) him not me	(5) him	(5) him	(5) God	(5) God
(6) rewards	(6) [receiving God]	(6) salvation from enemies	(6) eternal life	(6) repentance forgiveness	(6) positive judgment

THE KERYGMATIC COVENANT

		LETTERS: Paul		
Rom 10:8-9	2 Cor 5:19-20	Gal 4:4-7	Eph 2:4-10	Phil 2:5-11
(1) God	(1) God	(1) God	(1) God	(1) God
(2) raised	(2) raised	(2) sent forth	(2) raised us up	(2) exalted
(3) Jesus	(3) Christ	(3) his son	(3) with Christ	(3) him
(4) believe that	(4) reconciled	(4) cry	(4) walk in	(4) not grab/hold, obedient
(5) God	(5) to God	(5) Abba Father	(5) God's good works	(5) equality with God [to God]
(6) be saved	(6) reconciled world	(6) to redeem	(6) salvation by grace	(6) named "Lord"

		LETTERS: Paul		
Col 2:12-13 (see 1:25-28)	1 Thess 1:5-10	1 Tim 3:16, 4:7-8	2 Tim 2:8-15	Titus 3:4-8
(1) God	(1) God	(1) God	(1) God	(1) God
(2) raised	(2) raised	(2) took up	(2) raised	(2) [exalted]
(3) Christ	(3) Jesus	(3) him	(3) Jesus Christ	(3) Jesus Christ
(4) faith in working	(4) believing in	(4) hope in	(4) present self	(4) trusted
(5) of God	(5) God	(5) living God	(5) to God	(5) God
(6) enlivened pardoned	(6) rescue from wrath	(6) salvation	(6) salvation	(6) regeneration / renewal of Holy Spirit

	LETTERS: Catholic		APOCALYPSE
Heb 13:20-21 (see vv. 15-16)	1 Pet 1:18-21, 25	1 John 4:7-10	Rev 12:1-11, 17 (see 1:1-2)
(1) God	(1) God	(1) who	(1) God
(2) led from dead	(2) raised	(2) sent	(2) caught up
(3) Jesus	(3) Jesus	(3) only son	(3) child
(4) to do, confess	(4) believe hope	(4) to know	(4) keep commands
(5) God's will God's name	(5) in God	(5) God	(5) of God
#(6) covenant bond	#(6) redemption	#(6) salvation atoning sacrifice	#(6) no accusation defeat Satan

 # Through Jesus' death

8

Rehabilitating Good Works

The Meaning of ἔργον

Kent L. Yinger

"Good Works": Their Largely Negative Flavor among Protestants

IN WESTERN BIBLICAL-THEOLOGICAL USAGE the concept of a "work" or "deed"—there is no significant difference in meaning between these two English terms—is associated primarily with soteriology. Human beings are saved by unmerited grace through faith; they cannot earn salvation by legalistic human performance (= good works).

This strongly negative connotation is easily documented. Rudolf Bultmann understood works in Paul's theology as the Jewish condition for justification. "The Jew takes it for granted that this condition [for justification] is keeping the Law, the accomplishing of 'works' prescribed by the Law."[1] Bultmann is following Luther's lead, for whom such works (even as obedience to God's commands) are, in fact, themselves sinful acts because they "are not of such intensity and purity as the Laws requires . . . Thus we sin even when we do good, unless God through Christ covers this imperfection and does not impute it to us."[2]

---

1. Bultmann, *Theology of the New Testament*, 1:279.
2. Luther, "Lectures on Romans," 25.276. In fairness, Luther does not disparage the

For Bultmann, as also apparently for Martin Luther, even some parts of the NT put undue stress on good works—in Bultmann's terms they evince early catholicism—and no longer understand the Pauline contrast between faith and works (e.g., James, Pastorals, Hebrews, 1 Peter; see also Ignatius).

This has led some to assert that Christians, in fact, perform no works. Rather, they "bear fruit"; that is, a "work" (sg.) of grace is produced in them. "Paul differentiates consciously between 'work' and 'works.' He refers to ἔργον only in a positive sense, and to ἔργα only in a negative one. Christians never perform ἔργα; a Christian's work is exclusively ἔργον," argues Mattern.³

In contrast, and as a proponent of the holiness tradition, our honoree has not been timid about calling for Christian good works.

> This [the saving work of God in Christ] is the supreme and only source of Christian ethics that is enabled by grace and received in faith thereby bringing about the *divine expectation of and ability for good works* in the community of faith. From the covenant perspective, this reflects the *biblical necessity for faith to find expression in obedience (Epistle of James),* which is the appropriate response to the expectations of the covenant relationship established at Creation.⁴

This, of course, brings him and other Wesleyans under suspicion of being soteriological synergists, at least as far as the more Lutheran and Reformed branches of Protestantism are concerned.⁵

Since at least part of this debate revolves around the connotation of words—do good works carry a positive or negative resonance—this essay

---

doing of good works *per se*, but only such obedience which does not spring out of justifying faith. Nevertheless, his negative statements on good works were a major source of controversy. See Luther's "Against Latomus," 32.159–162.

3. Mattern, *Das Verständnis des Gerichtes bei Paulus*, 144, author's translation.

4. Shelton, "A Covenant Context," 232, emphasis added.

5. See the defense of Wesley's synergism in Rakestraw, "John Wesley," 193–203. For a defense of Arminian or evangelical synergism as authentically Protestant, see Olson, *Mosaic*, 277–86; Olson, *Arminian Theology*, 18: "When conservative theologians declare that synergism is a heresy, they are usually referring to those two Pelagian forms of synergism [Pelagianism and semi-Pelagianism] . . . Contrary to confused critics, classical Arminianism is neither Pelagian nor semi-Pelagian! But it *is* synergistic. Arminianism is *evangelical synergism* as opposed to heretical, humanistic synergism" (original emphasis).

will seek clarity through an assessment of the history of lexical study of ἔργον.

Brief History of Western Lexical Study of ἔργον / ἔργα

Although not a lexicon of Koine or NT Greek, Liddell-Scott-Jones [LSJ], *A Greek-English Lexicon* (1843–1996)[6] is typically consulted for foundational background as to the meaning of words in the NT. It has gone unnoticed by many that the classical connotations of ἔργον do not correspond to the negative assessment noted above.

- ἔργον was an *ancient* and *widely used* term.
- It was simply the *generic term* for a deed, an action, and the product of work.
- The term itself suggested *neither positive nor negative connotations*, but could be associated with a wide variety of positive or negative concepts such as:

  (a) deeds of war

  (b) peaceful contests

  (c) works of industry such as tilling the soil or weaving (i.e., occupations)

  (d) the product (rather than the activity) of (c), thus wealth or possessions

  (e) a thing or matter

  (f) and in idiomatic phrases such as to "give someone trouble [ἔργον τινι]"

We find an early and influential move away from LSJ's more neutral conclusions in D. Hermann Cremer, *Biblisch-theologisches Wörterbuch* (1866–1886).[7] As the title indicates, this is more a theological dictionary than a strictly lexical treatment. Its primary aim is to illumine the (theological) meaning of Greek words in the biblical tradition. Toward this end, Cremer notes that ἔργα (pl.) are "achievements [*Leistungen*] *which are contrasted with grace as a principle of salvation*, and which validate a claim to

---

6. Liddell and Scott, *Greek-English Lexicon*, 682–83.
7. Cremer, *Biblisch-theologisches Wörterbuch*, 363–64.

value and recognition [in judgment] or put the lie to such a claim."[8] The plural functions in Paul as a *terminus technicus* for works of self-justification opposed to grace. Note that a lexeme which is inherently neither positive nor negative is given a clearly negative theological value in biblical usage. This is due to Cremer's interpretation of passages containing the lexeme. Of particular interest for this essay, Cremer is an early instance of strong theological influence upon NT lexicography and of a move away from understanding ἔργον within its larger Hellenistic environment.

Unlike Cremer, Walter Bauer's *A Greek-English Lexicon*[9] is a strictly lexical treatment, and, unlike LSJ, it focuses exclusively upon word-meanings in the NT and in early Christian literature. It remains the most influential lexicon for NT study. In agreement with the larger Hellenistic environment, as seen in LSJ, BDAG shows clearly the breadth of meaning:

1. "that which displays itself in activity of any kind, *deed, action*"
2. "that which one does as regular activity, *work, occupation, task*"
3. "that which is brought into being by work, *product, undertaking, work*"
4. "something having to do with something under discussion, *thing, matter*"

Thus, overall, BDAG documents the same broad and generic range of meaning for work as was seen for the classical period in LSJ.

Of particular interest, however, is the lengthy section [1.c.β] on "the deeds of humans, exhibiting a consistent moral character, referred to collectively as τὰ ἔργα." In opposition to a strict distinction between work (sg.) as positive and works (pl.) as negative, mentioned briefly above, BDAG argues that the *singular is used collectively for the plural* (Gal 6:4; Heb 6:10; Rev 22:12). And against the largely negative theological assessment of works, the lexeme itself *does not connote negative or positive moral value*. "The ἔργον or ἔργα is (are) characterized by the context as good or bad," or "by an added word" (e.g., adjective, genitive). Bauer's lexical treatment does not find Cremer's theological connotation of self-righteousness to be inherent in the lexeme itself. Interestingly, however, this more moderate judgment does not seem to have had due impact in biblical-theological discussion.

---

8. Ibid., 363, emphasis added.

9. Danker, *Greek-English Lexicon*, s.v. ἔργον, 390–91; based on Bauer, *Griechisch-deutsches Wörterbuch*.

Begun before WWII by editor Gerhard Kittel and continued in the post-war years after Kittel's death by Gerhard Friedrich, the *Theological Dictionary of the New Testament* [*TDNT*] has guided countless pastors and scholars as to the theological significance of NT words. Georg Bertram's entry on ἔργον appeared in volume two in 1935.[10]

In commenting on "General Usage" (more lexical in nature), Bertram agrees with LSJ and others that ἔργον was "in common use from the time of Homer and Hesiod" and showed a very broad range of meaning.[11] He acknowledges that the term itself remains (morally) neutral; any associated moral value is described by adjectives and genitives rather than being inherent in ἔργον. That is, one could speak of good or evil works, works of virtue, vice, etc.

He also notes that ἔργον was widely used in philosophy, especially by Plato and Aristotle. "The *arete* of every creature, e.g., the eye or the race-horse, consists in fulfilling properly its specific *ergon*, i.e., seeing or running . . . *ergon* is the form of things, the fulfilment of the disposition inherent in matter."[12] This will become central to some later studies of the term. Like some earlier studies, Bertram thus notes that in general Greek usage ἔργον / ἔργα *function as a sign of inner reality*. He quotes, for instance, Xenophon's use of the phrase ἐκ τῶν ἔργων γιγνώσκειν [to know (for instance, another's character) by deeds].[13]

However, Bertram at this point makes this sense of "revealing inward reality" subsidiary to the sense of meritorious achievement: "The thought of achievement *sometimes* retreats into the background."[14] That is, only *sometimes* does the primary sense of achievement retreat behind the otherwise secondary revelatory meaning. This crystallization of the secondary nature of the revelatory meaning over against the primarily meritorious meaning will have major ramifications in future NT studies.

In his treatment of ἔργον used for "Human Labour and the Work of Man," Bertram begins a much stronger theologizing of the lexeme with an almost exclusive view toward its negative connotations.[15] Viewing human labor as a curse had become "almost completely dominant in Hellenistic Ju-

10. Bertram, "ἔργον, ἐργάζομαι," 631–49; English translation 635–52.
11. Ibid., 635.
12. Ibid., 636, citing Aristotle, *Ethica Nichomachea* I, 1.
13. Bertram, "ἔργον, ἐργάζομαι," 636.
14. Ibid., emphasis added.
15. Ibid., 643–52.

daism," he suggests.[16] In the LXX, ἔργον refers to that which "stands under the curse."[17] "Judaism of the Hell[enistic] period could never speak of ἔργον without disparagement,"[18] Bertram argues: "Everything called ἔργον in the life of man is sin. When the actions of man are measured by the final criterion, they are shown to be sin."[19]

Thus, from a strictly lexicographical perspective, ἔργον is acknowledged to be a broad term, capable of reference to many aspects of work—positive, negative, neutral, holistic, etc. However, when Bertram considers human work(s) *soteriologically*, he finds that the idea of works-righteousness inheres in the word itself. This is an example of what James Barr has called "illegitimate totality transfer." Bertram sees this negative (meritorious) connotation reflected in the works-righteousness of later Judaism: "The righteousness of casuistically ordered cultic and legal action is the decisive content of later Jewish piety."[20]

Roman Heiligenthal's 1981 Heidelberg dissertation appeared in 1983 as *Werke als Zeichen* [Works as Signs].[21] His was the first scholarly monograph devoted to a careful study of the meaning of human works. It has not been translated into English, which has reduced its impact on English-language scholarship to date.

Although previous lexical studies had noticed the formula "to know one by one's works [ἐκ τῶν ἔργων γιγνώσκειν]," Heiligenthal shows that this *allgemeine Erfahrungsregel* [principle of common experience] was widespread in Greek literature and expressed the chief function of works in Hellenistic texts. Because English-speakers may not as readily associate the term with this principle, I will give a number of Heiligenthal's examples.

---

16. Ibid., 643.
17. Ibid., 644.
18. Ibid.
19. Ibid.
20. Bertram, "ἔργον, ἐργάζομαι," 645; see esp. the section "The Righteousness of Works in Later Judaism" (645–47). This view of Judaism as wholly legalistic has a long history in NT scholarship. As one example, from a scholar who is not generally accused of being anti-Jewish: "The commonly-held ethical viewpoint of ancient Judaism was dominated by the thought of merit... Moral behavior is a piling-up of merits which one gains through the keeping of commandments and voluntary good deeds. At no other point is it so clear that Pharisaic Judaism is a religion of performance [*Leistungsreligion*]" (Jeremias, *Neutestamentliche Theologie*, 208f).
21. Heiligenthal, *Werke als Zeichen*.

- Aristotle, *Eudemian Ethics* II.xi.12[22]

    "Moreover because it is not easy to see the quality of a man's purpose *we are forced to judge his character from his actions . . .*"

    . . . ἐκ τῶν ἔργων ἀναγκαζόμεθα κρίνειν ὁποῖός τις

    Note how inward character ("the quality of a man's purpose") is only seen through observable works. For this reason, one is forced to "judge character from actions."

- Aristotle *Ethica Nicomachea* X.12[23]

    ". . . *it is by the practical experience of life and conduct that the truth is really tested*, since it is there that the final decision lies."

    τὸ δ'ἀληθὲς ἐν τοῖς πρακτοῖς ἐκ τῶν ἔργων καὶ τοῦ βίου κρίνεται

    Here also is an instance of knowing ("discerning" κρίνειν) a truth or principle from the resulting deeds; in this case it refers to the inward truth about a person (i.e., their unseen character).

- Xenophon *Agesilaus* 1, 6[24]

    ". . . for I believe that his deeds will throw the clearest light on his qualities."

    ἀπὸ γὰρ τῶν ἔργων καὶ τοὺς τρόπους αὐτοῦ κάλλιστα νομίζω καταδήλους ἔσεσθαι

- Dio Chrysostom *Discourses* 2.26[25]

    ". . . to give proof by his very conduct of a character that is humane, gentle, just."

    ἐνδεικνύμενον αὐτοῖς τοῖς ἔργοις φιλάνθρωπον ἦθος καὶ πρᾷον καὶ δίκαιον

    Here, clearly, one's inward character is proven or demonstrated by works.

---

22. Aristotle, *Eudemian Ethics*.
23. Aristotle, *Nicomachean Ethics*.
24. Xenophon, *Agesilaus*
25. Dio Chrysostom, *Discourses*.

- Isocrates *Evagoras* 65[26]

    "In truth, how could one reveal the courage, the wisdom, or the virtues generally of Evagoras more clearly than by pointing to such deeds and perilous enterprises?"

    Καίτοι πῶς ἄν τις τὴν ἀνδρίαν ἢ τὴν φρόνησιν ἢ σύμπασαν τὴν ἀρετὴν τὴν Εὐαγόρου φανερώτερον ἐπιδείξειεν ἢ διὰ τοιούτων ἔργων καὶ κινδύνων;

Here, the inner virtues and wisdom of Evagoras are "revealed" by "pointing to [his] deeds."

Thus, Heiligenthal underlines that ἔργα in extra-biblical Greek "are understood primarily not as a demonstration of achievement [*Leistungsausweis*] but as a means of knowing and judging [*Erkenntniswert*]."[27] This sharpens considerably the diffuse and misleading treatment offered by Bertram and others,[28] and moves the perspective away from a heavily negative view of ἔργον / ἔργα (= curse, sin, merit) toward a varied usage with primary emphasis on works as external signs of internal reality rather than meritorious achievements.

To give some sense of the potential impact of this lexical point on "judgment according to works," Heiligenthal concludes, "In Paul's thought works only superficially signal achievements in the sense of fulfilling divine demands; rather they should be seen as *signs of the inner reality of the person which become manifest in the judgment*."[29] "The Spirit's working . . . becomes visible as a sign in the activity of the body. *The final judgment reveals this unseen reality* (2 Cor 5:10) and confirms the justification given to the Christian."[30]

Conclusion

Any suggestion that the term work(s) of itself connotes something evil, something to be disparaged, something fleshly, self-righteous, or legalistic, should be rejected. This is the consistent finding of strictly lexical treatments (LSJ, BDAG, Heiligenthal). Studies which find an inherently negative connotation

26. Isocrates, *Evagoras*.
27. Heiligenthal, *Werke*, 25; cf. also 13.
28. See, for instance, Hahn, "Work," 1147–52.
29. Heiligenthal, *Werke*, 195, emphasis added.
30. Ibid., 201, emphasis added.

generally confuse a particular interpretation of NT texts with the meaning of the word (Cremer, *TDNT*). While ἔργον may certainly be used to speak of evil deeds, self-righteous behavior, works springing from human flesh, etc., these connotations must be shown to arise from the context and associated terms (genitives, adjectives, etc.) rather than from a falsely attributed meaning of the lexeme itself.

Rather than works and faith standing in contrast, works are, in fact, a manifestation of inward reality, including the unseen reality of faith. This does not, of course, exclude the possibility of hypocrisy (where works and inward reality do not coincide), nor a momentary or temporary disjunction between works and inward reality (i.e., one acts out of character or backslides). It does mean that the term and concept "(good) works" should be rehabilitated in Protestant usage. It should not normally be used to imply self-righteousness or the attempt to earn grace via doing; rather it should be used to note the outward and visible manifestation of the unseen inner reality of the person, that which is often called the heart in Scripture.

Directions for Future Study

"Works" and the Totality of a Person's Behavior

That one's works were seen as a unity, a whole way of life, rather than individual atomistic or disparate acts, was noted marginally in earlier studies. Bertram suggests, "Naturally, then, a man is judged by his works, his achievements, his deeds, his *total conduct*."[31] He adds, "[M]any words which denote *conduct in general* are brought under the concept of work, e.g., *derek* in Job 34:21."[32]

Since many studies still interpret works in the NT against the foil of a supposed Jewish atomization of works, instead of recognizing the generally holistic sense, this remains an area for further research and emphasis.

---

31. Bertram, "ἔργον, ἐργάζομαι," 636, emphasis added.
32. Ibid., 637, emphasis added. See also Job 36:23; Prov 16:5, 7; Sir 10:6; 11:21; Job 13:27; Sir 3:17.

Meaning of Perfection Vis-à-Vis Works

Protestant interpretation assumes the need for perfect keeping of the law if one were to be justified by works. A look at Luther's *Small Catechism* makes this clear.

> QUESTION: "What was the original design of the law?"
>
> ANSWER: "To secure perfect obedience to all its precepts, and thus confer eternal life."
>
> QUESTION: "Can any man be saved by the law?"
>
> ANSWER: "He cannot; because no man has perfectly obeyed . . ."[33]

This line of reasoning appeals to a number of Pauline texts, including the following: "For all who rely on the works of the law are under a curse; for it is written, 'Cursed is everyone who does not observe and obey all the things written in the book of the law.'" (Galatians 3:10 NRSV)

Although some dispute continues,[34] it is now generally accepted that most forms of Second-Temple Judaism did not, in fact, require perfection in our sense (= 100% error-free obedience).[35] That is, one could be called perfect, even perfect in deeds or in righteous behavior, and still commit sins needing atonement or repentance. Perfection refers to the totality of one's way of life, the unseen heart, which God judges according to one's works or path of life.

---

33. Luther, *Luther's Small Catechism*, 49–50.
34. Schreiner, "Is Perfect Obedience Possible," 151–60.
35. For a recent look at "perfection" = "integrity," see Hartin, *A Spirituality of Perfection*, esp. 17–32.

9

Suffering, Creation, and Luther's *Theologia Crucis*[1]

by Daniel L. Brunner

AFTER THE FLOOD, GOD spoke to Noah: "This is the sign of the covenant [*berith*] that I make between me and you and every living creature that is with you, for all future generations: I have set my bow in the clouds, and it shall be a sign of the covenant between me and the earth" (Gen. 9:12–13, NRSV). The Noahic covenant is unique to other covenants initiated by God, in that it includes the whole Earth community. Like other covenants, however, humankind assumes covenantal responsibility.[2] To keep or to fail to keep covenant has ramifications for the whole created world. Bernhard Anderson writes: "The Noahic covenant, then, is universal in the widest sense imaginable. It is fundamentally an ecological covenant that includes not only human beings everywhere but all animals."[3] The biblical theology of covenant declares that human well-being and the welfare of the planet are inexorably connected.

---

1. This essay is adapted from my presentation, "The Suffering of the Earth in Dialogue with Luther's Theology of the Cross," for the Quaker Theological Discussion Group, AAR-SBL, Chicago, Illinois, November 16, 2012. That presentation, in a shorter form, was also adapted for publication in *Quaker Religious Thought* 121. This festschrift seems an appropriate place for its publication, since Larry Shelton knew suffering firsthand, loved fishing and the outdoors, and, though a Wesleyan, holds a soft spot in his heart for Luther. This chapter will also be published in a forthcoming issue of *Quaker Religious Thought* on creation care. Used with permission.

2. Shelton, *Cross and Covenant*, 19.

3. Anderson, *From Creation to New Creation*, 157.

I am convinced that the world's ecological crisis is indeed the next "great work" facing humanity, demanding that Christians confront ecotheological issues we have had the privilege to ignore for decades.[4] As a Lutheran, I have found a helpful resource for engaging ecotheology in Martin Luther's theology of the cross, *theologia crucis*. Since I first encountered it in seminary I have been captured by the idea of God's concealed self-revelation, of our Western fixation on a theology of glory, and of unearthing God in suffering and pain, weakness and foolishness. To be honest, Luther's "ecological legacy"—an anachronistic expression, to say the least—is ambiguous. Like other reformers he was gripped by "soteriological-anthropocentric themes," and it would be unfair to expect otherwise.[5] Yet, many scholars, including Lutheran and non-Lutheran, women and men, feminist and Minjung, are discovering a resource for ecotheology in *theologia crucis*.[6]

Beyond scholarship, though, I have a personal motivation for this paper. One of our former students, someone who committed hours to helping craft the Christian Earthkeeping program at our seminary, decided when he left seminary to go to Mozambique to live and work among the poor instead of pursuing doctoral studies. In a recent email he said:

> I struggle for the poor and forgotten here in Mozambique. I have spent the last days with people dying from famine due to climate change. Some days I feel that I have chosen wrongly [by not going into academics]. I stand with the poor, but the world could care less. Money goes to the places with the most people dying. Since we only have hundreds dying, we do not count. We have no voice.[7]

Nathan knows the theology of the cross—he has studied it and now he is even experiencing it.

Walther von Loewenich wrote, "For Luther the cross is not only the subject of theology; it is the distinctive mark of all theology."[8] *Theologia*

---

4. Berry, *The Great Work*, 7, writes: "For the success or failure of any historical age *is the extent to which those living at that time have fulfilled the special role that history has imposed upon them.*"

5. Santmire, *The Travail of Nature*, 132f.

6. See, for example, Chung, "Discovering the Relevance of Martin Luther for Asian Theology"; Hall, *The Cross in our Context*; Moe-Lobeda, "A Theology of the Cross for the 'Uncreators'"; Rasmussen, "Returning to Our Senses."

7. Email. Used by permission.

8. Loewenich, *Luther's Theology of the Cross*, 18.

crucis is the "essence of true theology," said Paul Althaus.[9] Luther himself declared: *Crux sola est nostra theologia*, or "the cross alone is our theology."[10] And yet, as Mary Solberg emphasizes, "[T]here is a kind of restlessness in Luther's theology."[11] Centuries before Kirkegaard, Luther was an existentialist, someone whose writing defies systematization because it arose primarily out of his lived experience. That is its wonder and its hell. Our goal in this paper then is not to schematize Luther, but to draw ecotheological ramifications from three of the 28 theses in his Heidelberg Disputation of 1518.[12] In this early, groundbreaking defense at an Augustinian monastery, Luther presents the heartbeat of *theologia crucis*.

A Theology of Reality

First, the theology of the cross is a theology of reality. In Thesis 21 of the Heidelberg Disputation, Luther states: "A theology of glory calls evil good and good evil. A theology of the cross calls the thing what it actually is."[13] Dietrich Bonhoeffer, whose own life was an exposition on *theologia crucis*, was only too aware of how evil could "masquerade" as good and "appear in the form of light, good deeds, historical necessity, [or] social justice."[14]

Scientists and climatologists, ethicists and humanitarians, poets and artists, the marginalized and the earth itself are all pleading with the developed and the developing world to see reality, to see what actually is. In the words of Cynthia Moe-Lobeda, we in the first world have become "uncreators," destroying the ecosystems of this planet and "building a soul-shattering gap between the rich and the impoverished."[15] The World Meteorological Organization and the United Nations Environmental Program warn that humanity is "conducting an unintended, uncontrolled, globally

---

9. Althaus, *The Theology of Martin Luther*, 30.

10. Luther, *D. Martin Luthers Werke*, 5, 176, 32–33; Solberg, *Compelling Knowledge*, 68.

11. Solberg, *Compelling Knowledge*, 13.

12. Rasmussen, "Returning to Our Senses," 41, notes that to apply *theologia crucis* to ecojustice and the ecological crisis is also to respond to the challenge that James Cone issued to Lutheran churches "to extend Luther's theology of the cross to society" (*For My People*, 182).

13. Luther, "Heidelberg Disputation," 31:53.

14. Bonhoeffer, *Letters and Papers from Prison*, 38.

15. Moe-Lobeda, "A Theology of the Cross for the 'Uncreators,'" 183.

pervasive experiment," by which "Earth's atmosphere is being changed at an unprecedented rate."[16] Bill McKibben calls global warming "the deepest problem that human beings have ever faced."[17] Recently, *The Guardian* reported that climate change "is likely to be more severe than some models have implied."[18]

The "reality" is that we, the economically privileged, are disproportionately responsible for climate change, from which we disproportionately benefit and are disproportionately protected, and from which the underprivileged will disproportionately suffer. The ecological crisis and worldwide economic inequality are inseparably connected. Methodist Bishop Bernardino Mandlate of Mozambique, when speaking of the debt of impoverished nations, declared, "African children die so that North American children may overeat."[19]

Luther once stated, "If I profess with the loudest voice and clearest exposition every portion of the truth of God except precisely that little point which the world and the devil are at that moment attacking, I am not confessing Christ, however boldly I may be professing Christ."[20] What might it mean, then, to confess Christ in the midst of our ecological and economic tragedy, that place where the world and the devil are at this moment attacking? It can only start by entering reality, by fighting against the denial of our own participation in the sinful structures of our world.[21] By resisting denial, we move beyond numbness and isolation only to confront the disillusionment that inevitably results from coming to know how things actually are.[22] It opens the door to pain and grief, to becoming aware of how our anthropocentric mastery over creation has a created distance from creation. Facing reality and disillusionment begins to break down that detachment. We experience creation's groaning, and we are driven to the cross. In his *Ethics*, Bonhoeffer summarized a theology of reality: "What matters is *participating in the reality of God and the world in Jesus Christ today*, and

---

16. Statement by World Meteorological Organization, United Nations Environmental Programme, and Environment Canada at "The Changing Atmosphere," cited in Moe-Lobeda, "A Theology of the Cross for the 'Uncreators,'" 183.

17. McKibben, "Do the Math."

18. Harvey, "Climate Change."

19. Mandlate, cited in Moe-Lobeda, "A Theology of the Cross for the 'Uncreators,'" 184.

20. Luther cited in Hall, *Confessing the Faith*, vi.

21. Moe-Lobeda, "A Theology of the Cross for the 'Uncreators,'" 186f.

22. Solberg, "All That Matters," 150.

doing so in such a way that I never experience the reality of God without the reality of the world, nor the reality of the world without the reality of God."[23]

A Theology of Descent

Secondly, *theologia crucis* is a theology of descent. Luther makes this proposal in Thesis 20: "One deserves to be called a theologian . . . who comprehends the visible and the 'back' of God [*posteriora Dei*] seen through suffering and the cross."[24] The perspective that the Christian life is about leaving this world and climbing a ladder — where "every round goes higher, higher" — is a dominant theme, if not *the* dominant theme, in the history of Christian spirituality. Paul Santmire calls it a "metaphor of ascent."[25] Luther, however, in his cross theology polemicizes against any dualistic separation of the spiritual from the material and disavows "the great chain of being."[26] He stresses that in the Incarnation God descended the ladder to this earth.[27] God is embodied and materialized in Jesus. Luther contended that in the humanity of Jesus, we encounter the fullness of God's divinity.[28]

Luther insisted that the finite carries the infinite (*finitum capax infiniti*), that the transcendent is wholly immanent. His is an incarnational theology of descent, earthbound and bodily. Rasmussen states that Luther is "boldly pan-*en*-theistic," citing this down-to-earth passage from Luther: "For how can reason tolerate it that the Divine majesty is so small that it can be substantially present in a grain, on a grain, over a grain, through a grain, within and without, and that, although it is a single Majesty, it nevertheless is entirely in each grain separately, no matter how immeasurable numerous these grains may be?"[29]

23. Bonhoeffer, *Ethics*, 55.

24. Luther, "The Heidelberg Disputation," 31:52. The translation used here is from Mannermaa, *Two Kinds of Love*, 28. McGrath, *Luther's Theology of the Cross*, 148, translates *posteriora Dei* as "rearward parts of God." Both McGrath's and Mannermaa's translations are better than Harold J. Grimm's "manifest things of God" (*Luther's Works* 31:51).

25. Santmire, *The Travail of Nature*, 18f. Luther responded in particular to the "ascent" metaphor he saw in Thomas à Kempis's *The Imitation of Christ*.

26. Rasmussen, "Returning to Our Senses," 189 n. 22.

27. Forde, *Where God Meets Man*, 8.

28. Rasmussen, *Earth Community, Earth Ethics*, 282.

29. Luther, "Dass disese Worte Christi . . . (1527)." Cf. Rasmussen, *Earth Community, Earth Ethics*, 273.

This theme is often overlooked in Luther, that God became incarnate as *both* a human being *and* a created being. Elsewhere, he wrote that the power of God "must be essentially present at all places, even in the tiniest leaf."[30] Korean theologian Paul Chung states that we need to revitalize Luther's doctrine of ubiquity, so contentious in the sixteenth century, to cope with the ecological crisis.[31] Luther wrote, "God is substantially present everywhere, in and through all creatures, in all their part and places, so that the world is full of God and He fills all, but without His being encompassed and surrounded by it."[32] The transcendent is indeed immanent.

Much more controversial is Luther's conviction that a theology of the cross unavoidably involved suffering, that "the 'back' of God [is] seen through suffering and the cross." Luther underscored *Deus absconditus*, that God was hidden in suffering and in God's seeming absence. This preoccupation with the necessity of suffering—that "being a Christian is to have to suffer"—has caused numerous feminists to reject the whole idea of the theology of the cross, since it seemingly fails to recognize the systemic nature of sin and evil.[33] Holocaust survivor Elie Wiesel remarked: "a religion that glorifies suffering will always find someone to suffer."[34] Luther indeed seemed fixated on the psychological suffering of *Anfechtung*, to the exclusion of structural oppression, illustrated in his response to the Great Peasants' Revolt.[35] Yet many feminists and ecotheologians alike argue that the answer is not to reject all discourse about suffering. Korean feminist theologian Chung Hyun Kyung remarks, "Asian women cannot define humanity apart from their suffering."[36] She emphasizes that to be human is

30. Luther, "That These Words of Christ," 37:57. Luther, in "The Sacrament of the Body," 321, also wrote, "[Christ] is present in all creatures, and I might find him in stone, in fire, in water, or even in a rope, for he certainly is there." Cf. Moe-Lobeda, "A Theology of the Cross for the 'Uncreators,'" 193f.

31. Chung, "Discovering the Relevance of Martin Luther," 44.

32. Luther, *D. Martin Luthers Werke*, 23:134.34–23.136.36.

33. Thompson, *Crossing the Divide*, 112f.

34. Cited in ibid., 128.

35. *Anfechtung* is a difficult word to translate and is often left in its original German. Even though it could be translated as "temptation," McGrath, *Luther's Theology of the Cross*, 170, notes that "assault" is more revealing, since the world, despair, death, doubt, calamity, and the devil come together in a "terrifying assault" on the human conscience. Luther (infamously) sided with the (oppressive) nobility and princes against the peasants in the Great Peasants' Revolt of 1524–1525 through his tract, "Against the Murderous, Thieving Hordes of Peasants" (1525).

36. Kyung, *Struggle to be the Sun Again*, 39.

both to suffer and to resist the oppression that causes suffering, although she acknowledges that trying to find meaning in suffering is thorny because it "can be both a seed for liberation and an opium for . . . oppression."[37]

Larry Rasmussen observes that not all suffering is negative; some suffering is part of what it means to be finite and to struggle as creatures in the process of becoming. The cross, however, opposes any disintegrative suffering "that negates life and destroys the realization of creation."[38] The cross, Rasmussen insists, is rooted in reality, neither justifying suffering nor denying it. But where the cross "finds suffering caused by the culture of death, it willingly enters into it for the sake of life . . . [R]edeeming the planet . . . means going to the places of suffering to find God and God's power there."[39]

A Theology of Engaged Hope

Finally, a theology of the cross is a theology of engaged hope. Luther's last thesis in the Heidelberg disputation says, "God's Love does not find, but creates, that which is lovable to it. Human Love comes into being through that which is lovable to it."[40] Here, at the end of his defense, Luther lifts up hope rooted in God's love. This resurrection hope is not to be found in eschatological escapism; it arises out of clear-eyed reality and incarnational descent.

Luther wrote in explanation of Thesis 28, "Therefore sinners are beautiful because they are loved; they are not loved because they are beautiful."[41] God is not *primarily* a receiver of love, but a giver of love, a giver of a love that creates love. It is, in the words of Tuomo Mannermaa, "a characteristic of God to create something out of nothing."[42] It is the work of God to engage that which is broken and wrecked by sin, both personal and structural, and then to create out of love that which is loved and good and beautiful. Aquinas taught that as humans we are attracted to beauty and to what is more beautiful, and ultimately to God.[43] And, of course, we do see God's majesty

---

37. Ibid., 54.
38. Rasmussen, *Earth Community, Earth Ethics*, 289.
39. Ibid., 290.
40. Luther, "Heidelberg Disputation," 31:57. The translation used here is from Mannermaa, *Two Kinds of Love*, 1, and his translator.
41. Mannermaa, *Two Kinds of Love*, 3.
42. Ibid., 51.
43. Ibid., 10–25.

and presence in creation's wonder: the world is indeed "charged with the grandeur of God."[44] But what do we do with pain and degradation? How are we to understand the "suffering" of rainforests and mountaintops as they surrender to the bulldozers of human greed? It is precisely here that Luther's theology of the cross speaks boldly. When the creation—human or other-than-human—suffers any kind of degradation, God suffers. God enters the negation of suffering, and in suffering we meet God. Douglas John Hall affirms that Luther's *theologia crucis* "is not the good news of *deliverance from* the experience of negation so much as it is the permission and command to enter into that experience with hope."[45]

Luther's theology of the cross speaks to an engaged hope that arises out of love. Rasmussen stresses that "only those who love the earth fiercely, *in* its distress, will effect whatever redemption it might know."[46] This fierce love knows that God is present in a creation that is too often "blighted and disgraced," and that we are called to the same love: if Christ-followers "were present only in a redeeming way to creation's beauty and not in its plunder and rape, then broken creation would never be healed."[47] This love calls us as human beings to solidarity with everyone and everything suffering from exclusion and marginalization, to be, in the words of Moe-Lobeda, "God's embodied presence in and with responsible actions . . . on behalf of life."[48] When Bonhoeffer was faced with the rise of fascism and anti-Semitism in 1932, when the world was suffering, he wrote these words: "The hour in which we pray today for God's kingdom is the hour of the most profound solidarity with the world, an hour of clenched teeth and trembling fists."[49]

Martin Luther's theology of the cross challenges us today to face daringly into the reality of the earth's crisis. It reminds us of Jesus whose incarnate descent immersed him in the wonder and suffering of humanity and creation. And it invites us to an engaged hope that loves fiercely all that God loves fiercely, in solidarity and even in suffering. In the smallest of responsive action is the hope of creation's restoration and renewal. Luther said that divinity could be present in a grain. Chung Hyun Kyung cites a poem

---

44. Hopkins, *God's Grandeur*, 15.
45. Hall, *Lighten Our Darkness*, 123.
46. Rasmussen, *Earth Community, Earth Ethics*, 304.
47. Ibid., 287f.
48. Moe-Lobeda, "A Theology of the Cross for the 'Uncreators,'" 193.
49. Bonhoeffer, *Berlin*, 269; cf. Rasmussen, *Earth Community, Earth Ethics*, 304.

from an anonymous Indian woman who, in her famine-stricken area, also encounters Jesus Christ in the grain that makes her gruel:

> Every noon at twelve
> In the blazing heat
> God comes to me
> in the form of
> Two hundred grams of gruel.
>
> I know Him in every grain
> I taste Him in every lick.
> I commune with Him as I gulp
> For He keeps me alive, with
> Two hundred grams of gruel.
>
> I wait till next noon
> and now know He'd come:
> I can hope to live one day more
> For you made God to come to me as
> Two hundred grams of gruel.
>
> I know now that God loves me—
> Not until you made it possible.
> Now I know what you're speaking about
> For God so loves this world
> That He gives His beloved Son
> Every noon through You.[50]

---

50. Anonymous, "From Jaini Bi—With Love," 11.

10

Covenantal Responses after Nine Minutes of Horror in Newtown

by Susie C. Stanley

THE DETAILS OF DECEMBER 14, 2012 are still fresh in our minds. We were traveling on the day of the massacre and saw images and heard countless reports repeated over and over on televisions located throughout the hallways in the waiting areas of the airports. Earlier in the day, misinformation filled the airwaves, but gradually the facts began to emerge. It was horrendous and almost impossible to fathom. We stood watching televisions with strangers and shared the horror as newscasters pieced the story together. Twenty-year-old Adam Lanza, armed with an assault rifle and two handguns, broke glass windows in Sandy Hook Elementary School about 9:30 a.m. He carried enough ammunition to kill every student in the school located in Newtown, Connecticut, a town of 27,000 located about sixty miles from New York City.[1] In less than ten minutes, he killed twenty first-graders and six adults before shooting and killing himself as first responders arrived.

One may ask, "What does this horrifying event have to do with 'covenant?'" This chapter will briefly summarize the divine-human covenantal relationship and then apply it to the covenant we are called as humans to keep with each other. Then I will consider the theological meaning of

---

1. "Newtown Shooting." Due to time constraints, research for this paper was extremely limited, with only two exceptions, in terms of time frame and scope. I consulted a national paper, *The New York Times*, and *The Harrisburg Patriot-News* for a local perspective on the tragedy at Newtown.

covenant in light of the covenantal language and behavior that emerged in response to this terrifying incident.[2] President Barack Obama's public comments on two occasions provide excellent descriptions of a covenantal relationship. His statements following the shooting in Newtown inspired my examination of the responses to the tragedy incorporating the context of covenant.

Even though the word "covenant" was absent from most articles covering the mass killings, it quickly became obvious that covenant is an appropriate representation of what was evident in the aftermath of the shooting. My primary focus will be on the understanding and expression of covenant between families of the victims and those who responded to their grief and pain.

Larry Shelton defines covenant as "a formal or informal agreement between two parties that stipulates the nature and purpose of the agreement, the expectations of the arrangement, and the accountability of the parties for the consequences of failure to fulfill the terms of the agreement . . . Covenant is more of an interpersonal agreement based on the goodwill and trust that exists between those involved in it." Shelton suggests substituting "divine expectations" for "covenant" as a way to better understand the meaning of this theological term.[3] Theologians such as Shelton generally consider the covenant God has established with humans. But he, and others, also recognize that the divine-human covenant has implications for the covenant between humans, because it calls for love of neighbor. It also provides the model for relationships between humans.

Shelton selects the theological theme of covenant as the best way to understand the atonement. While "atonement" denotes an extremely complicated aspect of theology, one way to simplify the meaning of the word is to literally break it down into syllables as follows: at-one-ment. The atonement restores the divine-human relationship broken by sin. Because of the atonement, God and humans can be "at-one" again. Shelton speaks of the

2. Working on this chapter, I became aware of another covenantal relationship. This is the covenant we share with the mentally ill. Martin E. P. Seligman editorialized in "Don't confuse crazy with evil," making a clear distinction between the two categories. They are not identical. It is an unfair stereotype to label all those who commit mass murders as crazy or insane, since most crazy people are not evil. In fact, Christopher Gordon contends: "people with mental illness are far more likely to be victims of violence than perpetrators (letter to the editor). To keep our covenant with neighbors who are mentally ill, we must not paint them with a broad brush that scapegoats all of them as potential serial killers.

3. Shelton, *Cross and Covenant*, 19–20.

"covenant renewal concept of atonement" and maintains that the covenant understanding of relationship is "God's way of working."[4]

While the covenant between humans is not Shelton's main focus, he does mention it several times. Specifically, he relates the two in terms of love by paraphrasing Scripture: "the covenant relationship entails the divine expectations of love of God and love of neighbor."[5] God expects us not only to honor our covenant with God by loving God, but also to reflect that love in our human relationships by loving each other.

Jesus succinctly stated the demands of the divine-human covenant in the Greatest Commandment: "You shall love the Lord your God with all your heart, and with all your soul, and with all your strength, and with all your mind; and your neighbor as yourself" (Luke 10:27, NRSV. See also Matt 22:34–40 and Mark 12:28–31, which repeat this saying). Jesus did not stop with a definition of our relationship with God. He also explained the covenant between humans in terms of love.

Of course, the divine-human model of the covenant characterized by love is our blueprint for relationships among humans. The Wesleyan emphasis on God's nature as love supports this notion of covenant.[6] How could it be otherwise? Since God is love, that love is infused in every aspect of our covenant with God. Love is the defining quality of God and covenant. While not using the term, clergy described the love present in the God-human covenant when speaking of the tragedy in Newtown. Rev. Meg Boxwell Williams, who preached at the funeral for Victoria Soto, one of the teachers, declared that it is "God who consoles us in our affliction."[7] God's love provides solace to humans when they suffer.

Jesus also provides the example of love for us to emulate. Jesus' expression of love extends beyond a narrow conception of neighbor. Examples abound—Jesus reached out to the Samaritan woman, a tax collector, and the sick, all of whom who were not only outside the generally accepted boundaries of "neighbor," but were shunned by all those who knew them. The covenant is not confined to a closed, narrowly defined group, but encompasses everyone.

As Christians, our goal is to be more Christ-like. We speak of this theologically as sanctification or holiness. Being more Christ-like entails

4. Ibid., 7, xvii.
5. Ibid., 99. See also 3, 98.
6. Ibid., 107, 110.
7. Berger, "Remembering the Passion."

being more loving. It is a process of growing in our experience of God's love and in sharing that love with others. Sometimes, we have limited our expression of holy love to God. We have neglected our responsibility in terms of our covenant to others, but the application is appropriate. As a Wesleyan, I identify God's presence and the love of God in the world as the Holy Spirit. Wesleyans believe that the Holy Spirit inspires and empowers us to engage in acts of love toward others. The Holy Spirit enables us to fulfill the obligations of our covenant with others. However, the Holy Spirit is present wherever love manifests itself. The Holy Spirit's expression of love is not limited to Christians. I rely on experience as my source of theology to support this statement. There have been times in my life when this has been the case. My encounter with the Holy Spirit's love, sometimes in the most unexpected of places, is not unique.

Columnist Maureen Dowd asked Father Kevin O'Neil to reflect on the theological implications of what happened at Newtown. *The New York Times* published his remarks in her column. O'Neil's focus was on God's presence in the world through our actions. He ruminated on the nature of relationships that reflect our covenantal obligation to each other. In this case, he also was defining the human-human covenant not just in terms of reflecting God's love but as involving God's very presence. O'Neil wrote:

> I really do believe that God enters the world through us . . . But how we are with one another in that suffering and dying makes all the difference as to whether God's presence is felt or not and whether we are comforted or not.
>
> One true thing is this: Faith is lived in family and community, and God is experienced in family and community. We need one another to be God's presence . . . I am pulled out of myself to be love's presence to someone else, even as they are love's presence to me.
>
> . . . What I do know is that an unconditionally loving presence soothes broken hearts, binds up wounds, and renews us in life. This is a gift that we can all give, particularly to the suffering.[8]

O'Neil's words capture the essence of what it means to model God and God's covenant as we relate to each other.

The adults who died at Sandy Hook Elementary School imitated Christ when they gave their lives for the students. Dawn Hochsprung, the principal, and Mary Sherlach, the school psychologist, were the first to encounter Adam Lanza after he entered the school. Authorities reported that

---

8. Dowd, "Why, God?"

the women had been "rushing toward Lanza in an attempt to stop him."[9] They gave no thought to their personal safety. They instinctively fulfilled a covenantal responsibility to their students. Their action reflected their priority to put the students' safety ahead of their own.

Family and friends spoke of Victoria Soto's devotion to her students. Authorities confirmed her efforts to protect the first-graders in her class. Gary MacNamara, chief of the Fairfield Police Department, reported that ". . . she took action to save the life of the students. I know, because I've spoken to children in that class who are alive because of what she did."[10] Lanza shot her as she tried to hide the children from the killer by shielding them.[11] At Soto's funeral, Rev. Meg Boxwell Williams made the comparison to Christ explicit: "Her last act was selfless, Christ-like in laying down her life for her children."[12] Soto, and the other adults shot in the school, sacrificed their lives in their attempts to meet their covenantal commitment to the students.

Cardinal Timothy M. Dolan spoke at the funeral for Anne Marie Murphy, a teacher's aide at the school. He eulogized her by also comparing her action to Christ: "Like Jesus, Annie was an excellent teacher. Like him, she had a favored place in her big, tender heart for children, especially those with struggles. Like Jesus, Annie laid down her life for her friends." Like Jesus' death, he added, Mrs. Murphy's death "has brought together a community, a nation, a world, now awed by her own life and death."[13] Mrs. Murphy's father reported that "the authorities had informed him that his daughter's body was found covering a group of children's bodies, as if she were trying to shield them."[14] The family of Dylan Hockley corroborated this in a printed statement: "Dylan had died in the loving arms of his favorite teacher. We take great comfort in knowing that Dylan was not alone when he died but was wrapped in the arms of his amazing aide, Anne Marie Murphy."[15] A woman at the funeral noted: "When you're an aide, the kids become your own . . . they become your family."[16] Her words echoed

9. "Coroner: Newtown Gunman." Lanza killed his mother before going to the elementary school.
10. Berger, "Remembering the Passion."
11. "Coroner: Newtown Gunman."
12. Berger, "Remembering the Passion."
13. Berger, "Cardinal Finds."
14. Ibid.
15. Ibid.
16. Ibid.

President Obama's emphasis that we are to act as the parents of all children in our concern for their well-being.[17]

President Obama's comments Friday afternoon following the murders in Newtown illustrated an application of the covenantal understanding of relationship. Even though he did not use the term "covenant," his language reflected a covenantal view of how he as an individual and as a representative speaking for the whole country responded to the incident. President Obama's words defined him as a parent as well as the president. He positioned himself as a member of the covenant by explicitly speaking as a father when he stated: "I know there's not a parent in America who doesn't feel the same overwhelming grief that I do." The print version of President Obama's comments did not begin to do justice to the depth of his response to the killings. The live or video version showed him wiping tears from his eyes as he spoke, and pausing several times to regain his composure. His tears reinforced the authenticity of his words. This was not a detached formal speech. It reflected the unity of his mind and his heart. President Obama spoke for millions when he sympathized: "So our hearts are broken today for the parents and grandparents, sisters and brothers of these little children, and for the families of the adults who were lost." He further elaborated, "these children are our children" and stressed that their families "need all of us right now. In the hard days to come, that community needs us to be at our best as Americans." He concluded: ". . . all of us can extend a hand to those in need, to remind them that we are there for them, that we are praying for them, that the love they felt for those they lost endures not just in their memories, but also in ours."[18] President Obama defined the covenantal relationship between the families of the victims and everyone else when he identified their children as our children. He outlined the covenantal responsibilities of those, like himself, whose grief was once-removed and who realized that the extent of their grief could not compare with that of the parents of Newtown. He infused his speech with covenantal language by urging us to extend helping hands, love and prayer.

President Obama was one of those who addressed the audience at the Sunday-evening prayer vigil in Newtown on December 16. He continued the theme from his Friday-afternoon address. Again, his speech was replete with covenantal language and bore the earmarks of a sermon in tone and content. He began and ended with Scripture. Like the other speakers, he

17. "President Obama's Speech."
18. "Full Text of Obama Speech."

repeated the word "love" frequently. He stated: "I come to offer the love and prayers of the nation." He was not referring to just a personal covenant between him and the residents of Newtown, but expanded it by speaking on behalf of the whole country. He also specifically addressed the love shared among those who lived in Newtown. His primary emphasis was on the relationship between not only parents, but all other adults and our children. He referred to the "boundless love" we have for our own children, but also extended that love beyond our immediate families to embrace everyone. President Obama was explicit regarding the covenantal responsibilities to protect and care for all our children: "It comes as a shock at a certain point where you realize no matter how much you love these kids, you can't do it by yourself, that this job of keeping our children safe and teaching them well is something we can only do together, with the help of friends and neighbors, the help of a community and the help of a nation. And in that way we come to realize that we bear responsibility for every child, because we're counting on everybody else to help look after ours, that we're all parents, that they are all our children."

Maintaining his focus on children, President Obama continued: "We know we're always doing right when we're taking care of them, when we're teaching them well, when we're showing acts of kindness. We don't go wrong when we do that." In his remarks, President Obama outlined the covenantal responsibilities all adults bear for children. Yet he also personally promised to meet his obligation to fulfill the covenant: "I'll use whatever power this office holds to engage my fellow citizens . . . in an effort aimed at preventing more tragedies like this."[19]

President Obama also recognized the covenantal responsibilities of everyone for the families of the bereaved as he identified with them. The covenantal relationship extended beyond the children: "I am very mindful that mere words cannot match the depths of your sorrow, nor can they heal your wounded hearts. I can only hope it helps for you to know that you're not alone in your grief, that our world, too, has been torn apart, that all across this land of ours, we have wept with you. We've pulled our children tight. And you must know that whatever measure of comfort we can provide, we will provide. Whatever portion of sadness that we can share with you to ease this heavy load, we will gladly bear it. Newtown, you are not alone." President Obama concluded his comments by calling on God's covenantal relationship with us: "May He grace those we still have

19. "President Obama's Speech."

with His holy comfort, and may He bless and watch over this community and the United States of America."[20] Without once mentioning the word "covenant," President Obama managed to include numerous references to covenant and descriptions of various covenantal relationships. His remarks were a sermon permeated by the theme of covenant. The presidential seal was attached to the podium and President Obama was speaking as the president of the United States. Yet his words reflected a parent calling the nation to accept our covenantal obligations.

While the focus thus far has been on words that define covenants, symbols additionally convey the meaning of covenant and represent its reality. The biblical symbol for the Christian covenant between God and us is communion. Jesus created this symbol at the Last Supper when he identified the wine he was sharing with his disciples as "the blood of the covenant" (Luke 22:20, NRSV). The book of Hebrews repeats this statement in reference to Moses' inauguration of the first covenant when he purified the people and everything used in worship: "This is the blood of the covenant that God has ordained for you" (Heb. 9:20, NRSV).

Just as Jesus consecrated the wine symbolizing the New Covenant, individuals and groups designated their covenantal commitment to the residents of Newtown by utilizing numerous symbols. They represented the shared grief of those both near and far away. People knew the symbols would not make the pain of the horror go away, but they wanted to indicate in a tangible way that they sympathized with the townspeople. Objects filled the town square. Individuals placed flowers, teddy bears, and other items in the square that formed huge piles. Mourners took the time to make snowflakes, angels, and Japanese birds which were visible everywhere. Symbols expressing care and concern overwhelmed the town. Some symbols represented each life that had been lost, including a life-sized Santa with a scroll listing the names of the victims. Someone made ornaments with names of the victims written on them.[21]

Contributors donated an estimated 60,000 teddy bears. So many toys arrived that every child in Newtown could select one, with toys left over. Postmaster Cathy Zieff observed: "This is just the proof of the love that's in this country."[22] Amy Mangold, a local mother, attended the toy give-away with her twelve-year-old daughter. Her comments reflected the positive

---

20. Ibid.
21. "People from All Over."
22. Eaton-Robb and Washington, "This Is Bringing."

impact of the covenantal symbols: "'This means people really care about what's happening here. They know we need comfort and want to heal.' She pointed to two people across the room. 'Look at that hug, that embrace. This is bringing people together. Some people haven't been getting out since this happened. It's about people being together. I see people coming together and healing.'"[23] Dennis Stratford, who was organizing the gifts with a forklift, signified the personal effect of the abundance of toys: "This is therapy for me."[24] Ann Spillane, a townsperson, expressed appreciation for the outpouring of gifts, saying: "People are just so good. We understand. They just want to do something."[25] They recognized the symbolic meaning embodied by the thousands of donated objects sent from both near and far. They became unmistakable symbols of covenantal love, shared grief, and initial steps toward healing.

The number of toys sent to Newtown was so massive that a spokesperson for the local United Way requested that donors refrain from further contributions and instead "send those teddy bears to a school in your community or an organization that serves low-income children, who are in need this holiday season, and do it in memory of our children."[26] Speaking for the community, she extended the covenant with Newtown to others with different needs.

In some cases, worshippers physically embodied the covenant with the residents of Newtown in religious gatherings by conducting candlelight prayer vigils throughout the country. Jodi and John Glass attended a service in central Pennsylvania. They explained that their reason for being there "was about making a direct connection, one community to another." John Myers, another participant in the same service, noted the symbolism of the event by describing it as a way for "members of the community here [to] show how much they care for those devastated by the massacre in Newtown."[27]

Citizens demonstrated their desire to fulfill the covenant with Newtown in numerous other ways. They contributed to a Sandy Hook School Support Fund to assist community members.[28] A woman from Alaska gave

23. Ibid.
24. "People from All Over."
25. Ibid.
26. Eaton-Robb and Washington, "This Is Bringing."
27. Miller, "Local Residents Gather."
28. "How You Can Help."

$500 to the Newtown General Store so food and drinks could be distributed for free. Another man gave $2,000 for the same purpose.[29] Amish families whose daughters were killed while attending school at West Nickel Mines in Lancaster County, Pennsylvania in 2006 sent letters to the victims' families.[30] They could truly empathize with the grief these family members faced.

Some fulfilled the covenant by coming to Newtown just to be a supportive presence. Cars with license plates not only from New England, but from as far away as Washington and Florida, crowded the streets.[31] Hundreds came to show their covenantal concern. One account was particularly moving. At the first funeral to be conducted for a victim, a carload of young African-Americans who had traveled from Huntsville, Alabama stood at the side of the funeral home and sang "Amazing Grace." Then they drove to the funeral home where the second funeral was being held and sang there as well.[32]

Caregivers with specialized training also came to Newtown. Massage therapists, acupuncturists, and art therapists shared their skills. One of the most unlikely, yet perhaps one of the most effective, means of reaching out (particularly to the children of Newtown) was the presence of comfort dogs. Trained to work with victims of natural disasters as well as situations like the one in Newtown, the dogs allowed children to pet them.[33] As one child broke into a smile while petting a dog, a newscaster marveled that it was the first smile he had seen in Newtown.

Seven dogs subsequently joined everyone else who welcomed the Sandy Hook Elementary School students when they gathered at their new school building for the first time in January 2013. The golden retrievers received their specialized training as K-9 Parish Comfort Dogs under the auspices of Lutheran Church Charities (LCC), which partners with the Lutheran Church-Missouri Synod. Referring to the dogs, LCC president Tim Hetzner commented on this highly unusual ministry: "They are safe. They show unconditional love. And dogs have a unique ability to sense hurt in people." The mission of the organization is to "bring the mercy, compassion, presence and proclamation of Jesus Christ to those who suffer." Handlers

29. Eaton-Robb and Washington, "This Is Bringing."
30. "A Shared Grief."
31. "People from All Over."
32. Barry, "With a Why No Closer."
33. "People from All Over."

demonstrate covenantal love by making their dogs available to those who will benefit from the presence of dogs who have been trained not to bark, lick, or get upset when hugged by strangers.[34]

The myriad responses to the mass shooting in Newtown represented the covenant that God established with humans and the covenantal behavior we are to exhibit toward each other. While not generally described in covenantal language, people responded to the massacre by identifying the victims' families, friends and other inhabitants of Newtown as neighbors, in the broader sense, who merited an outpouring of our love. We responded to their grief. We shared in their suffering. As a country, we were at our best. But time has passed and most people seem to have moved on. There are exceptions. Lapel ribbons are a remembrance. Groups have mobilized to seek to reduce violence caused by guns. Is the expression of covenantal identification with the townsfolk of Newtown a passing phase? One could easily become discouraged and frustrated that covenantal relationships emerge during times of catastrophe only to recede soon into the background and even disappear. Life goes back to normal for everyone else but the families who continue to live with their grief. At first, this appears to be a depressing scenario. But a different picture emerges when the situation is examined eschatologically. Many Wesleyans affirm an inaugurated eschatology in which the kingdom or realm of God is both "already" and "not yet." Through the life, death, and resurrection of Jesus, God inaugurated the new kingdom rather than making us wait for a future realm. Instead of becoming discouraged when the covenantal moments recede into the past, we can take hope in the fact that these expressions of love are glimpses of God's realm in our midst now. At Newtown, we had a glimpse of the vision of God's realm, where love will ultimately reign over all.

---

34. De Santis, "Lutheran 'Comfort Dogs.'"

11

Marriage as a Metaphor for God's Covenant Love and Faithfulness

by Clifford W. Berger

WRITING A CHAPTER THAT includes the topics of "marriage" and "covenant" involves some risk of being misunderstood. This is partly because marriage currently is at the center of heated cultural conflicts, and partly because the concept of "covenant" today is understood poorly or simply not at all. *Covenant* is not a word one frequently reads or hears in general conversation. It has, in fact, something of a quaint and even Elizabethan ring to it. Larry Shelton, whom we honor with this festschrift and who has devoted much of his scholarly attention to the topic of covenant, writes, "But although the term *covenant* is a central and well-known concept within biblical theology, the broader unchurched twenty-first-century culture does not recognize it."[1]

    The purpose of this chapter is to revisit this biblical concept of covenant in light of marriage as a metaphor, and to suggest implications for effective pastoral theology and practice. I'm quite aware that marriage is not exactly a fresh metaphor for God's covenant love, nor is it a flawless one. The institution of marriage itself has become rather controversial, at least in Western culture, and marriage is too frequently imperfectly modeled—at best—by imperfect human beings. But it is a metaphor employed in Scripture itself and, for that reason among others, it merits our attention and

---

1. Shelton, *Cross and Covenant*, 19.

re-consideration—perhaps especially so in this time when our culture is struggling to come to terms with the meaning and significance of marriage.

A central theme of Shelton's book, *Cross and Covenant: Interpreting the Atonement for 21st Century Mission* is a call for fresh motifs and metaphors for understanding the biblical doctrine of the atonement.[2] Other writers recently also are calling attention to the need for fresh metaphors to explain various aspects of Christian belief and practice. R. Anderson Campbell speaks of the need to develop networks of fresh metaphors, rather than just words or statements, that will "carry the freight" of re-describing complex topics in fresh ways.[3] The idea is to avoid simplistic metaphors that function as little more than illustrations. Campbell observes, "Metaphoric networks that offer the most space in which to find new meaning are those which are culturally appropriate. There is a certain fittingness to them because they exist in the shared cultural-linguistic space of the speaker and hearer. As such, there is a constant need for new metaphors and metaphoric networks. The space is always changing, always shifting."[4] There is little doubt that marriage as a metaphor has the substance to "carry the freight" of describing or re-describing God's covenant love. The question is whether the concept of marriage is currently too disputed and battle-worn to effectively serve this role—and thus whether it provides the culturally appropriate vessel Campbell calls for. It is the thesis of this chapter that re-examining marriage as a metaphor for God's covenant love will provide us a better understanding and appreciation of both of these themes. I should further note that this chapter will generally consider marriage as an ideal, rather than focusing on the realities and complexities of actual experience. It is thus beyond the scope and intent of this Chapter also to address issues of divorce and re-marriage, same-sex relationships, etc. Part of the challenge of creating or re-introducing metaphors is to understand the limits of a given metaphor so that the point of the comparison is not lost in the process.

---

2. Ibid., 29 ff. Shelton offers his own fresh motif by examining the doctrine of the atonement in light of his own experience with a heart transplant. He utilizes the heart-transplant image throughout his book.

3. Campbell, "Realms and Redescription," 72. While drawing attention to the need for fresh metaphors, Campbell himself offers a book-length metaphor of home-brewing beer as a way of gaining new insights into Christian spiritual formation.

4. Ibid., 73.

What is Covenant?

Recalling that 21st-century culture has little or no familiarity with the concept of covenant, Shelton describes it in straightforward, non-theological terms: "It is a formal or informal agreement between two parties that stipulates the nature and purpose of the agreement, the expectations of the arrangement, and the accountability of the parties for the consequences of failure to fulfill the terms of the agreement."[5] He further notes that in cases of an impersonal, more businesslike, arrangement it may be called a contract. It is easy to see how a marriage relationship exhibits characteristics of a covenant thus defined. I would add that a contract—versus a covenant—generally is considered not as a lasting mutual commitment, but as a temporary arrangement based on satisfaction of mutual needs. The arrangement can be ended once the terms of the contract are fulfilled, or if one or the other of the parties breaches the agreement. Unfortunately, it is easy for a marriage to exhibit more of the characteristics of a contract than of a covenant. Marriage, in 21st-century culture, could benefit from the chance to embrace a renewed understanding of what it means to be in covenant. Likewise, understanding God's ideal for the marriage relationship can help us envision in a personal and intimate way what it means to live under the covenant love of God.

The basis for the concept of covenants in the First and Second Testaments is that God desires to have a relationship with persons.[6] God is described in Genesis as the creator, the one who called forth life and who breathed life into God's human creation (Gen 1:1, 2:7). Human beings were created to be in relationship with one another, in intimate communion as male and female (Gen 1:27, 2:18). This creation of humanity reflected something important and unique as the image or reflection of God: "When God created humankind, he made them in the likeness of God. Male and female he created them, and he blessed them and named them 'humankind' when they were created" (Gen 5:1–2). God later commanded his people not to make any carved images or idols—even in an attempt to represent God himself (Exod 20: 4). From God's point of view, humanity itself was the only image required. Men and women could gaze upon one another and see in themselves an image and reflection of God. Christopher Roberts observes, "In and through their male and female differences, humans

---

5. Shelton, *Cross and Covenant*, 19–20.
6. Ibid., 23.

are commanded to be and do something no other animals do, which is to witness to God's own form of relational life.[7]

Ray Anderson develops a theological anthropology in his book *On Being Human*, asserting that "humanity is determined as existence in covenant relation with God."[8] He goes on to connect the concept of covenant to human and family relationships, considering these relationships as a type of "co-humanity." In a later book with Dennis Guernsey (1985), Anderson connects the concept of covenant to marriage and family even more directly: "It is covenant love that provides the basis for family. For this reason, family means much more than consanguinity, where blood ties provide the only basis of belonging. Family is where you are loved unconditionally, and where you can count on that love even when you least deserve it."[9]

This relational dimension of creation, between God and humanity and between human beings themselves, was carried forward as the basis of God's choosing a people with whom to be in relationship. The nature and the boundaries of that relationship were often described in "covenant" language, and frequently included references to God's love, grace and faithfulness to his people.[10]

Much attention has been given to framing an understanding of covenant in light of ancient Near Eastern culture. The literature is extensive, in fact, and it is beyond the scope of this paper to attempt a thorough review.[11] I will suffice with a brief overview highlighting some key characteristics of ancient Near Eastern covenants or treaties, and how they contribute to our purposes here.

---

7. Roberts, *Creation and Covenant*, 143. Roberts writes this as part of a study of Karl Barth's work on the concept of *Imago Dei*.

8. Anderson, *On Being Human*, 37.

9. Anderson and Guernsey, *On Being Family*, 40.

10. Exod 34: 6–7, 10 expresses these characteristics of God's commitment: "The Lord, the Lord, a God merciful and gracious, slow to anger, and abounding in steadfast love and faithfulness, keeping steadfast love for the thousandth generation, forgiving iniquity and transgression and sin ... I hereby make a covenant ..." Other references to covenant and to God's love and faithfulness to his people include Deut 7:6–9; 2 Sam 7:11–16; Pss 98:3, 100:5, 136:1; Jer 31:31–34; Luke 22: 20.

11. For sources on biblical and ancient Near Eastern covenants such as provided background for this paper, see: Birch et al., *A Theological Introduction to the Old Testament*; Hillers, *Covenant*; Hugenberger, *Marriage as a Covenant*; Hvidberg, "The Canaanitic Background of Gen. I–III"; Kittel and Bromiley, s.v. "diatheke" in *TDNT*; Mendenhall, "Covenant"; Roberts, *Creation and Covenant*; Stackhouse, *Covenant and Commitments*.

More than forty years ago, Delbert Hillers provided a classic synopsis of the principal elements of an ancient Near Eastern treaty:[12]

1. The preamble. This consists of a description of the parties involved in the covenant.

2. The historical prologue, which personalized the narrative of the covenant to fit the partners involved. This prevented it from becoming a generic, fill-in-the-blank type of contract.

3. Stipulations—this includes a recital of the obligations agreed upon by the parties in the treaty.

4. Provisions for deposit of the text and for public reading. Max Stackhouse describes this characteristic thus, "A body of sanctions, positive and negative, that on the one hand detail what benefits may be realized if the bond is kept and on the other hand define what is likely to happen if one or the other of the parties fails to fulfill the promises or live up to the standards. Blessings and woes are specified."[13]

5. Witnesses to the treaty. The treaty or covenant has implications for the community and is not to be done in secret. The public and communal nature of the covenant recognizes religious and social importance of what takes place.

6. Blessings and curses. This element also may include "sworn oaths or solemn promises that make the covenant binding."[14]

It is easy to see how the basic parts of the traditional western wedding ceremony in many ways mirror these elements of the ancient covenant or treaty as described by Hillers (among other influences[15]). The ritual nature of wedding ceremonies, especially in their origin prior to government-issued and archived marriage licenses, was essential to establish the legality of the marriage.[16] The word "wed" or "wedding" itself comes from the

12. Hillers, *Covenant*, 29ff.
13. Stackhouse, *Covenant and Commitments*, 146.
14. Ibid.
15. See Chesser, "Analysis of Wedding Rituals," 204. Chesser traces the development of the rituals of the wedding ceremony as a publicly conducted covenant, including exchange of rings, transfer of ownership of the bride, the kiss, etc. The history of the wedding covenant has been closely tied to the legal and economic transfer of dependence of women; see Encyclopedia Britannica Online, s.v. "family law."
16. Chesser, "Analysis of Wedding Rituals," 206.

Anglo-Saxon for pledge or promise, "something deposited as security for a payment or the fulfillment of an obligation."[17] In keeping with these ritual elements of historical covenants, the biblical covenants also are expressed through ritual such as seen in the Passover (Exod 12), the Christian Eucharist (Matt 26: 26–30; Luke 22:14–20) and baptism (Matt 28:19; Acts 2:38; Rom 6:3–4). As with marriage, the regular repetition and near-universality of these rituals—the Eucharist and baptism in particular—could be seen as affirming the binding nature of the covenant between God and his people.

Based on this broader context for near eastern covenants as described by Hillers, the Hebrew word for "covenant" used in the First Testament (286 times), *b'rit*, generally represents an agreement that formally yoked together two persons or groups with both agreeing to certain benefits and responsibilities.[18] Sometimes *b'rit* is viewed alongside the companion concept of *hesed*. The term *hesed* may be "translated variously as 'covenant,' 'steadfast love,' 'loyalty' or 'devotion' (Ps 42:8; Prov 3:3; Lam 3:22; Sakenfeld 1985). Steadfast love and faithfulness are thus at the heart of covenant relationships."[19] Such covenants are entered voluntarily, not conditioned on what each party is to gain from the arrangement. The *b'rit*, or covenant, rests on the foundation of steadfast love and commitment that is inherent in *hesed*.[20] Ruth and Naomi, for example, shared life together for a number of years following the deaths of their husbands. They created their family covenant based on this loving relationship (Ruth 1:4–7). David and Jonathan shared a deep friendship and love for one another, out of which they created a formal covenant (1 Sam 18:1–4).[21] Likewise, a couple pledging wedding vows are making an enduring commitment, but in our culture at least, the wedding covenant develops out of the love and affection that they have already been nurturing.

In addition to the biblical terminology and concepts for covenant, we can take note of various other linguistic forms of covenant. In Latin we see the *testamentum*, the covenant term for Old and New "Testaments," and *foedus*, from which we derive *federation*. From Latin we also see the terms *pactum* and *compactum*, which denote a binding agreement, often

---

17. Oxford English Dictionary Online, s.v. "Wed, n."
18. Garland, *Family Ministry*, 333.
19. Ibid., 333–334.
20. Ibid., 335.
21. Ibid.

of a political or commercial contract.[22] Also consider *institutio*, implying an agreement based on established practice, or *religio*, which can have the sense of "binding," especially toward spiritual and ethical obligation.[23] In French we see *alliance*, and in German *bund*, both of which imply covenanting together in a federation or a league. This rich variety of terminology for various aspects of "covenant" demonstrates the depth of the human impulse to join and ally together for various social purposes. One of the oldest and most deeply-rooted of these covenant alliances, of course, is that of marriage.

The Marriage Metaphor in Scripture

It is no surprise that Scripture freely makes use of marriage—this most intimate of human covenant relationships—as a metaphor for God's covenant relationship with his people, in both the First and Second Testaments (see Prov 2:17; Jer 2:2; 3:1–8; Ezek 16:8–32; Hosea; Matt 2:14; Mark 2:18–20; 2 Cor 11:2; Eph 5:21–33). Hosea, in particular, presents marriage as a vivid case study of God's covenant love.[24] In Hosea 1–3 the prophet is directed by God to marry a promiscuous or adulterous woman.[25] Hosea is expected by

---

22. Stackhouse, *Covenant and Commitments*, 143. Consider for example the "Mayflower Compact" of 1620, which established the basis for government in the Plymouth, MA settlement.

23. Ibid.

24. For a challenge to this more traditional view see Bauman, *Love and Violence*. Bauman offers a feminist theological interpretation, asserting that the marriage metaphor, rather than demonstrating God's caring and loving commitment to his people, actually represents YHWH as the violent and abusive husband/lord of his "wife." Ehud Ben Zvi acknowledges the marital relationship in Hosea 1–3, but contends that it represents an asymmetrical perspective from the point of view of the male literati; see Ben Zvi, "Observations on the Marital Metaphor" 363–384. John J. Schmitt, on the other hand, denies altogether the marital relationship metaphor in the Hebrew Bible, contending that the wife of God in Hosea 2 is the city of Samaria. See Schmitt, "The Wife of God in Hosea 2." For an affirmation of the traditional view of marriage in the Hebrew Bible as covenant, and as representative of God's commitment to his people, see Hugenberger, *Marriage as a Covenant*, 27, 47–48, 122ff., etc.

25. Ben Zvi argues that there is no reason to translate or to assume that Hosea's wife was an actual prostitute, a woman who was expected to have sexual relations for money. Such encounters did not breach the prostitute's accepted but frowned-upon social role. The text in Hosea rhetorically associates the promiscuous and adulterous behavior of a married woman with the socially stigmatized behavior of a prostitute ("Observations on the Marital Metaphor," 379).

God to remain faithful and committed to his wife in spite of her adultery and betrayal, metaphorically reflecting the religious unfaithfulness of the Israelites. His personal life is to serve as a living illustration of the relationship between God and his people, a moving example of covenant love that endures and restores. "God is envisioned as a faithful spouse pursuing an unfaithful lover and as a loving parent who continually pursues the children of Israel."[26] Building on the commitment of Hosea to his unfaithful wife, God says to the people of Israel: "I will take you for my wife forever; I will take you for my wife in righteousness and in justice, in steadfast love, and in mercy. I will take you for my wife in faithfulness; and you will know the Lord" (Hos 2:19-20). "These expressions of God's final will for Israel provide an alternative model of marriage and family relationships shaped not by inequality, shame, and violence but by justice and love."[27] The Hosea text presents challenges for the interpreter, of course, such as the images' being informed by a generally patriarchal culture. But in spite of these difficulties, Hosea 1-3 affirms commitment and faithfulness as virtues in both the marriage relationship and that between God and his people.

The prophecy of Malachi contains another of the well-known First-Testament marriage metaphors. As with Hosea, the use of the metaphor here presents challenges for the interpreter. Malachi 2:16 is too often taken at face value and out of context: "For I hate divorce, says the Lord, the God of Israel, and covering one's garment with violence, says the Lord of hosts. So take heed to yourselves and do not be faithless." As such, it can be seen as simply as elevating the marriage covenant and condemning human divorce. Cautions against this approach abound.[28] David Peterson acknowledges the metaphoric language around marriage and divorce here and in Hosea and Jeremiah, but argues that the author uses human relationships to reflect Israel's unfaithfulness to Yahweh.[29] There is certainly no doubt as to this first-level meaning of the text. And yet, the fact that the human relationship of marriage was chosen to make this point ought to tell us something about the subject of the metaphor itself. Elizabeth Achtemeier makes the case that

---

26. Balswick and Balswick, *A Model for Marriage*, 40.

27. Olson, "Family Relationships as Metaphor," 220.

28. C. C. Torrey, making that argument more than 100 years ago, warned against a simplistic and literalistic interpretation of these images: Torrey, "The Prophecy of 'Malachi,'" 9.

29. Peterson, *Zechariah 9-14 and Malachi*, 205.

Malachi 2:14–16 presents a high view of the human marital relationship.[30] Contrary to Bauman's study of the text as representing patriarchal "violence" toward the wife, Achtemeier writes, "The wife here is described as the husband's 'companion,' and that description accords with Genesis 2:18, in which the woman is termed a mutual helper, and with Ephesians 5:21, in which male and female are 'subject to one another' in mutual service out of love for Christ. There is no rule of the husband over the wife here. There certainly is no thought of the woman as a material object, to be bought and sold, as is sometimes erroneously said of the Old Testament's view of the marital relation. No. Marriage here is to be characterized by companionship, mutuality, and lifelong covenant faithfulness to one another."[31] She further argues that the nature of the marital relationship has direct bearing on one's worship of God. God was as grieved with the faithlessness of the Judeans' worship as he was with the faithlessness of their marriages. "In other words, we can deny our relation to God in our bedrooms and living rooms and dining rooms as surely as we deny it in our failure to minister to the poor or in our failure to act justly . . . Faithfulness in marriage is part of what it means to be faithful in our discipleship. And God desires faithfulness in our marriage covenant as surely as he asks it in all our service and in our worship of him."[32]

Second-Testament references to the marriage covenant metaphor, while not as numerous, exhibit a generally positive view of the marriage covenant. Paul alludes to this metaphor in 2 Cor 11:2, but develops it much more robustly in Ephesians 5.[33] Markus Barth provides an extensive examination of Eph 5:21–33, considering linguistic, cultural, and theological issues.[34] He describes Paul's use of the marriage metaphor as having First-Testament parallels in passages such as those from Hosea and Malachi, which we have just considered. Barth notes that "The OT speaks of the 'Yahweh-Israel' covenant; Eph 5 describes the 'Messiah's' covenant with a people composed of 'Jews and Gentiles.'"[35] Further, the "special and

---

30. Achtemeier, *Preaching from the Minor Prophets*, 129–30.

31. Ibid., 130.

32. Ibid.

33. Paul also addresses the marriage relationship in 1 Cor 7:10–11, although more from the perspective of appropriate expressions of the human sexual relationship than from the overall sense of covenant commitment.

34. Barth, *Ephesians*, 607–753.

35. Ibid., 670.

intimate relationship between husband and wife has its basis, model, criterion—and limit—in the grace of God and the Messiah."[36] As with ancient Israel, the early church functioned in a culture of male superiority. Paul here avoids embracing an extreme patriarchy, although the Household Codes (*haustafeln*) that he advocates here and in Col. 3:18–4:1 would have been approved by contemporary Greek moral philosophers.[37] But Paul goes further than the prevailing Greco-Roman household codes, by urging husbands to love their wives (Eph 5:25ff.). This speaks to the nature of the marriage covenant as going beyond a contractual societal arrangement to protect property and provide for child-rearing. Rather, he calls for an unconditional, self-sacrificing love (*agapate*), comparable to the passionate descriptions of covenant love in the prophets, and in particular to the sacrificial love that Christ has for the church. Even though Paul does not here use the Greek word for covenant (*diatheke*, with its parallel the Hebrew term *b'rith*), both the marriage relationship and the relationship of Christ with his people is one of complete and unreserved commitment. On this basis, Markus Barth argues that "it makes sense to use the biblical term 'covenant' (despite its quaintness and legal associations) as the most fitting description of the structure of marriage, as proclaimed by Eph 5."[38]

The Historical Development of Marriage

Our current understandings of the marriage covenant are, of course, shaped by much more than just the biblical perspective. This is true no matter how much we might search for a "biblical pattern" for marriage today. Marriage has continued to evolve in response to historical developments, legal oversight, and theological trends. John Witte, Jr., has insightfully outlined the western understanding of marriage as having passed through five eras or models: 1) as a sacrament in the Roman Catholic tradition, 2) as social estate in the Lutheran Reformation, 3) as covenant in the Calvinist tradition, 4) as commonwealth in the Anglican tradition, and 5) as contract in the Enlightenment tradition.[39] One could make the case that today's understanding of marriage has assimilated aspects of all

36. Ibid., 712.

37. Liefeld, *Ephesians*, 143. First Peter 3:1–7 reflects a somewhat more patriarchal structure than does Paul in Eph 5.

38. Barth, *Ephesians*, 752.

39. Witte, *From Sacrament to Contract*, 77–287.

of these traditions, as well as that of a "biblical" perspective. This perhaps has contributed to marriage's being such a misunderstood and contentious institution. One can see the influence of the different theological traditions throughout, but what is remarkable is how the locus of political and legal authority has shifted from the church (in the Catholic model) to the state (in the Enlightenment model). One could further make the case that within these models there is no single "golden age" for marriage and family in the western tradition.[40] We are simply left to deal with the realities of these historical developments, for better or for worse. While it is not the purpose of the First and Second Testaments to provide a comprehensive perspective on marriage, neither can we leap from the pages of the Testaments to the present without realizing these influences over time. And yet, it is the thesis of this chapter that, while we can benefit from assimilating the positive aspects of many of these perspectives on marriage, we have the most to gain by re-emphasizing the biblical model of covenant faithfulness.

The general acceptance or at least tolerance of divorce in western culture is of concern to many students and observers of marriage and family. Some propose to remedy this by making divorce more difficult to obtain, abandoning "no-fault" divorce laws, etc.[41] But addressing the problem of divorce from the point of dissolution can be fruitless without addressing it from the point of marital formation. What is entered lightly can be dissolved lightly just as well. Many people "get married" today, but often with vastly different understandings of the commitment they make. Many people may repeat the same marriage vows and pledges, but how it works out in practice varies from one marriage to another. An understanding, and embracing, of the concept of "covenant" (as Christ loves the church) may lead to a more healthy and committed approach to the human marriage relationship. This has been most evident in the "Covenant Marriage" movement, which allows couples the option of a "covenant marriage" over the more common civil, contractual-style arrangement.[42] I am not advocating broad implementation of the Covenant Marriage movement as such; that approach seems to focus more on re-shaping the legal options. Rather, I am suggesting a more pastoral approach through teaching and counseling

---

40. Ibid., 216.

41. Butler, "Iowa GOP."

42. Felkey, "Will You Covenant Marry Me?" Felkey analyzes the covenant-marriage movement, currently adopted by three states (Louisiana, Arkansas, and Arizona). This is essentially a different level of state-regulated marriage, making it more difficult both to enter into marriage and to obtain a divorce.

during marriage preparation. A pastoral focus on the nature of biblical covenant can create a framework both for healthier marriage and for greater depth of spiritual formation.

A Pastoral Perspective on Covenant and Marriage

Pastors and counselors who teach and work with couples could benefit from revisiting the basic elements of biblical covenant in light of marriage. Drawing from the above survey of covenant and marriage in biblical and historical perspective, we can outline certain characteristics of covenants. These characteristics may provide an initial framework for more effective engagement in the pastoral task of teaching, counseling, and spiritual formation. Some of these characteristics are adapted from Diana Garland's book, *Family Ministry*, and from Jack and Judith Balswick, *A Model for Marriage*. Both of these sources have effectively bridged biblical and theological perspectives with an applied approach to marriage and family ministry.

Covenants Are Based on Commitment

Couples reciting wedding vows may be unable to comprehend the challenges ahead. Nor can we reasonably expect that they should. A contractual approach to a relationship is based on mutual fulfillment of needs; in its most base form, there may be an unspoken understanding that one will stay in the relationship as long as needs are met. The increasingly common practice of cohabitation apart from marriage seems designed to create trial relationships that resemble a marriage, but lacking the commitment. If one partner finds the arrangement not to his or her liking, walking away becomes an acceptable option. The lesson of covenant love from Hosea's experience, however, emphasizes a perseverance and commitment in the face of incredible relational challenges. Understanding that this is the same kind of commitment that God showed to Israel, or that Christ has for the church, can give individuals and couples a firm platform on which to develop a commitment of their own.

Covenants are Meant to Last

A contract is meant to be temporary, but a covenant endures. A couple pledging marriage vows typically has every intention, at that moment, of remaining in the relationship "until death do us part." And yet—realities of human sin and imperfection occur, and sometimes the relationship does end. When Jesus said, "Therefore what God has joined together, let no one separate" (Matt 19:6), was he teaching that a person should continue in a destructive or even abusive relationship? I am not suggesting that is what he meant. Even so, those who have experienced painful divorces or family separations can attest that even when no longer living with the other person, a part of the relationship based on that original covenant remains with them for the rest of their lives. One cannot simply roll back time as if the relationship had never happened. One's personality, ideas, and habits are forever shaped by the covenant once made, even if one separates never to see that person again. This is part of the power of the marriage metaphor—a relationship that can be legally ended, but never entirely undone.[43]

We Grow into the Marriage Covenant over Time

On their wedding day, a couple may be signing the equivalent of a promissory note, but with very little collateral. Their promises grow out of a relationship already begun, of course. But it is in the daily rhythm of living and relating, sharing acts of loyalty and love, that "deposits" are made giving substance to the promises. In the same way, a couple conceives a child and their love relationship with the baby grows throughout gestation. A lasting bond is created in the birthing process, and a covenant of care and love is made. A covenant is created from a developing relationship, but requires time to mature.

Covenants Can Be Costly

The focus of a contract is generally on the benefits one gains from the relationship. There are obligations, of course, but the negotiations of a contract typically are on gaining the greatest personal advantage at the least personal cost. A covenant, however, is the very opposite. The focus is on what one gives, not what one gains. The relationship itself is the currency of value.

---

43. Garland, *Family Ministry*, 336.

When the people of Israel made covenant with Yahweh, they had to make choices. They could not follow both Yahweh and the foreign gods they had served previously. Joshua called on them to "choose this day whom you will serve" (Josh 24:15), requiring that the covenant relationship cost them something. In Ephesians 5, Paul calls on husbands to love their wives with a love that costs their life—just as Christ did for the church. When Jesus said, "This cup that is poured out for you is the new covenant in my blood" (Luke 22:20), he was talking about a covenant relationship that would call for his life. Covenants are costly.

Covenants Are Uniquely Personal

As Diana Garland observes, "Covenants are defined by the participants, not by the expectations of others."[44] Yahweh's covenant with Israel was particular and unique. It was not a generalized covenant with all of humanity at once; rather, it was personal to them and is what made them his people. The covenant relationship of Christ with the church is uniquely based on Christ's sacrificial love, and the faith-response of his people. The participants themselves agree upon the terms of the covenant. Likewise, the covenant life of a family or marriage must be fleshed out in ways unique to that relationship. A covenant cannot function by a cold set of rules and terms; it is intensely relational. How a couple relates to one another is not defined by gender-specific rules and expectations, but by gifts and needs exercised in dynamic and loving relationship.[45]

Covenants Exist for a Greater Purpose

One does not wake up to find him- or herself bound in a covenant relationship. It isn't something that happens randomly and accidentally. One enters a covenant intentionally and with purpose.[46] The covenant of God with his people reflected such a purpose. The children of Abraham were to be "blessed to be a blessing" (Gen 12:2). The church is called to "Go therefore and make disciples of all nations" (Matt 28:19). Likewise when a married couple can gain a vision of their marriage and their family serving a

---

44. Ibid., 340.
45. Ibid., 341.
46. Ibid.

larger purpose of ministry and service, it can have a transforming effect on their relationship. A sense of mission beyond personal satisfaction reflects the concept of biblical covenant, and is essential to an ultimately fulfilling marriage covenant. Our marriage and family covenants have not only to do with our private lives, but also have a bearing on relationships with all those around us. This may be why weddings are typically public events, or at least must be performed in the presence of witnesses. In marriage and in family life we are in relationship and on mission, bound by a covenant with a purpose.

12

Theologians *in* Covenant
WHAT THEY DO, WHY THEY DO IT, AND WHAT GETS IN THEIR WAY

A. J. Swoboda

> "Unless there is within us that which is above us,
> we shall soon yield to that which is about us."
> —SCOTTISH THEOLOGIAN PETER FORSYTH (1848–1921)

Introduction

A THEOLOGIAN, AMONG OTHER things, is a bit like a chauffeur. First and foremost, good theologians fulfill the task of helping people along on their Christian journey. The primary objective, thus, is not to insert themselves as the central character in any person's faith development. Rather, theologians strive to work tirelessly in assisting others to get where they are going safely, on time, whilst keeping things appropriate along the way. Secondly, good theologians know when to vacate themselves and get out of the way. This metaphor may not be appreciated by all because, as it suggests, a chauffeur plays the part only some of the time. Any theologian is *helpful*, yet essentially *not necessary*. Anyone inspired by the lasting spirit of Luther's theology of the "priesthood of all believers" not only recognizes, but strives to attain, the dream that every Christ-follower might know God and serve Him faithfully in their world. And once a theologian has helped this dream come to fruition, his or her role changes. With the spirit of sensitivity, at the right time, the theologian/chauffeur knows how to get out of the way and allow the two parties do what they are intended to do on a date. Good theologians know well their place in the drama of salvation.

Dr. R. Larry Shelton has served as my theological chauffeur for some seven years along my faith journey. Both as his student and as a fellow colleague, I've had the distinct pleasure of knowing Larry on a personal and professional level as well as in the classroom and faculty gatherings. I first came to know Larry during my initial semester in seminary when I enrolled in his graduate course on biblical theology. His nuanced theological perspective honed over nearly four decades of scholarship (which was keenly constructed through the hermeneutical lens of his own personal story of receiving a heart transplant) made the Bible dance in a way I'd never imagined possible. The God of the Bible was a God who constantly extended Himself in covenant to people by promising to make them new.

Years later, I joined Shelton to co-teach a course on Christian history during what became his next to final semester before retirement. Until the very end, he pushed me to academic excellence. One of the more humbling experiences was having Larry sit in on a class I taught. The day's lecture was on the "Road to the Reformation." Prepped and ready to deliver, I commenced my lecture in secret hopes of making a hero proud. As he listened attentively, nodding and giving affirmative comments, I was sure my goal had been met. Just following the dismissal of class, Larry pulled me aside in the hallway. After he encouraged me and was about to walk away, he stopped, turned around, and thought. Then, as if an afterthought, he said: "Oh, A.J., by the way, Luther posted the 95 theses on Wittenberg Door in 1517, *not* 1511. But, hey, those are just details, right? Great work." Never is it easy to broadcast your failures before a hero. But God still has a knack for making even the most proud humble.

This short piece will add to the growing polyphonic chorus of voices raising in unison honoring Shelton's theological brilliance. Covenant, as the theme of this *festschrift*, is appropriately chosen as a lens through which to view the scope of Shelton's work. Even more so, covenant is an apt field of study for any serious theologian. The Bible teems with the theme: in Hebrew Scripture, God takes Israel upon a covenant journey to become a light among the Gentiles, and the New Testament writings depict Jesus gathering a covenant community to Himself who will witness to the world of the saving power of His cross and resurrection. In this chapter, I should like to take covenant as a theme in a different direction. For our purposes here, I believe covenant *as a way of being a theologian is equally as integral as the theme itself.* Let us inquire: what is a theologian in covenant with God, and what does this look like practically? What does a theologian in covenant do?

Theologians in Covenant

What does a professional theologian actually do with her or his time? What practices does the craft of theology entail? The Swiss theologian Karl Barth once reflected upon this: "If there is any branch of learning that both inwardly and outwardly can aspire only to serve, it is theology."[1] Theology, for Barth, was the engine of Christian service and action. The story of Ezra comes to mind. The Israelites, after a long journey of travel to their Promised Land from exile, encounter a small but motivated group of discouragers of their efforts rebuild the temple. Led by Tattenai, a governor from their community, the locals offer a sustained, critical voice in seeking to inhibit the work of the Lord being done by the newly re-established Israelites. Speaking before the discouraged and distraught people, they tell the Israelites that, despite Tattenai's discouragement, the time has come to build. Ezra tells us that the "prophets of God were with them, *supporting them*" (Ezra 5:2). The prophets, given the task of hearing from God, put down their prophetic messages and pick up their shovels and hammers to help the work. Or, to be more precise, their hammering is their message. The theologian isn't just one with an opposing view to the people. A theologian is one who knows how to pick up a shovel.

Hammering, shoveling, and carrying rocks as theologian is clearly a different way of imagining God-talk in an age where everyone can pontificate, blog, and tweet their most recent theological ideas. More often than not, people *say* theology more than they *do* theology. An old statement hangs over the dining hall at a church I've visited: "everyone wants to change the world, but no one wants to do the dishes." Theologians should hear this. A slight problem arises in that in a postmodern and information-infused world, everyone—Christian, scientist, garbage hauler, Democrat,

---

1. Barth, *Fragments Gray and Gay*, 27.

and novelist—is a theologian. No one does *not* think about or discourse on the nature of God. Personally, the awareness of the universality of theologians came as a bit of a let-down once I had, exhausted and half-dead, finished my doctoral work in theology in Britain. Believing these three shiny new letters behind my name gave me the authority to be God's appointed thinker at any after-dinner party, I came across some frustrating words from a hero. "Theology," Jürgen Moltmann once wrote, "is the business of all God's people."[2] Everyone considers God. And everyone has an opinion.

Every human, for sure, is a theologian. Some of them are paid and some of them are amateurs (lat. "lovers"). The sort of theologian I have in mind here are professional theologians whose burden in life is teaching pastors, academics, and lay-people the nature of God in places like a seminary where Shelton instructs. What is the actual purpose of a professional theologian when everyone else is a theologian? Old Testament scholar Bernard Anderson writes that, "Standing within the circle of faith, a theologian articulates and elaborates the faith of the believing and worshipping community so that members of the community, or others interested, may understand who God is, God's relationship to the world and all that is in it, and the unfolding purpose of God from creation to consummation."[3] Quite simply, a theologian of this regard articulates, re-tells, and proclaims that of the community. Within this is something profound worth noting. A professional theologian, in a sea of theologians, is one who faithfully articulates the story of God in the past for the future. The theologian *is not* someone tasked primarily with profundity or even novelty.

A theologian *in* covenant is one first and foremost enthralled with the Subject of his or her proclamation. In the end, what Shelton has modeled for the church, the seminary, and the larger academic world has not been strictly as a theologian *of* covenant but as a theologian *in* covenant. Why is this distinction important? In our current academic climate, what lacks is often the integration of knowledge and real life. Academia, in general, has the propensity to create a guild of scholars who know a great deal *about* their subjects without having personal knowledge *of* those subjects. This can be due to many factors. For one, contemporary academics increasingly rely on literature, libraries, and technology to gather information, quotations, and anecdotes about their subjects. This certainly has changed anthropological epistemology, or the way humans *know* something. Today,

---

2. Moltmann, *Experiences in Theology*, 11.

3. Anderson, *Contours*, 3.

no longer must an evolutionary scientist visit the Galapagos Islands to learn about what Darwin discovered. Nor must a scholar in French literature visit the region of her or his literature's origination. The Internet, libraries, and a proliferation of literature have removed the cumbersome task of actually going somewhere to know about a subject. Before the availability of these technologies, humans were required to go, or know someone who personally went, in order to know something.

Thus the death of what Michael Polanyi famously called "personal knowledge."[4] However, this academic problem of not knowing our subjects in fidelity over great deals of time goes much deeper than blaming it on the Internet. A theologian in the academy today is not assumed to believe in the Living God they study and teach. Now, we must be careful here. I admit in total humility that non-confessional theologians have and will play crucial roles in their work as scholars and fellow contributors in their disciplines. Some of these are friends with whom I have had the joy of working over the years, whether in the academy or elsewhere. Whether in biblical studies, hermeneutics, or Christian history, we are indebted to any who have forwarded their fields' knowledge, no matter *what* their confessional identity. But, equally as humbly, I believe non-confessional theologians can take us only as far in knowing God as the Internet can take us to the Galapagos or a French village. Information, in Christian theology, has never equated to revelation. Theology free of "personal knowledge" is nothing more than a webpage about heaven. Jesus' community is not those who know information *about* heaven, but those who *enter* the Kingdom of heaven. As Rodney Clapp has brilliantly observed, there is a drastic difference between *theologians* ("knowers of God") and *theologian-logians* ("knowers of knowers of God").[5] Some theologians can articulate with brilliance the names, dates, and stories of those in the past who studied God and the ideas they taught. Other theologians do theology by knowing, loving, and worshipping the Great Subject. We stand before someone (Shelton) who has mastered both.

Disciplines of a Theologian in Covenant

A theologian *in* covenant is marked by a number of fundamental traits, a few of which I have observed in the work of Larry Shelton. First, a theologian in covenant is not primarily concerned with originality, innovation, or

4. Polanyi, *Personal Knowledge*.
5. Clapp, *Border Crossings*, 54.

novelty, as much as he or she is with *faithfulness* to God. The enemy of this kind of faithfulness can come in many forms: drive, academic anxiousness, the need for innovation in one's particular field of study. A Christian theologian, however, rests in God's love. The theologian, like the biblical reader, must deal first with what has already been uttered rather than making up something new. Brevard Childs, the famed father of the biblical-theology movement, taught a widely loved course on exegesis and hermeneutics at Yale University for decades. Most students would be required to take his course at some point in their seminary journey to hone their reading skills to rightly interpret a given passage of Scripture. As a project, Childs would often give them a biblical text with which they would be required to exegetically wrestle. After receiving the finished projects, Childs would grade them. On many occasions, Childs would give students a mediocre grade, some poor grades, and others good grades. Rarely, Childs would give a student "brilliant" as a grade. One might think that "brilliant" was a sign of theological brilliance. To the contrary, Childs was quick to remind his students that in terms of exegesis, "brilliant" was not a form of praise and that he was certainly not happy with "brilliant." He would tell those students who received this grade that if their exegesis was "brilliant," it probably *wasn't in the text*.[6]

Now, clearly, this call for faithfulness is not intended to convey a need to kill all fresh readings of Scripture. The Bible demands to be read afresh in each generation through the abiding Spirit of God. Historically, it is only because of the valiant efforts of those who were willing to read the Bible afresh that segregation, slavery, and the degradation of women were put in their right place in cultural history. No, this call to faithful proclamation is by no means the death of creativity. Faithfulness is not the absence of creativity; rather, it is a presence of an unending responsibility to a Creator above all else. A theologian humbly admits she or he has nothing to add to the Incarnation. The whole alphabet of salvation, Alpha to Omega, has been written with the blood of Jesus Christ on the hearts of people. The gospel is complete and needs neither footnotes nor peer-reviewed articles to be acceptable. The gospel is a final word. It is in this context of the gospel that a theologian is free from being tasked to articulate anything new. Rather, a theologian is tasked to say it freshly for today. The empty tomb can never be more relevant. This is exactly what Stanley Hauerwas means

6. This story was conveyed by professor Sondra Ely Wheeler at a meeting of the Association of Theological Schools in Pittsburgh, PA (Feb. 23–25, 2013).

when he perceptively writes that a theologian's primary role is faithfulness and not ingenuity.[7]

Conjurors of innovation and pushers of progress to "improve" the doctrinal proclamation of the orthodox community (like the Enlightenment fathers Kant, Schleiermacher, and von Harnack attempted) for the sake of pleasing the modern mind fail to recognize that it is in innovation itself that the world broke *shalom*, or peace, with God in Eden. Innovative theologians could make a great deal of ruckus (and money, for that matter) telling us that Jesus' church and all her beliefs throughout antiquity are wrong, outdated, and nonsensical. "Did God really tell you that?" they might echo. And to that, theologians in covenant must boldly proclaim, yes, God did say that! A nuanced reading of Scripture reminds us how little joy it takes in innovation or entrepreneurship. In fact, that was Adam and Eve's greatest sin. The fall was about being *too* innovative.

Secondly, a theologian in covenant is devoted to a life of discipline. Every once in a while, a theological thinker or author will come along who seems to exhibit a kind of eternal creativity that is faithful to the church's history *and* the world's needs. The challenge remains: creativity within the confines of orthodox Christianity. Orthodox theologians must learn to color within the lines. Yet, at the same time, a theologian sometimes prophetically reminds us that the lines within which we've been coloring for some time were the wrong lines. The best theologians do both: reminding us of the faith and prodding us to question false idols in our faith. Meeting a theologian like this is not an everyday occurrence, nor are these kinds of theologians made overnight. I would argue that history's best theologians pursued devotional practices that gave them the God-inspired ability to know what words to say, how to say them, and what the human heart desires. In short, what marks this engine of theological genius? I would argue at the heart of this creative theologian's life is a set of disciplines.

Creativity, we are finding, depends on rote, tireless, disciplined living. The bourgeoning academic field of creativity studies seeks to examine this engine of genius apparently present in certain individuals. In his book, *Creating Minds*, Howard Gardner examines the historical/sociological phenomena that made it possible for individuals such as Einstein, Picasso, Stravinsky, and Gandhi to be as creative as they were.[8] Mihaly

---

7. Hauerwas, *Christian Existence Today*, 1.
8. Gardner, *Creating Minds*.

Csikszentmihalyi's work has added a groundbreaking voice to the conversation.[9] Creativity research appears to indicate a rather fascinating piece of data: people are not born creative; they *become* creative through disciplines. One abiding practice that continues to appear is that of continuing to show up to their particular problem, or area, or thought. Robert Grudin, a scholar on the study of creativity, reflects on this and sees the ongoing, never-ending, fidelity to one's creative work a key to the process. Grudin writes, "Inspiration tends to visit people who renew contact with the major challenges of some ongoing project every day and who set no time limit on their involvement. Such people can accept the failure of a day's effort or a week's enterprise, confident at once that the past has brought better results and the future will offer new opportunities. Their confidence in turn gives them the calm attention which is open to new ideas. *They belong to their work, and it rewards their commitment with unexpected discovery.*"[10] Theological creativity is, I would argue, a similar process. Theologians who have made major contributions to their area of study were not freaks of nature or born as great minds; they were faithful to certain ways of discipline.

What is a theologian in covenant faithful to do? The normal assignments demand constant attention: writing, delivering papers, creating networks, talking to pastors. However, these disciplines are dependent upon the theologian's life in Christ. Which is why, first, the practice of prayer is a key discipline. Why? It centers the theologian into their goal of personally knowing God. In teaching through the history of the church, one finds that the most influential theologians (e.g., Augustine, Luther, Bonheoffer) all had one thing in common: their fathers were disappointed that their children went into theology as a profession. In many cases, their fathers had wished their sons would go into law where the real action was. At times, assuredly, theologians may be tempted to leave their work for brighter fields that await them elsewhere. But prayer reminds us of the importance of our work and our calling before God and His people. Prayer gets us at the heart of our work. When we are working in reaction, in anger, and in protest, usually there are unhealed hearts that God is seeking to touch. Theology in protest rarely works anyway. Grudin writes, "rebels and mavericks driven by dissatisfaction and anger, however justifiable, generally make poor

---

9. See, for instance, his text, Csikszentmihaly, *Creativity: Flow and the Psychology of Discovery and Invention.*

10. Grudin, *Grace of Great Things*, 13, emphasis mine.

discoverers. To gain valid insights, we must love truth more than we hate error."[11]

Along with prayer, the discipline of self-examination comes to mind. Continual re-questioning of old assumptions and values for the purpose of greater knowing keeps the theologian from getting stuck in the ruts of life that can be so comfortable. Humans have always constructed meaningful theologies about God from various sources and in diverse ways. Philosopher Ken Wilber has said that we know reality in three ways: the "eye of the senses" (empirical science), the "eye of reason" (philosophy, logic, mathematics), and the "eye of contemplation" (systematic and disciplined faculties of the real).[12] But, as Shelton would remind us, John Wesley first taught us this. Through the faculties of reason, experience, tradition, and Scripture, we arrive at vistas of faith whereupon we can gaze with wonder afresh at the world God has created.

A theologian in covenant is faithful, disciplined, and finally, humble. In reality, this will be one of the lasting legacies of the work of Larry Shelton, yet I do not believe he found humility on his own. The remarkable spirit of John Wesley has not gone unnoticed by Wesleyan historians and theologians, especially his humility. Randy Maddox, for instance, discusses the "epistemic humility" of Wesley. In the years leading up to Wesley's maturation into a traveling evangelist, theologians were debating vigorously the nature of knowledge. Three theologians in particular (William Chillingsworth, John Tillotson, and Edward Stillingfleet), while believing in the truth of reality and even in absolute truth, called for a "common-sense" approach to knowing such truth. Their central conviction was that while absolute truth did exist, absolute certainty was not a possibility. Wesley, Maddox points out, was introduced to the concept of epistemic humility in his years at Oxford. Over time, the implications of such humility took root in his theology and practice. "Ultimately, this convinced Wesley," writes Maddox, "that *all* human understandings of our experience, tradition, and Scripture itself are 'opinions.'"[13] Interpretations, even of infallible truth, is always fallible in the human mind and must always remain open to new perspective and modification.

Wesley was known for saying in Sermon 39 that we learn *humanum est errare et nescire*. Translated, this means, "To be ignorant of many things,

---

11. Ibid., 31.
12. Discussed throughout Wilber, *Eye to Eye*.
13. Maddox, "John Wesley's Precedent," 24.

and to mistake in some, is the necessary condition of humanity."[14] For the Enlightenment crowd who lusted for the allure of certainty, Wesley became a fascinating voice. They were intrigued with, if not enthralled by, a theologian of such influence who was ready to admit his epistemic fallibility. What upset them most, Maddox pointed out, was that Wesley extended this call for humility even to the scientists who arrogantly believed that their infallible knowledge was real. What a "humility theology" does is remind us of the ever-pressing fact that no matter how great our knowledge may be today, how much we know about God and the world, there is always something new.[15] Humility theology is one of wonder, which awaits us under every rock of certainty.

I learned a humility theology through Shelton, but again, he got it from somewhere—through years of studying Wesley, who got it from three theologians I've never heard of. They probably learned humility elsewhere. Humility, unlike our ability to swallow or breathe, is not built-in. It is a sort of special apostolic succession that is passed down from generation to generation, person to person. Humility is a learned virtue.

Humility can be a challenging pursuit in the face of academic renown, as Dr. Morse's chapter opening this book has illustrated. When we do not find a way to balance students' encouragement and the publications and speaking opportunities that beckon, this can be detrimental to a theologian's personal development. Faithfulness to pleasing the crowds or stoking one's reputation does not nurture a way of thinking that pleases the Living God. In so doing, we taste hell for what C. S. Lewis said it really is: a life of "ruthless, sleepless, unsmiling concentration on self."[16]

Humility, mind you, is not the loss of one's voice into an abyss of selflessness. Nor is humility being beckoned into the waters of calmness so that no one's feelings are hurt. Such false humility only places one at the epicenter of the cultural status quo where no one says anything with value, bite, or critique. True humility isn't being nice. Godly humility can be loud, persuasive, and have a bite. It can buckle down and say the hard word. Pluralism will lure us to believe that the differences between the Christian gospel and other religious traditions must be minimized and muted in an almost "Will Rogers pluralism" where every theologian has "never met a

---

14. Wesley, "Catholic Spirit," 84.
15. On "Humility Theology", see Hermann, *God, Science and Humility*.
16. Lewis, *Screwtape Letters*, vii.

position they didn't like."[17] That kind of humility is heresy. This heresy seeks to reduce all difference and offense, both in the theologian's own voice and from the Christian gospel. But this cannot be the approach of a theologian in covenant. A theologian humbly proclaims the words of God and the particularities of the Christian gospel. David Tracy's arresting words sum this up: "Each of us contributes more to the common good when we dare to undertake a journey into our own particularity . . . than when we attempt to homogenize all differences in favor of some lowest common denominator."[18] A theologian knows the particularity of his position, the power of her gospel, and the love of God. It is a sin to tone it down.

Conclusion

The late Paul Achtemeier once said, "the seminary is the place where the church loves God with all its mind." The seminary is the place where, ideally, true education is possible: to know and love God.[19] A theologian's primary assignment, especially in the context of the evangelical world, is to help others know God and love God through the gospel of Jesus Christ. Shelton has been faithful to this. He has shown us what it means to love the Lord with all his mind and taught us how we might do the same.

As the church-history course I taught with Larry came to a close on the final day, we approached the final fifteen minutes of class. Having ended a lecture on neo-orthodoxy and the contributions of Barth, I turned around to see Larry sitting on the side still nodding and engaged. Knowing the sacredness of the moment, I told him, with the class watching, what an honor it was to teach alongside him at this stage in his theological journey. When the final word of thankfulness came from my mouth, the entire class, in total unison, stood to give Larry a one-minute-long standing ovation. Standing up and putting his hands together like the Dalai Lama, he took a bow. He stood, proud, before the students he loves. He then shed a tear. Gracefully, Larry thanked me for helping that semester and we closed up shop for the night.

---

17. Tracy, "Defending the Public Character of Theology," 355.
18. Ibid., 353.
19. Markides, *Mountain of Silence*, 52.

For all of us who have watched you become a true covenant theologian, thank you, Larry. You've been a great chauffeur. We know the Living God more because of you.

Now enjoy your well-deserved rest.

Afterword

SINCE LARRY SHELTON CONCLUDED his "official" career teaching at a Quaker and Wesleyan seminary, let me start with a story about the 20th century's most influential Quaker theologian, D. Elton Trueblood (1900–1994). It's a story that so inspires me personally that I have taken to keeping this Trueblood tradition going in my own academic life and faith practice.

Trueblood had a signature way of introducing quotes: "as my friend George Fox says," or "as my friend John Wesley demonstrates," or "as my friend William Penn proves." One day William Albritton interrupted him and reminded him that Samuel Johnson was a contemporary of the Wesley brothers. Trueblood smiled and said, "Walter, that is the great value of books. When we read and digest the writings of people like Samuel Johnson, they become our friends through their writing."

Larry Shelton approaches all of church history as the story of "his friends." We join our ancestors in a community of inquiry. Our arguments take place in the true Cloud, the original and ongoing cloud of witnesses. Our theories and theses are not things that just reverberate in our heads; they are things that are being conducted in conversation with a host of others, some living, some dead. As his masterful *Cross and Covenant* (2006) reveals, Shelton quotes ancient writers as if he had just talked to them, and he encourages his students to treasure the privilege of becoming "friends" of a wide cast of characters that populates the past.

Too wide a cast for some, Larry is not afraid to quote anyone, which has always made him feel like a kindred spirit. I am not loquacious but I am quotatious, which makes me theologically litigious, as my bounty of hate sites reveals. Like Larry, I will quote anyone in my books (I even quoted Miss Piggy once) if they have something insightful to contribute to my learning.

Both of us have been criticized for quoting suspicious characters, for the promiscuous referencing of people who don't get everything right, for citing someone who in other areas of their life made big mistakes and said outlandish things but who provides alternative views and fresh vantage points. I wish I had learned earlier the shrewdness of David Seamands, so I could have followed in his steps. Seamands pastored Wilmore (KY) United Methodist Church after serving for almost 20 years as a missionary in India. In his sermons, Seamands would sometimes begin a quote with "As Wesley has said . . ." then in a couple of minutes, after his congregation had opened their minds and evaluated the quote for its content, he would retract his citation by saying something like "Sorry. Wesley didn't say that. That was Freud."

I have been more prone to take the advice of pastor Mark Cain: "Quote whom you wish—bees make honey from weeds as well as orchids." Or as the founder of Methodism John Wesley put it about Egyptian gold, "plunder the Egyptians." Wesley himself may have found support for his position in his "friend" Thomas à Kempis, whose classic devotional text *Imitation of Christ* (chapter 5), says "Let not the authority of the writer offend you, whether he be of great or small learning; but let the Love of pure truth draw you to read. Search not who spoke this or that, but mark what is spoken."

The parable of the dishonest servant (Luke 16:1–13), which some have called the most repugnant and startling story Jesus ever told, provides primary evidence that Jesus wasn't just about telling stories of people who were "better" than we are, good and moral people we should try to imitate in some tradition of Aesop's fables. In fact, the servant in this parable is bad to the bone. Yet he still has a message to bring that we can learn from. Jesus shows how even the worst have something of the best to teach us if we will be willing to receive wisdom from a tainted source, just as the servant received tainted wealth from a tainted world.

Jesus cared less about pedigree than destiny. In fact, Jesus even told the disciples not to stop those who were speaking even though they "were not one of us" (Luke 9:49–50). Paul echoed this sentiment to the church at Philippi in an equally amazing portion of Scripture: "It is true that some preach Christ out of envy and rivalry, but others out of goodwill. The latter do so out of love, knowing that I am put here for the defense of the gospel. The former preach Christ out of selfish ambition, not sincerely, supposing that they can stir up trouble for me while I am in chains. But what does it matter? The important thing is that in every way, whether from false motives or true, Christ is preached. And because of this I rejoice. Yes, and I will continue to rejoice" (Phil 1:15–18).

Augustine and Aquinas took the best thinkers of their time and used them to introduce Christ to their culture. Augustine used Neo-Platonism; Aquinas used Aristotle. When criticized for lifting up the thinking and insights of non-Christians, Thomas Aquinas said: "Do not heed by whom a thing is said, but rather what is said you should commit to memory." Or in the words of the great philosopher Alfred North Whitehead, "Great ideas enter into reality with evil associates and with disgusting alliances. But the greatness remains."

Bridging Augustine and Aquinas, my 12th century "friend" Abelard, a French theologian, insisted that quoting authorities was not sufficient, if we dared not think for ourselves. The 20th-century German literary critic Walter Benjamin dreamed of one day composing a book entirely of quotations—a collage of the urbane, the arcane, the quotidian, and the contemporary. Abelard not only had the same idea eight centuries before Benjamin, but he produced the book. His volume of contrasting quotations, *Sic et Non* ("Yes and No"), allowed opposing opinions and disagreements without resolution. When Abelard did delurk, it was not to referee the fight or choose a winner but to bridge the two sides or bring into relationship the two positions. For this reason Tony Blair, President of Evangelical Seminary (Myerstown, Pa), calls Abelard his candidate for patron saint of the 21st century academy, and the church.

Larry Shelton is the closest thing to an Abelard I'll ever meet. In his heart, head, and hands, which in good Wesleyan tradition are never disconnected, he is in the harmony business. Scholastic theology is a world of "distinctions" and "differences." Shelton, in the tradition of Abelard, has always been in search of arpeggios of creative harmony and dissonance rather than union and consonance. These arpeggios always have, and always will, send shivers up and down my spine.

Leonard I. Sweet
September 27, 2013

Bibliography

"A Shared Grief." Harrisburg Patriot-News, December 19, 2012. http://blog.pennlive.com/midstate_impact/print.html?entry=/2012/12/amish_near_nickel_mines_school.html.

Achtemeier, Elizabeth. *Minor Prophets I*. New International Biblical Commentary. Peabody, MA: Hendrickson, 1996.

———. *Preaching from the Minor Prophets: Texts and Sermon Suggestions*. Grand Rapids: Eerdmans, 1998.

Achtemeier, Paul J. *Romans*. Interpretation. Atlanta: John Knox, 1985,

Aland, Kurt, et al., eds. *Novum Testamentum Graece*. 27th ed. Stuttgart: Deutsche Bibelgesellschaft, 1998.

Althaus, Paul. *The Theology of Martin Luther*. Translated by Robert C. Schultz. Philadelphia: Fortress, 1966.

Anderson, Bernhard W. *Contours of Old Testament Theology*. Minneapolis: Fortress, 1999.

———. *From Creation to New Creation*. Minneapolis: Fortress, 1999.

Anderson, Herbert, et al., eds. *The Family Handbook*. The Family, Religion, and Culture. Louisville, KY: Westminster John Knox, 1998.

Anderson, Ray Sherman. *On Being Human: Essays in Theological Anthropology*. Grand Rapids: Eerdmans, 1982.

Anderson, Ray S. and Dennis B. Guernsey. *On Being Family: A Social Theology of the Family*. Grand Rapids: Eerdmans, 1985.

Anonymous. "From Jaini Bi—With Love." In *Voices of Women: An Asian Anthology*, edited by Alison O'Grady, 11. Singapore: Asian Christian Women's Conference, 1978.

Aristotle. *Aristotle in Twenty-Three Volumes, vol. XIX, The Nicomachean Ethics*. 2nd ed. Translated by Harris Rackham. Loeb Classical Library 73. Cambridge, MA: Harvard University Press, 1975.

———. *The Athenian Constitution, The Eudemian Ethics, On Virtues and Vices*. Rev. ed. Translated by Harris Rackham. Loeb Classical Library 285. Cambridge, MA: Harvard University Press, 1952.

Bailey, Kenneth E. "The Pursuing Father." *Christianity Today* 42/12 (October 26, 1998) 34–40.

Balswick, Jack O., and Judith K. Balswick. *A Model for Marriage: Covenant, Grace, Empowerment and Intimacy*. Downers Grove, IL: InterVarsity, 2006.

Barr, James. *History and Ideology in the Old Testament: Biblical Studies at the End of a Millennium*. The Hensley Henson Lectures for 1997 delivered to the University of Oxford. Oxford: Oxford University Press, 2000.

Barry, Dan. "With a Why No Closer, Two Boys, 6, Two Burials." *New York Times*, December 18, 2012, A24.
Barth, Karl. *Fragments Grave and Gay*. The Fontana Library. New York: HarperCollins, 1971.
Barth, Markus. *Ephesians: Translation and Commentary on Chapters 4–6*. The Anchor Bible. Garden City, NY: Doubleday, 1974.
Barton, John, and John Halliburton. "Story and Liturgy." In *Believing in the Church: The Corporate Nature of Faith*, edited by the Doctrine Commission of the Church of England, 79–207. London: SPCK, 1981.
Bass, Bernard M., and Ronald E. Riggio. *Transformational Leadership*. 2nd ed. Mahweh, NJ: Laurence Erlbaum, 2006.
Bass, Bernard M., and Ralph M. Stogdill. *Handbook of Leadership: Theory, Research, and Managerial Applications*. New York: Free Press, 1990.
Bauer, Walter. *Griechisch-deutsches Wörterbuch zu den Schriften des Neuen Testaments und der frühchristlichen Literatur*. 6th ed. Edited by Kurt Aland et al. Berlin: W. de Gruyter, 1988.
Bauman, Gerlinde. *Love and Violence: Marriage as Metaphor for the Relationship between YHWH and Israel in the Prophetic Books*. Translated by Linda M. Maloney. Collegeville, MN: Liturgical, 2003.
Ben Zvi, Ehud. "Observations on the Marital Metaphor of YHWH and Israel in Its Ancient Israelite Context: General Considerations and Particular Images in Hosea 1.2." *Journal for the Study of the Old Testament* 28/3 (2004) 363–84.
Bennis, William G., and Robert J. Thomas. *Geeks and Geezers: How Era, Values, and Defining Moments Shape Leaders*. Cambridge, MA: Harvard University Press, 2002.
Berger, Joseph. "Cardinal Finds a Biblical Parallel in a School Aide's Selfless Life and Death." *New York Times*, December 21, 2012, A24.
———. "Remembering the Passion of a Teacher Who Died Protecting Students." *New York Times*, December 20, 2012, A29.
Bergquist, William R., and Kenneth Pawlak. *Engaging the Six Cultures of the Academy*. San Francisco, CA: Jossey-Bass, 2008.
Berry, Thomas. *The Great Work: Our Way into the Future*. New York: Bell Tower, 1999.
Bertram, Georg. "ἔργον, ἐργάζομαι." In *Theologisches Wörterbuch zum Neuen Testament*. Vol. 2. Stuttgart: Kohlhammer, 1935. English translation in the *Theological Dictionary of the New Testament*. Vol. 2. Translated by Geoffrey Bromiley. Grand Rapids: Eerdmans, 1964.
Best, Ernest, ed. *1 Peter*. New Century Bible. London: Oliphants, 1971.
Birch, Bruce C., Walter Brueggemann, Terence E. Fretheim, and David L. Peterson. *A Theological Introduction to the Old Testament*. Nashville: Abingdon, 2005.
Bird, Michael. "New Testament Theology Reloaded: Integrating Biblical Theology and Christian Origins." *Tyndale Bulletin* 60/2 (2009) 161–87.
Bohm, David. *On Dialogue*. London: Routledge, 1996.
Bonhoeffer, Dietrich. *Berlin: 1932–1933*. Translated by Isabel Best, David Higgins, and Douglas W. Stott. Edited by Larry L. Rasmussen. Minneapolis: Fortress, 2009.
———. *Ethics*. Edited by Clifford Green. Translated by Reinhard Kraus, Douglas W. Stott, and Charles C. West. Minneapolis: Fortress, 2005.
———. *Letters and Papers from Prison*. Edited by John W. de Gruchy. Translated by Lisa E. Dahill, Isabel Best, Reinhard Krauss, and Nancy Lukens. Minneapolis: Fortress, 2010.

Brown, Brené. "Daring Greatly." Session 6. Willow Creek Global Leadership Summit, South Barrington, IL. August 9, 2013.
Brown, Raymond E., Joseph A. Fitzmyer, and Roland E. Murphy, eds. *The New Jerome Biblical Commentary*. London: Geoffrey Chapman, 1990.
Browne, Ray B., and Arthur B. Neal, eds. *Ordinary Reactions to Extraordinary Events*. Bowling Green, OH: Bowling Green State University Popular Press, 2001.
Brueggemann, Walter. *The Bible Makes Sense*. Atlanta: John Knox, 1985.
———. *The Prophetic Imagination*. Philadelphia: Fortress, 1978.
———. *Theology of the Old Testament*. Minneapolis: Augsburg Fortress, 1997.
Brunner, Daniel. "The Suffering of the Earth in Dialogue with Luther's Theology of the Cross." For the Quaker Theological Discussion Group, AAR-SBL. Chicago, IL, November 16, 2012.
Bultmann, Rudolf. *Theology of the New Testament*. 2 vols. Translated by Kendrick Grobel. New York: Scribner's, 1951, 1955.
Burns, James MacGregor. *Leadership*. New York: Harper & Row, 1978.
Butler, Kristen. "Iowa GOP: No More No-fault for Parents, Divorce Too Damaging." UPI, March 5, 2013. No pages. http://www.upi.com/blog/2013/03/05/Iowa-GOP-No-more-no-fault-for-parents-divorce-too-damaging/6711362525611/.
Campbell, R. Anderson. "Realms and Redescription in Ricoeur: Discovering Fresh Metaphoric Networks for Spiritual Formation in a Postmodern Consumer Culture." DMin diss., George Fox University, 2013.
Chalke, Steve, and Alan Mann. *The Lost Message of Jesus*. Grand Rapids: Zondervan, 2004.
Chesser, Barbara Jo. "Analysis of Wedding Rituals." *Family Relations* 29 (April 1980) 204–9.
Chesterton, G. K. *Orthodoxy*. Wheaton, IL: Harold Shaw, 1994.
Chung, Paul S. "Discovering the Relevance of Martin Luther for Asian Theology." *Dialog: A Journal of Theology* 44/1 (Spring 2005) 38–49.
Clapp, Rodney. *Border Crossings: Christian Trespasses on Popular Culture and Public Affairs*. Grand Rapids: Brazos, 2000.
Coles, Robert. *The Call of Stories: Teaching and the Moral Imagination*. Boston: Houghton Mifflin, 1989.
Collins, Jim. *Good to Great: Why Some Companies Make the Leap . . . and Others Don't*. New York: Harper, 2001.
Collins, Robin. "Understanding Atonement: A New and Orthodox Theory." Unpublished paper, 1995. Online: www.home.messiah.edu/~rcollins/Atone.htm.
Cone, James. *For My People: Black Theology and the Black Church*. Maryknoll, NY: Orbis, 1984.
"Coroner: Newtown Gunman Adam Lanza Shot Mom Repeatedly in Head." December 16, 2012. http://www.pennlive.com/midstate/index.ssf/2012/12/coroner_newtown_gunman_adam_la.html.
Cremer, D. Hermann. *Biblisch-theologisches Wörterbuch der neutestamentlichen Gräcität*. 4th ed. Gotha: Friedrich Andreas Perthes, 1886.
Csikszentmihalyi, Mihaly. *Creativity: Flow and the Psychology of Discovery and Invention*. New York: Harper Perennial, 1997.
Daniels, T. Scott, and Marty Michelson. "Passing the Peace: Worship That Shapes Non-Substitutionary Convictions." Unpublished paper presented at the Wesleyan Theological Society Conference, Seattle, WA, March 2005.

Danker, Frederick William, ed. *A Greek-English Lexicon of the New Testament and Other Early Christian Literature* [BDAG]. 3rd ed. Chicago: University of Chicago Press, 2000.

De Santis, Solange. "Lutheran 'Comfort Dogs' Welcome Students Back to Newtown School." *Christian Century* (February 6, 2013) 21.

Dio Chrysostom. *Discourses. Dio Chrysostom in 5 vols. Vol. I.* Translated by J. W. Cohoon. Loeb Classical Library. Cambridge. MA: Harvard University Press, 1949.

Dodd, Charles H. *Historical Tradition in the Fourth Gospel.* Cambridge: Cambridge University Press, 1963.

Dowd, Maureen. "Why, God?" *New York Times*, December 26, 2012. http://www.nytimes.com/2012/12/26/opinion/dowd-why-god.html.

Dunn, James D. G. *Unity and Diversity in the New Testament.* Philadelphia: Westminster, 1977.

Dziczkowski, Jennifer. "Mentoring and Leadership Development." *The Educational Forum* 77/3 (2013) no pages. http://www.tandfonline.com/doi/full/10.1080/00131725.2013.792896.

Eaton-Robb, Pat, and Jesse Washington. "This Is Bringing People Together." *Harrisburg Patriot-News*, December 23, 2012. http://bigstory.ap.org/article/conn-town-mourning-inundated-gifts-money.

Ehrman, Bart D. *The New Testament: A Historical Introduction to the Early Christian Writings.* 4th ed. New York: Oxford University Press, 2008.

Elliott, John H. *A Home for the Homeless: A Sociological Exegesis of 1 Peter, Its Situation and Strategy.* Philadelphia: Fortress, 1981.

Felkey, Amanda J. "Will You Covenant Marry Me? A Preliminary Look at a New Type of Marriage." *Eastern Economic Journal* 37/3 (2011) 367–89.

Fernando, Ajith. *Jesus and the World Religions: Is Christianity Just Another Religion?* Kent: STL, 1988.

Fiddes, Paul S. *Participating in God: A Pastoral Doctrine of the Trinity.* Louisville: Westminster John Knox, 2000.

Forde, Gerhard O. *Where God Meets Man: Luther's Down-to-Earth Approach to the Gospel.* Minneapolis: Augsburg, 1972.

Friedman, Edwin. *A Failure of Nerve: Leadership in the Age of the Quick Fix.* New York: Seabury, 2007.

Fryer, Bronwyn. "The Ethical Mind." *The Harvard Business Review* (March 2007) n.p. http://hbr.org/2007/03/the-ethical-mind/ar/1.

"Full Text of Obama Speech after Connecticut School Shooting," December 14, 2012. http://www.denverpost.com/breakingnews/ci_22194021/full-text-obama-speech-after-connecticut-school-shooting

Fullen, Michael. *Leading in a Culture of Change.* San Francisco: Jossey-Bass, 2001.

Gardner, Howard. *Creating Minds: An Anatomy of Creativity Seen through the Lives of Freud, Einstein, Picasso, Stravinsky, Eliot, Graham, and Gandhi.* New York: Basic Books, 1993.

———. *Five Minds for the Future.* Boston: Harvard Business Review, 2006.

Gardner-Smith, Percival. *St. John and the Synoptic Gospels.* Cambridge: Cambridge University Press, 1938.

Garland, Diana S. *Family Ministry: A Comprehensive Guide.* Downers Grove, IL: InterVarsity, 1999.

Gordon, Christopher. "Letter to the Editor." *New York Times*, January 28, 2013. http://www.nytimes.com/2013/02/03/opinion/sunday/sunday-dialogue-treating-the-mentally-ill.html.

Grenz, Stanley J., and John R. Franke. *Beyond Foundationalism: Shaping Theology in a Postmodern Context*. Louisville: Westminster John Knox, 2001.

Grudin, Robert. *The Grace of Great Things: Creativity and Innovation*. New York: Ticknor & Fields, 1990.

Guelich, Robert. *Mark 1–8:26*. Word Biblical Commentary 34. Dallas: Word Books, 1989.

Gunton, Colin. *The Actuality of Atonement*. London: T. & T. Clark, 1998.

Hahn, Hans-Christoph. "Work." In the *New International Dictionary of New Testament Theology* 3, edited by Colin Brown, 1147–52. Grand Rapids: Zondervan, 1978. Translation of (with revisions and additions) *Theologisches Begriffslexikon zum Neuen Testament*. Wuppertal: Brockhaus, 1971.

Hall, Douglas John. *Confessing the Faith: Christian Theology in a North American Context*. Minneapolis: Fortress, 1996.

———. *The Cross in Our Context: Jesus and the Suffering World*. Minneapolis: Fortress, 2003.

———. *Lighten Our Darkness: Toward an Indigenous Theology of the Cross*. Philadelphia: Westminster, 1976.

———. *The Steward: A Biblical Symbol Come of Age*. Grand Rapids: Eerdmans, 1990.

Hartin, Patrick J. *A Spirituality of Perfection: Faith in Action in the Letter of James*. Collegeville, MN: Liturgical, 1999.

Harvey, Fiona. "Climate Change 'Likely to Be More Severe than Some Models Predict.'" *The Guardian*, November 8, 2012. http://www.guardian.co.uk/environment/2012/nov/08/climate-change-severe-models?intcmp=122.

Hauerwas, Stanley. *Christian Existence Today: Essays on Church, World and Living in Between*. Grand Rapids: Baker, 1988.

Heiligenthal, Roman. *Werke als Zeichen, Untersuchungen zur Bedeutung der menschlichen Taten im Frühjudentum, Neuen Testament und Frühchristentum* [*Works as Signs: Studies on the Meaning of Human Deeds in Second Temple Judaism, the New Testament and Early Christianity*]. Wissenschaftliche Untersuchungen zum Neuen Testament 2/9. Tübingen: J. C. B. Mohr [Paul Siebeck], 1983.

Hermann, Robert L., ed. *God, Science and Humility: Ten Scientists Consider Humility Theology*. Philadelphia: Templeton, 2000.

Hillers, Delbert R. *Covenant: The History of a Biblical Idea*. Baltimore: Johns Hopkins University Press, 1969.

Hirsch, Alan. *The Forgotten Ways: Reactivating the Missional Church*. Grand Rapids: Brazos, 2006.

Hopkins, Gerard Manley. *God's Grandeur and Other Poems*. Mineola, NY: Dover, 1995.

"How You Can Help." Harrisburg Patriot-News, December 18, 2012, n.p.

Hugenberger, Gordon P. *Marriage as a Covenant: Biblical Law and Ethics as Developed from Malachi*. Biblical Studies Library. Grand Rapids: Baker, 1998.

Hvidberg, Flemming. "The Canaanitic Background of Gen. I-III." *Vetus Testamentum* 10/1 (1960) 285–94.

Isocrates. *Evagoras. Isocrates in Three Volumes.* Vol. III. Translated by Larue Van Hook. Loeb Classical Library 373. Cambridge, MA: Harvard University Press, 1968.

Jeremias, Joachim. *Neutestamentliche Theologie. Erster Teil: Die Verkündigung Jesu*. 4th ed. Gütersloh: Mohn, 1988.

Kaiser, Walter C. *Malachi: God's Unchanging Love*. Grand Rapids: Baker, 1984.
Keller, Evelyn Fox. *Reflections on Gender and Science*. New Haven, CT: Yale University Press, 1995.
Kitchen, Kenneth A. "The Fall and Rise of Covenant, Law, and Treaty." *Tyndale Bulletin* 40/1 (1989) 118–35.
Kittel, Gerhard, and Geoffrey William Bromiley, eds. *Theological Dictionary of the New Testament*. Grand Rapids: Eerdmans, 1964.
Kraft, Charles N., and Tom N. Wisley. *Readings in Dynamic Indigeneity*. Pasadena, CA: William Carey, 1979.
Kyung, Chung Hyun. *Struggle to be the Sun Again: Introducing Asian Women's Theology*. Maryknoll, NY: Orbis, 1990.
Lemcio, Eugene E. "Ephesus and the New Testament Canon." *Bulletin of the John Rylands Library* 69/1 (Autumn 1986) 210–34.
———. *The Past of Jesus in the Gospels*. Society for New Testament Studies Monograph Series 68. Cambridge: Cambridge University Press, 1991.
———. "The Unifying Kerygma of the New Testament [part 1]." *Journal for the Study of the New Testament* 33 (1988) 3–17.
———. "The Unifying Kerygma of the New Testament [part 2]." *Journal for the Study of the New Testament* 38 (1990) 3–11.
Levison, John R. *Filled with the Spirit*. Grand Rapids: Eerdmans, 2009.
Lewis, C. S. *Screwtape Letters*. New York: Macmillan, 1961.
Lewis, Robert, and Rob Wilkins. *The Church of Irresistible Influence*. Grand Rapids: Zondervan, 2003.
Liddell, Henry George, and Robert Scott. *A Greek-English Lexicon*. Revised and augmented by Henry Stuart Jones and Roderick McKenzie. Oxford: Clarendon, 1996.
Liefeld, Walter L. *Ephesians*. Edited by Grant R. Osborne. InterVarsity New Testament Commentary. Downers Grove, IL: InterVarsity, 1997.
Lodahl, Michael. *The Story of God: Wesleyan Theology and Biblical Narrative*. Kansas City: Beacon Hill, 1994.
Luther, Martin. "Against Latomus." In *Luther's Works*, edited by George W. Forell. Translated by George Lindbeck. Philadelphia: Muhlenberg, 1958.
———. "Against the Murderous, Thieving Hordes of Peasants." (1525). No publisher (pamphlet).
———. "Dass disese Worte Christi... (1527)." In *D. Martin Luthers Werke*, 23.134.34–23.136.36.
———. *D. Martin Luthers Werke: Kritische Gesamtausgabe*. Weimar: Hermann Böhlaus Nachfolger, 1883.
———. "Heidelberg Disputation." In *Luther's Works*. Translated by Harold J. Grimm Philadelphia: Muhlenberg, 1957.
———. "Lectures on Romans." In *Luther's Works*, edited by Hilton C. Oswald. Translated by Jacob A. O. Preus. St. Louis: Concordia, 1972.
———. "That These Words of Christ, 'This is My Body,' etc., Still Stand Firm Against the Fanatics." In *Luther's Works* 37, edited by Robert H. Fischer. Saint Louis: Concordia, 1972.
———. "The Sacrament of the Body and Blood of Christ—Against the Fanatics." In *Martin Luther's Basic Theological Writings*, edited by Timothy F. Lull. Minneapolis: Fortress, 1989.

Luther, Martin, and Frederick W. Conrad. *Luther's Small Catechism: Explained and Amplified for Use in Classes, Schools, and Families.* Rev. ed. Philadelphia: Lutheran Publication Society, 1886.

Loewenich, Walter von. *Luther's Theology of the Cross.* Translated by Herbert J. A. Bouman. Belfast: Christian Journals, 1976.

Maddox, Randy. "John Wesley's Precedent for Theological Engagement." In *Divine Grace and Emerging Creation: Wesleyan Forays in Science and Theology of Creation*, edited by Thomas Jay Oord, 1–36. Eugene, OR: Pickwick, 2008.

Mandlate, Bernardino. Presentation to the United Nations PrepCom for the World Summit on Social Development Plus Ten. New York, February 1999.

Mangham, Iain. "Leadership, Ethics, and Integrity." In *Leadership in Organizations: Current Issues and Key Trends*, edited by John Storey, 41–55. 2nd ed. New York: Taylor & Francis, 2010.

Mannermaa, Tuomo. *Two Kinds of Love: Martin Luther's Religious World.* Translated and edited by Kirsi I. Stjerna. Minneapolis: Fortress, 2010.

Markides, Kyriacos C. *The Mountain of Silence: A Search for Orthodox Spirituality.* New York: Doubleday, 2001.

Mattern, Liselotte. *Das Verständnis des Gerichtes bei Paulus.* Abhandlungen zur Theologie des Alten und Neuen Testaments 47. Stuttgart: Zwingli, 1966.

McGee, Michael Calvin. "The 'Ideograph': A Link Between Rhetoric and Ideology." *The Quarterly Speech Journal* 66/1 (1980) 1–16.

———. "Text, Context, and the Fragmentation of Contemporary Culture." *Western Journal of Speech Communication* 54 (1990) 274–89.

McGrath, Alister E. *Christian Theology: An Introduction.* 2nd ed. Oxford: Blackwell, 1997.

———. *Luther's Theology of the Cross.* Cambridge, MA: Blackwell, 1985.

———. *The Reenchantment of Nature: The Denial of Religion and the Ecological Crisis.* New York: Doubleday, 2002.

McKerrow, Raymie E. "Critical Rhetoric: Theory and Praxis." *Communication Monographs* 56 (1989) 91–111.

McKibben, Bill. "Do the Math" Seminar. Portland, Oregon. November 8, 2012.

McLaren, Brian. *Finding Faith: A Self-Discovery Guide for Your Spiritual Quest.* Grand Rapids: Zondervan, 1999.

———. *More Ready Than You Realize.* Grand Rapids: Zondervan, 2002.

Meeks, M. Douglas. "Introduction." In *On Human Dignity: Political Theology and Ethics*, by Jürgen Moltmann, ix–xiv. Philadelphia: Fortress, 1984.

Mendenhall, George E. "Covenant." In *The Interpreter's Dictionary of the Bible* 1. Nashville: Abingdon, 1980.

———. *Law and Covenant in Israel and the Ancient Near East.* Pittsburgh: Presbyterian Board of Colportage, 1955.

Miller, Dan. "Local residents gather to show support for Newtown families." December 17, 2012. http://www.pennlive.com/midstate/index.ssf/2012/12/newtown_shooting.html.

Moe-Lobeda, Cynthia. "A Theology of the Cross for the 'Uncreators.'" In *Cross Examinations: Readings on the Meaning of the Cross Today*, edited by Marit Trelstad, 181–95. Minneapolis: Augsburg Fortress, 2006.

Moltmann, Jürgen. *Experiences in Theology: Ways and Forms of Christian Theology.* Minneapolis: Fortress, 2000.

Morris, Leon. *The Atonement.* Leicester, UK: InterVarsity, 1983.

Neal, Arthur. *National Trauma and Collective Memory: Extraordinary Events in the American Experience*. London: M. E. Sharpe, 2005.

———. *National Trauma and Collective Memory: Major Events in the American Century*. London: M. E. Sharpe, 1998.

Neuhaus, Richard John. *Freedom for Ministry*. Grand Rapids: Eerdmans, 1992.

"Newtown Shooting Victims' Funerals Begin Today; School is Closed and May Not Reopen," Harrisburg Patriot-News, December 17, 2012. http://www.pennlive.com/midstate/index.ssf/2012/12/newtown_shooting_victims_funer.html

Notting Hill. Directed by Roger Michell. Written by Richard Curtis. MCA/Universal Pictures, 1999. DVD.

Nouwen, Henri J. M. *Return of the Prodigal Son*. New York: Bantam Dell, 1994.

Olson, Dennis T. "Family Relationships as Metaphor (Hosea 1–3)." In *The Family Handbook*, edited by by Herbert Anderson et al. Louisville: Westminster John Knox, 1998.

Olson, Roger E. *Arminian Theology: Myths and Realities*. Downers Grove, IL: InterVarsity, 2006.

———. *The Mosaic of Christian Belief: Twenty Centuries of Unity and Diversity*. Downers Grove, IL: InterVarsity, 2002.

"People from All Over Gather in Newtown, Grieve for Those Killed in School Shooting." December 24, 2012. http://www.pennlive.com/midstate/index.ssf/2012/12/people_from_all_over_gather_in.html.

Peterson, David L. *Zechariah 9-14 and Malachi: A Commentary*. Old Testament Library. Louisville: Westminster John Knox, 1995.

Plantinga, Cornelius, Jr. *Not the Way It's Supposed to Be: A Breviary of Sin*. Grand Rapids: Eerdmans, 1995.

Polanyi, Michael. *Personal Knowledge: Towards a Post-Critical Philosophy*. Chicago: University of Chicago Press, 2000.

Ponzetti, James J., and Barbara Horkoff Mutch. "Marriage as Covenant: Tradition as a Guide to Marriage Education in the Pastoral Context." *Pastoral Psychology* 54/3 (January 2006) 215–30.

Postman, Neil. *Amusing Ourselves to Death Public Discourse in the Age of Show Business*. New York: Viking, 1985.

"President Obama's Speech at Prayer Vigil for Newtown Shooting Victims (Full Transcript)," Washington Post, December 16, 2012. http://articles.washingtonpost.com/2012-12-16/politics/35864241_1_prayer-vigil-first-responders-newtown.

Raeisaenen, Heikke. *Beyond New Testament Theology*. 2nd ed. London: SCM, 2000.

Rakestraw, Robert V. "John Wesley as a Theologian of Grace." *Journal of the Evangelical Theological Society* 27 (1984) 193–203.

Rasmussen, Larry. *Earth Community, Earth Ethics*. Maryknoll, NY: Orbis, 1996.

———. "Returning to Our Senses: The Theology of the Cross as a Theology for Eco-Justice." In *After Nature's Revolt: Eco-Justice and Theology*, edited by Dieter T. Hessel, 40–56. Philadelphia: Fortress, 1992.

Ray, Paul H., and Sherry Ruth Anderson. *The Cultural Creatives: How 50 Million People Are Changing the World*. New York: Harmony, 2000.

Ritschl, Dietrich. *Memory and Hope: An Inquiry Concerning the Presence of Christ*. New York: Macmillan, 1967.

Ritzer, George. *The MacDonaldization of Society*. London: Pine Forge, 1996.

Roberts, Christopher Chenault. *Creation and Covenant: The Significance of Sexual Difference in and for the Moral Theology of Marriage*. New York: T. & T. Clark, 2007.

Robinson, John A. T. *The Priority of John*. Edited by James F. Coakley. London: SCM, 1985.

———. *Redating the New Testament*. London: SCM, 1976.

Santmire, H. Paul. *The Travail of Nature: The Ambiguous Ecological Promise of Christian Theology*. Philadelphia: Fortress, 1985.

Schmitt, John J. "The Wife of God in Hosea 2." *Biblical Research* 34 (1989) 5–28.

Schreiner, Thomas R. "Is Perfect Obedience to the Law Possible? A Re-Examination of Galatians 3:10." *Journal of the Evangelical Theological Society* 27/2 (1984) 151–60.

Segalla, Giuseppe. "La Testimonianza Dei Libri del Nuovo Testamento ad un Unico Kerygma/Evangelo, Buon Annuncio Dell'evento Originario." In *L'interpretazione della Bibbia nella Chiesa. Atti del Simposio promosso dalla Congregazione per la Dottrina della Fede*. Atti e Documenti 11. Rome: Libreria Editrice Vaticana, 1999.

Seligman, Martin E. P. "Don't Confuse Crazy with Evil." *Washington Post*, January 3, 2013. http://www.washingtonpost.com/opinions/in-debating-newtown-massacre-dont-confuse-crazy-and-evil/2013/01/03/4d12eb62-5136-11e2-8b49-64675006147f_story.html.

Shelton, R. Larry. "Covenant Atonement as a Wesleyan Integrating Motif." *Asbury Theological Journal* 59 (Spring 2004) 127–38.

———. "A Covenant Context for Wesleyan Ethics." In *Holiness as a Root of Morality: Essays on Wesleyan Ethics, Essays in Honor of Lane A. Scott*, edited by John Sungmin Park and Lane A. Scott, 209–44. Lewiston, NY: Edwin Mellen, 2006.

———. *Cross and Covenant: Interpreting the Atonement for 21st Century Mission*. Tyrone, GA: Paternoster, 2006.

———. "Justification by Faith in the Pauline Corpus." In *An Inquiry into Soteriology from a Biblical Theological Perspective*, edited by John E. Hartley and R. Larry Shelton, 97–132. Wesleyan Theological Perspectives. Anderson, IN: Warner, 1981.

———. "Sanctification in Romans 6." ThM thesis, Asbury Theological Seminary, 1967.

———. "Sharing from My New Heart." *Light and Life* (2003) n.p. http://www.freemethodistchurch.org/Magazine/Articles/Nov-Dec_2003/N-D_2003_Shelton.htm.

Solberg, Mary M. "All That Matters: What an Epistemology of the Cross Is Good For." In *Cross Examinations: Readings on the Meaning of the Cross Today*, edited by Marit Trelstad, 139–53. Minneapolis: Augsburg Fortress, 2006.

———. *Compelling Knowledge: A Feminist Proposal for an Epistemology of the Cross*. Albany: State University of New York Press, 1997.

Spaulding, Henry W., II. "Practicing Holiness: Consideration of Action in the Thought of John Wesley." *Wesleyan Theological Journal* 40/1 (Spring 2005) 132.

Stackhouse, Max L. *Covenant and Commitments: Faith, Family, and Economic Life*. Family, Religion, and Culture. Louisville: Westminster John Knox, 1997.

Sweet, Leonard. *SoulTsunami*. Grand Rapids: Zondervan, 1999.

Taylor, Vincent. *The Gospel According to St. Mark*. 2nd ed. Grand Rapids: Baker, 1966.

Thielicke, Helmut. *The Waiting Father*. New York: Harper, 1959.

Thompson, Deanna A. *Crossing the Divide: Luther, Feminism, and the Cross*. Minneapolis: Fortress, 2004.

Torrance, Thomas F. *The Christian Doctrine of God: One Being, Three Persons*. London: T. & T. Clark, 1996.

———. *The Mediation of Christ*. Colorado Springs: Helmers & Howard, 1992.

Torrey, Charles Cutler. "The Prophecy of 'Malachi.'" *Journal of Biblical Literature* 17 (1898) 9.

Tracy, David W. "Defending the Public Character of Theology." *The Christian Century* 98 (1981) 350–56.

Veblen, Thorstein. *The Instinct of Workmanship and the State of the Industrial Arts*. New York: Huebsch, 1914.

Visotzky, Burton L. *The Genesis of Ethics: How the Tormented Family of Genesis Leads Us to Moral Development*. New York: Crown, 1996.

Volf, Miroslav. "Soft Difference: Theological Reflections on the Relation Between Church and Culture in 1 Peter." *Ex Auditu: Journal of the North Park Symposium on the Theological Interpretation of Scripture* (June 2005) no pages. http://www.northpark.edu/sem/exauditu/papers/volf.html.

Wall, Robert W. *1 and 2 Timothy and Titus*. With Richard B. Steele. Two Horizons New Testament Commentary. Grand Rapids: Eerdmans, 2012.

Wennberg, Robert N. *Terminal Choices: Euthanasia, Suicide, and the Right to Die*. Exeter, UK: Paternoster, 1989.

Wesley, Charles. "And Can It Be That I Should Gain." 1738.

Wesley, John. "Catholic Spirit [Sermon 39]." In *The Works of John Wesley, Volume 2: Sermons II (34-70)*, edited by Albert C. Outler, 81–95. Nashville: Abingdon, 1985.

Wilber, Ken. *Eye to Eye: The Quest for the New Paradigm*. Garden City, NY: Anchor, 1983.

Willard, Dallas. *The Divine Conspiracy: Rediscovering Our Hidden Life in God*. New York: HarperCollins, 1998.

Wilson, David R. Review of *Cross and Covenant* by R. Larry Shelton. *Wesleyan Theological Journal* 43/1 (Spring 2008) 222–24.

Witte, John. *From Sacrament to Contract: Marriage, Religion, and Law in the Western Tradition*. Family, Religion, and Culture. Louisville: Westminster John Knox, 1997.

Wolff, Hans W. *A Commentary on the Book of the Prophet Hosea*. Hermeneia. Philadelphia: Fortress, 1974.

Woodley, Randy. *Shalom and the Community of Creation: An Indigenous Vision*. Grand Rapids: Eerdmans, 2012.

Wright, Christopher J. H. *The Mission of God: Unlocking the Bible's Grand Narrative*. Downers Grove, IL: InterVarsity, 2006.

———. *The Mission of God's People: A Biblical Theology of the Church's Mission*. Grand Rapids: Zondervan, 2013.

Wright, N. T. "On Becoming the Righteousness of God." In *Pauline Theology* 2, edited by D. M. Hay, 200–208. Minneapolis: Augsburg Fortress, 1993.

Xenophon. *Agesilaus* I.6 In *Xenophon, Vol. VII. Scripta Minora*. Translated by E. C. Marchant. Loeb Classical Library 183. Cambridge, MA: Harvard University Press, 1968.

Yukl, Gary A. *Leadership in Organizations*. 2nd ed. Englewoods Cliffs, NJ: Prentice Hall, 1989.

www.ingramcontent.com/pod-product-compliance
Lightning Source LLC
Chambersburg PA
CBHW051742230426
43670CB00012B/2127